FLEXIBLE REGIONAL ECONOMIC INTEGRATION IN AFRICA

This book examines the relationship between flexible regional economic integration in the East African Community (EAC), through its application of variable geometry, and the establishment of the African Continental Free Trade Area (AfCFTA) as a continent-wide form of integration. It uses a historical, political, legal and economic analysis of the processes that led to the adoption of flexible regional integration in Africa, with particular regard to the EAC. This takes place in the inescapable context of pan-Africanism, showing how regional integration efforts in Africa are based on pan-Africanist ideals, and how an evolution of these ideals has led to an evolution in the goals of integration. With growing awareness of the weaknesses and impracticality of consensus-based decision-making on a global level, it makes the case for the pursuit of flexibility in multilateral trade, drawing lessons from the experience of the AfCFTA and blocs in other regions.

This book is a historical evaluation of regional economic integration efforts in Africa. It follows the path of attempts to integrate the economies on the continent from colonial times to the birth of the AfCFTA. While it is a study in law, it relies heavily on politics, economics and history to weave together a more complete theory of economic integration based on the African experience.

Studies in International Trade and Investment Law: Volume 26

Winner of the 2020 SIEL–Hart Prize in International Economic Law.

Society of International Economic Law

Studies in International Trade and Investment Law

Series Editors
Gabrielle Marceau
Krista Nadakavukaren Schefer
Federico Ortino
Gregory Shaffer

This series offers a forum for publication of original and scholarly analyses of emerging and significant issues in international trade and investment law – broadly understood to include the whole of the law of the WTO, the public international law of foreign investment, the law of the EU common commercial policy and other regional trade regimes, and any legal or regulatory topic that interacts with global trade and foreign investment. The aim of the series is to produce works which will be readily accessible to trade and investment law scholars and practitioners alike.

Recent titles in this series:

Flexible Regional Economic Integration in Africa

Lessons and Implications for the Multilateral Trading System

Timothy Masiko

•HART•

OXFORD · LONDON · NEW YORK · NEW DELHI · SYDNEY

HART PUBLISHING

Bloomsbury Publishing Plc

Kemp House, Chawley Park, Cumnor Hill, Oxford, OX2 9PH, UK

1385 Broadway, New York, NY 10018, USA

29 Earlsfort Terrace, Dublin 2, Ireland

HART PUBLISHING, the Hart/Stag logo, BLOOMSBURY and the Diana logo are
trademarks of Bloomsbury Publishing Plc

First published in Great Britain 2022

A catalogue record for this book is available from the British Library.

Library of Congress Cataloging-in-Publication data

Names: Masiko, Timothy, author.

Title: Flexible regional economic integration in Africa : lessons and implications
for the multilateral trading system / Timothy Masiko.

Other titles: Studies in international trade and investment law ; v. 26.

Description: Gordonsville : Hart Publishing, an imprint of Bloomsbury Publishing, 2022. | Series:
Studies in international trade and investment law; v. 26 | Includes bibliographical references and index.

Identifiers: LCCN 2021056169 (print) | LCCN 2021056170 (ebook) | ISBN 9781509944965 (hardback) |
ISBN 9781509945009 (paperback) | ISBN 9781509944989 (pdf) | ISBN 9781509944972 (Epub)

Subjects: LCSH: East African Community. | International economic integration. | Trade blocs—
Africa. | Pan-Africanism—Economic aspects. | Africa, East—Economic conditions—21st century.

Classification: LCC HF1612.4 .M34 2022 (print) | LCC HF1612.4 (ebook) |
DDC 337.1676—dc23/eng/20220104

LC record available at https://lccn.loc.gov/2021056169

LC ebook record available at https://lccn.loc.gov/2021056170

ISBN: HB: 978-1-50994-496-5
       ePDF: 978-1-50994-498-9
       ePub: 978-1-50994-497-2

Typeset by Compuscript Ltd, Shannon

To find out more about our authors and books visit www.hartpublishing.co.uk. Here you will find
extracts, author information, details of forthcoming events and the option to sign up for our newsletters.

www.bloomsbury.com

For my mothers, Emily, Hilda and Mauda.

Foreword

THIS IS AN extremely welcome book. I first read this book as an external examiner. Then, as now, I found it extremely well researched and written. I was delighted to see my impressions confirmed when that thesis was subsequently awarded the 2020 SIEL-Hart Prize in International Economic Law by the Society of International Economic Law (SIEL) and Hart Publishing.

This book reads even better than that award-winning thesis. Timothy convincingly argues that flexible integration is a central feature in nearly, if not all, African integration initiatives. In the book, he convincingly shows that variable geometry is now regarded as a codified norm needing no definition in new African integration treaties. By flexible integration, he means instances in which there is non-uniform application of treaty provisions by, or to, all state parties. While acknowledging the difficulty of precisely defining flexible integration, Timothy notes that non-uniformity may relate to time, extent of application or scope, subject-matter or membership to which the rules are applicable. He demonstrates the centrality of flexible integration in treaty texts, but also with very persuasive illustrations and examples. The book powerfully combines doctrinal analysis with a social legal approach that allows focus on empirical realities on the ground. The archival and desk research is very insightful, especially in tracing for the first time how flexible design came to be embedded in African integration schemes. This is supplemented by interviews of officials involved in regional integration efforts.

The discussion of varying visions between Afrocentric versus Eurocentric visions of pan-Africanism, while probing the various layers of pan-African idealism and the changing content of this pan-Africanism over the decades, is very well done. The shifts in this pan-Africanism, for example from global black unity, to anti-colonialism, to reducing external dependence and back again to seeking African unity, is extremely well done. In addition, the book traces the contestations between the gradualists who overwhelmingly adopted flexibility in regional design, on the one hand, and those who sought immediate African economic unity in the decolonisation period, on the other. Among the many other virtues of the book is how it uncovers the history of the United Nations Economic Commission on Africa (ECA), and its leadership of integration efforts in Africa over the last several decades. The fact that the ECA, which is a significant neo-classical economics outpost on the continent, has provided a lot of the intellectual leadership for the African Continental Free Trade Agreement provides an important contribution to our understanding of the current moment of regional integration in Africa.

The socio-legal approach adopted in the book pays off very well. For example, the in-depth case-study of the Northern Corridor Integration projects in the East African Community powerfully illustrates Timothy's major claim. He does this in part by showing how historical differences and mutual suspicions among the region's Partner States created an environment 'that necessitates flexible economic integration.' Flexible integration in turn left behind some Partner States while it fast-tracked others in their cooperation on infrastructure, immigration, regulation, land ownership and fast-tracking political federation. However, although this project had its successes, it ultimately failed. The lessons that Timothy draws from this example are consistent with his overall approach of discussing African integration efforts on its own terms, in its context and against its history and experience. While he does not ignore comparative experiences, his analytical framework does not start with borrowed theoretical frameworks from other regions.

To achieve this African-centredness, Timothy's book is based on in-depth research of the treaty frameworks, but also of the day-to-day efforts of region building that in turn help him to trace the origins, justifications and the elements of the flexible design of African regional integration treaties. This approach helps Timothy unearth the elements of this flexible design including variable geometry and incremental integration both in the East African Community and in the African Continental Free Trade Area.

Drawing lessons from his excellent research, in the final chapter of the book Timothy draws lessons for the World Trade Organization (WTO). He argues that the practical difficulties in WTO decision-making and in the administration of its trade agreements is a major explanation for the WTO's inability to achieve its goals. Timothy argues that a WTO reform agenda can select from a range of options including the kind of flexibility embodied in African variable geometry or through types of differentiated integration.

There are at least two key contributions that Timothy makes to the ongoing discussions about WTO reform from his extensive study. First, because he looks to the flexible integration model in Africa for lessons that the multilateral trading systems can learn. Second, because he argues that WTO reforms should not merely improve decision-making, but rather that they should embrace flexibility to enable WTO members to meet the goals of the multilateral trading framework. As Timothy sees it, the stalemate in WTO decision-making can be accounted for by virtue of the static nature of its multilateral trading order. From that perspective, by adopting flexibility, the WTO could become more responsive to the constantly evolving international trading system.

This important book is part of a new stream of African international economic law scholarship that unlike the predominant literature in the field is not underpinned by non-African idioms, canons and institutions of international economic law as its point of departure. Rather, the book is based on a rich interdisciplinary mix of the history, politics and economics of African integration. Rarely have I seen such an original approach and methodology that does not imbibe lock, stock and barrel standard approaches developed elsewhere as a starting point for understanding African realities, interests, priorities and concerns. Readers have a lot to learn from this impressive, important and very welcome book whose approach I hope scholars of African international economic law, as indeed of other regions, will emulate and continue to nurture.

James Thuo Gathii
Evanston IL, February 2022

Acknowledgements

I AM GRATEFUL to the Society of International Economic Law (SIEL) and Hart Publishing, without whose support this book would not have been possible. I am thankful to the reviewers for their feedback and advice on how to improve the draft manuscript.

I thank my PhD supervisors, Mary Footer and Annamaria La Chimia. As far as supervision teams go, I hit the goldmine. Thank you for the support, guidance, correction, advice, encouragement, prodding, and perhaps most importantly, listening to and hearing me. This project went in the direction I wanted it to, and my supervisors helped get me there. Any errors in this work are my own. I am especially grateful for their support beyond the PhD, and their understanding when I have needed some coddling.

I am indebted to my PhD examiners, Jeff Kenner and James Gathii for reading this work, pointing out its strengths, and showing where I can do better. Your guidance at the viva and beyond have gone a long way in providing fuel for the research journey ahead.

I thank my family and friends, my support system, and the reason for my sanity. You kept me grounded, and you kept me going. I am immensely grateful to all the staff in the University of Nottingham School of Law for your encouragement, advice, mentorship, and support in all forms throughout the course of this project.

This entire research would not have been possible without funding from the University of Nottingham School of Law, and for that, I am eternally grateful. I am also grateful to the Faculty of Social Sciences, who funded my fieldwork research in Uganda and Tanzania in spring of 2017. Thank you for giving this Ugandan a chance.

Contents

List of Abbreviations

ACM	African Common Market
ACP	Africa, Caribbean and Pacific Regions
AEC	African Economic Community
AfCFTA	Africa Continental Free Trade Area
AU	African Union
CEMAC	Central African Economic and Monetary Community
CENSAD	Community of Sahel-Sahara States
CEPGL	Economic Community of Great Lakes Communities
COMESA	Common Market for Eastern and Southern Africa
COMTRADE	United Nations International Trade Statistics Database
CoW	Coalition of the Willing
EABC	East African Business Council
EAC	East African Community
EAC-CM	East African Community Common Market
EAC-CU	East African Community Customs Union
EACF	East African Cooperation Forum
EACJ	East African Court of Justice
EACSO	East African Common Services Organisation
EADB	East African Development Bank
EALA	East African Legislative Assembly
EASD	East African Statistical Department
ECA/UNECA	United Nations Economic Commission for Africa
ECCAS	Economic Community of Central African States
ECOWAS	Economic Community of West African States
EEC	European Economic Community

EFTA	European Free Trade Area
EPA	Economic Partnership Agreement
EU	European Union
EURATOM	European Atomic Energy Community
FAL	Final Act of Lagos
FDI	Foreign Direct Investment
GATT	General Agreement on Tariffs and Trade
GDP	Gross Domestic Product
IATA	International Air Transport Association
IGAD	Inter-Governmental Agency on Development
IOC	Indian Ocean Commission
ITA	Information Technology Agreement
IUCEA	Inter-University Council for East Africa
LAPPSSET	Lamu Port, South Sudan, Ethiopia Transport Corridor
LDCs	Least Developed Countries
LPA	Lagos Plan of Action
MERCOSUR	Mercado Común del Sur (Southern Common Market)
MFN	Most Favoured Nation
MOU	Memorandum of Understanding
MRU	Manu River Union
MULPOCs	Multilateral Programming and Organisational Centres
NBI	Nile Basin Initiative
NCIP	Northern Corridor Integration Projects
NIEO	New International Economic Order
NTB(s)	Non-Tariff Barrier(s)
OAU	Organisation of African Unity
PTA(s)	Preferential Trade Agreement(s)
PTCEAC	Permanent Tripartite Commission for East African Cooperation

REC	Regional Economic Community
RTA	Regional Trade Agreement
SACU	Southern African Customs Union
SADC	Southern African Development Community
SCT	Single Customs Territory
SGR	Standard Gauge Railway
TFTA	Tripartite Free Trade Area Among the Common Market for Eastern and Southern Africa, The East African Community, and the Southern African Development Community
TIFTEAI	Tripartite Initiative for Fast Tracking East African Integration
TRALAC	Trade Law Centre
TRIPS	Trade Related Aspects of Intellectual Property Rights
UDEAO	Union Douanière et Economique de L'Afrique de l'Ouest
UMA	Arab Maghreb Union
UN	United Nations
UNCTAD	United Nations Conference on Trade and Development
UNESCO	United Nations Educational, Scientific and Cultural Organisation
WACU	West African Customs Union
WAEC	West African Economic Community
WAECU	West African Economic and Customs Union
WAEMU	West African Economic and Monetary Union
WGI	World Governance Indicators
WITS	World Integrated Trade Statistics
WTO	World Trade Organisation

Table of Treaties and Statutes

1

Introduction

REGIONAL ECONOMIC INTEGRATION in Africa elicits one of two reactions: curiosity or lethargy. For some, it is a new subject, and gives rise to questions about how effective it is, how long it has been going on, and whether there are any success stories of note. For others, it is another reminder of another treaty waiting to be discarded in favour of a 'new and improved' one, hoping that the mistakes of the previous one will be remedied by the creation of a new bloc. Curiously, both perspectives are valid. Regional economic integration in Africa has existed longer than African countries in their current form have, so it is nothing new. And yet, there is still limited coverage of the issues surrounding regional economic integration in Africa.

The myriad of factors that have driven and hampered regional economic integration in Africa are a central theme of this book. Through all the highs and lows, the common thread of pan-Africanism remains ever present. Pan-Africanism is based on the belief in a shared heritage among Black Africans, and can be deduced from this famous quote from former Tanzanian president, Julius Nyerere:

> Africans all over the continent, without a word being spoken either from one individual to another, or from one African country to another, looked at the European, looked at one another, and knew that in relation to the European, they were one.[1]

This is, arguably, rooted in the same philosophy as 'Ubuntu' – the belief in a common and shared identity as humans.[2] Pan-Africanism is a race consciousness that is the result of the relationship between often-oppressive colonial masters and their former colonies. As Ali Mazrui explains, if class-consciousness in Africa is partly the result of the intensification of capitalism, race consciousness on the continent has been partly the result of the intensification of imperialism. Just as capitalist exploitation helps to make workers more collectively conscious of themselves as workers, so European imperialism over time has helped to make the colonised Africans more collectively conscious of themselves as a colonised people.[3]

---

[1] J Nyerere, *Africa's Place in the World,* in *Symposium on Africa* (Massachusetts Wellesley College, 1960).

[2] CBN Gade, *The Historical Development of the Written Discourses on Ubuntu* (2011) 30(3) *South African Journal of Philosophy* 303–329.

[3] A Mazrui, in A Mazrui and C Wondji (eds), *General History of Africa, Volume VIII – Africa Since 1935,* (Oxford, UNESCO/Heinemann Educational, 1993) 7.

Pan-Africanism, therefore, is an ideology that pushes for the unification of the African continent based on the common identity Africans share as against other races. To quote Minkah Makalani, it is the belief that African peoples, both on the African continent and in the Diaspora, share not merely a common history, but a common destiny.[4] As will be seen throughout this book, it drives the efforts to unify the continent, and indeed, a case can be made for the idea that integration in Africa is an attempt to return to pre-colonial, borderless times. Since independence, African leaders have advocated for a politically and economically united Africa. At the formation of the Organisation of African Unity, Kwame Nkrumah famously inspired the unity of African states:

> Here is a challenge which destiny has thrown out to the leaders of Africa. It is for us to grasp that golden opportunity to prove that the genius of African people can surmount the separatist tendencies in sovereign nationhood by coming together speedily, for the sake of Africa's greater glory and infinite well-being, into a Union of African States.[5]

Such ambitious rhetoric continues to underpin regional economic integration across Africa. This book reveals that since independence, there have been ceaseless attempts to unify the continent, using all kinds of approaches and based on various motivating factors. One of the approaches to integration has been flexible integration in different forms, with different names and even without being named. In the most general terms, flexible integration is the non-uniform application of treaty provisions by state parties to any given treaty. Like integration in Africa, it exists mostly as a footnote in literature, with limited efforts to define it in detail. This book is an attempt to fill both gaps simultaneously.

The history of the East African Community (EAC) illustrates the evolution of flexible regional economic integration in Africa, explaining how it is simultaneously a method and a consequence of integration efforts across the continent. This inevitably involves an examination of the ideological conflict between the unifying ideals of pan-Africanism and the nationalist and regional interests of African states. This book considers how, after trying multiple methods of integration, African states appear to have admitted that some fundamental differences will always exist, and rather than let those differences hamper integration, they should be accounted for in the process of integration. Indeed, without a specific form of flexible integration,[6] the African goal of continental integration may never have been set in motion. The Treaty Establishing the

---

[4] M Makalani, *Pan-Africanism, African Age: African and African Diasporan Transformations in the 20th Century*, available at http://exhibitions.nypl.org/africanaage/essay-pan-africanism.html (accessed 25 November 2018).

[5] K Kimbugwe, N Perdikis et al, *Economic Development Through Regional Trade: A Role for the New East African Community?* (New York, Palgrave Macmillan, 2012) 35.

[6] Disjointed incrementalism, explained in ch 2, section II.C.i, and illustrated in ch 5, section V.B and ch 7, section I.B in this volume.

Africa Continental Free Trade Area (AfCFTA)[7] is the direct result of the relative success of smaller units of integration on the continent. The EAC is one such unit, which has, more formally than any other, applied flexible regional economic integration to its own development.

The political, economic, and legal history of the EAC reveals the use of flexible integration in the liberalisation of trade between the bloc's Partner States. It is a stellar example of how the law is used to achieve balance between potentially opposing yet necessarily merging interests. This presents the paradox of flexible integration: integration as it is currently understood would necessitate some sort of convergence, if not in rules, then in policies and practice. Flexibility, on the other hand, would seek to accommodate differing levels of willingness and capacity to reach this convergence. Flexible integration, then, seems like a 'two steps forward, one step back' approach to economic liberalisation between states.

The pages that follow tell a story of decades of successes and failures, broken and reconstructed relationships, and a regularly renewed hope in the possibility of unity – a unity that takes account of diversity. It is the story of the EAC, a bloc that took the relatively bold step to admit that while consensus is admirable, the existing approaches that encourage a uniform application of rules are broken. It demonstrates how, based on the desire to unify a continent, states may design the rules in a way that allows them not to uniformly apply those rules. It questions where, how and why this idea was conceived, whether it is a good idea, and whether it is effective – whether for better or for worse.

The sections that follow contextualise the EAC and flexible regional economic integration, and present a summary of the methods and data relied on throughout the book.

I. THE EAST AFRICAN COMMUNITY (EAC)[8]

The EAC is the regional intergovernmental organisation of the Republics of Burundi, Kenya, Rwanda, South Sudan, Uganda, and the United Republic of Tanzania, with its headquarters in Arusha, Tanzania.[9] The Community in its current form is a third attempt at integration, with the first iteration being between Kenya and Uganda in 1917, later joined by Tanzania in 1927.[10] This only lasted until 1966, but was revived in 1967, only lasting until 1977.[11] The EAC as it is today started on 7 July 2000, and has adopted variable geometry, one

---

[7] Referred to in this book as 'the AfCFTA Treaty.'

[8] For a detailed review of the EAC and its history, see ch 4.

[9] EAC Website, www.eac.int/overview-of-eac (accessed 2 July 2018).

[10] Chapter 4 in this volume discusses a more detailed history of the EAC.

[11] A Hazlewood, *Economic Integration: The East African Experience* (London, Heinemann Educational Books, 1975) 21–22.

of several forms of flexible regional economic integration,[12] as an operational principle for its integration.

Even from this summarised history of the EAC that spans three alliances across a century, it is clear that the EAC's journey has been eventful. Its chequered history makes it the ideal focus of this book. At its beginning, the EAC was a matter of convenience for the colonial governments of British East Africa,[13] while the first post-independence reincarnation was an attempt by young states to cooperate in the absence of a central, external power.[14] With the revival of the EAC more than 20 years after its second collapse, this history was not disregarded, and the lessons of the past were incorporated into the 1999 treaty.

Both the second and third versions of the EAC reveal pan-Africanist nuances, whether expressly, as with the post-independence cooperation, or impliedly, as the current bloc shows. The 1967 EAC was consistent with the liberation-driven pan-Africanism of the time, focused on aiding the newly independent member states to establish themselves. The EAC today is therefore an essential building block of the AfCFTA, leading to continent-wide integration.[15] In both, the idea of an independent and unified Africa is a prominent driving factor.

Thus far, there appears to be considerable effort at convergence and deeper integration of the Partner States' economies.[16] However, starting in June 2013, the heads of state of Kenya, Rwanda, and Uganda engaged in several negotiations and made decisions to expedite the integration process among the three countries, to the exclusion of Burundi and Tanzania. These negotiations gave birth to the Tripartite Initiative for Fast Tracking the East African Integration (TIFTEAI), which was initially referred to as *the Coalition of the Willing*. This nomenclature is indicative of several factors, but most importantly, it reflects the attitudes of the different member states towards the integration process, highlighting the glaring disparity between Kenya, Rwanda and Uganda on the one hand, and Burundi and Tanzania on the other. In the months that followed, this initiative came to be formally known as the Northern Corridor Integration Projects (NCIP).[17]

The NCIP was the first, and so far most significant implementation of variable geometry in the EAC. There are several reasons for this state of play, not least of all being Tanzania's apparent reluctance to implement the treaty and its protocols, and Burundi's lack of capacity to make the relevant adjustments

---

[12] Chapter 3, section III details the different forms of flexible regional economic integration.

[13] Chapter 4, section I describes the establishment and operation of the EAC between 1917 and 1966.

[14] Chapter 4, section II shows how the independence of East African states hampered regional integration.

[15] Chapter 7 highlights the role of the EAC and other regional blocs as building blocks of the AfCFTA.

[16] Chapter 4, section III reviews the EAC's progress on policy harmonisation, common institutions, and the establishment of a common market.

[17] Chapter 6 in this volume discusses the evolution of the NCIP, and the reasons for its development.

for integration. Although South Sudan joined the EAC after all these events had taken place, its position is similar to Burundi's. However, unlike Tanzania, it appeared more willing to fast-track the integration of the bloc. Chapter four gives a more detailed history of the EAC, including a summary of the process of integration in the bloc at the time of writing, while the dynamics of regional relations are considered in detail in chapter six.[18]

Why, then, select the EAC? There are several reasons, with the first being the academic's old faithful: interest. As a citizen of an EAC Partner State, I was inspired to undertake this study because of a question that appeared to have no answer. In the early days of the NCIP, someone asked why Kenya, Rwanda and Uganda were cooperating more closely, to the exclusion of the other members of the EAC. A quick answer was found in Article 7(1)(e) of the EAC Treaty in the form of variable geometry. That sated the enquirer's curiosity, but only stirred mine. It seemed counter intuitive to have a disintegrative principle included in what appeared to be a treaty for economic integration. And like the proverbial Alice in Wonderland, down the rabbit hole I went in pursuit of answers.

Another reason for the selection of the EAC is just as practical as the first: expediency. Being born of the EAC, materials, offices and officials would be more readily accessible to me than any other regional bloc in Africa. I have benefitted from living, studying and working in both Tanzania and Uganda, and am familiar with the laws, politics and history of the region and its constituent Partner States. Prior to undertaking this study, I was a consulting associate in trade policy and trade law, and this led to a considerable interface with integration issues in the region and beyond. While this may seem like reaching for low-hanging fruits, it is, instead, pragmatic, since a study that imposed an inordinate burden on a limited budget would be undesirable.

Beyond the attractiveness of ease and convenience, the EAC is an ideal candidate for any study in African regional economic integration for several reasons. It has a long and eventful history, with only the Southern African Customs Union (SACU) being older.[19] It has experienced various upheavals, some stemming from the natural flow of a free market, and others being the result of policy and other considerations. The EAC has slowly expanded, from two members in 1917 to six members in 2018, although it is admitted that the bloc has not existed consistently throughout this period. The bloc also brings together a fine mixture of Partner States, ranging from some of the world's poorest nations like

---

[18] Chapter 6, section I.B.

[19] SACU was first established in 1889 as the Customs Union Convention between the British Colony of Cape of Good Hope and the Orange Free State Boer Republic. It expanded in 1910 to include the Union of South Africa and the British High Commission Territories of Basutoland (Lesotho), Bechuanaland (Botswana), Swaziland and South West Africa (Namibia), which was administered as part of South Africa. See SACU, *History of SACU*, available at www.sacu.int/show.php?id=394 (accessed 21 February 2019).

Burundi, Rwanda and Uganda[20] to lower middle income Kenya.[21] The differences resulting from the history of the bloc and its Partner States are covered extensively in the chapters that follow, and have created an environment that necessitates flexible economic integration.

The EAC is unique and therefore ideal for study because it was the first African regional bloc to expressly provide for flexible regional economic integration. As chapters five and seven demonstrate, the EAC's variable geometry is inextricably linked with continental integration efforts, going as far back as 1958. As this is a book on the evolution of flexible regional integration, especially in the African context, no other bloc would provide both a clear definition of the principle and sufficient demonstration of its application.

II. FLEXIBLE REGIONAL ECONOMIC INTEGRATION[22]

Defining flexible regional economic integration requires a deductive process due to the combination of concepts it includes. These can be placed into two broad categories of ideas: regional economic integration and flexibility.

Regional economic integration is the process of preferential trade liberalisation between states, usually in the same geographic region and more often than not, sharing common borders. It involves the gradual reduction of tariff and non-tariff barriers in order to facilitate free trade between the states participating in the integration process. As discussed in chapter two, regional economic integration also refers to the result of this process – a situation in which economic integration is complete, so that the economic significance of political boundaries is substantially diminished.[23] Flexibility, in the context of this book, refers to a situation in which rules are not applied uniformly and at all times by, or to, all parties to an agreement.

Flexible regional economic integration, therefore, is a method of regional economic integration in which member states are allowed to apply rules and policies non-uniformly. The non-uniformity may relate to time, extent of application or scope, subject matter or membership to which the rules are applicable. As explained further in chapter three, flexible regional economic integration takes various forms in different situations, which makes it a complex concept to define.[24]

---

[20] Burundi (1st, at US$771.2), Rwanda (16th, at US$2,214.0) and Uganda (20th, at US$2,297.2) are among the world's poorest nations (measured by GDP per capita, purchasing power parity) according to the World Bank (The World Bank, *International Comparison Program Database*, available at https://data.worldbank.org/indicator/NY.GDP.PCAP.PP.CD?year_high_desc=true (accessed 13 July 2021)).

[21] The World Bank, *International Comparison Program Database – Kenya*, available at https://data.worldbank.org/country/kenya (accessed 29 December 2018).

[22] For a detailed review of flexible regional economic integration, see ch 3.

[23] Chapter 2, section I explores multiple definitions of regional economic integration.

[24] Chapter 3, sections I and II consider the definitions of flexible regional integration.

Even so, it is necessary, at this stage, to highlight the definition of flexible regional economic integration as it is applied and understood in African integration efforts. This requires recourse to the East African definition of the concept, which is referred to as *the principle of variable geometry* in the EAC Treaty and other African treaties for regional economic integration. Article 7(1)(e) of the Amended Treaty for the Establishment of the EAC (the EAC Treaty) defines variable geometry as:

> a principle of flexibility which allows for progression in cooperation among groups within the Community for wider integration schemes in various fields and at different speeds.[25]

This definition was the earliest treaty definition of flexible regional integration in Africa, and this makes it a central part of this study. Any enquiry into flexible regional integration in Africa that does not study this definition, its implications and application would be incomplete and would not benefit from how it has shaped regional economic integration in Africa. This definition evolved over at least 20 years of negotiations and agreements, culminating in the EAC Treaty.[26] Beyond the EAC Treaty, it has been adopted by the Tripartite Free Trade Area between the EAC, SADC[27] and COMESA[28] (TFTA), and the AfCFTA Treaty. Given how central pan-African integration is to this study, it is essential to emphasise this version of flexible regional economic integration, if for no other reason than the possibility that it is the most effective method of unifying African economies.

Most literature on flexible regional economic integration is theoretical and attempts to provide a doctrinal justification and explanation of the concept. This book goes a step further and explores the socio-legal and empirical factors that led to the adoption of variable geometry in the EAC and other African integration efforts, and compares the use of the principle in the EAC and the rest of the African continent. This interdisciplinary approach should yield a more holistic understanding of the concept and enrich the existing literature on regional integration.

III. THE APPROACH

There is plenty of room for literature on regional economic integration in Africa, and even more room for the study of flexible regional economic integration in Africa and beyond. This book examines the relationship between flexible regional economic integration in the EAC, through its application of variable

---

[25] Article 7(1)(e) of the Amended Treaty for the Establishment of the East African Community.
[26] Chapter 5, Section I traces the history of Art 7(1)(e) in the context of African integration.
[27] The Southern African Development Cooperation.
[28] The Common Market for East and Southern Africa.

geometry, and the establishment of the AfCFTA, as a continent-wide form of economic integration. It does so by means of a historical, political, legal and economic analysis of the processes that led to the adoption of flexible regional integration in Africa, with particular regard to the EAC. This is guided by one central question:

> What is the relationship between flexible regional economic integration in the EAC and continental economic integration?

Establishing this relationship involves an assessment of the causes and effects of flexible regional economic integration in both Africa and the EAC. This requires a breakdown of the main research question into two further questions:

1.   What is the historical, political, legal and economic context that led to the adoption of variable geometry in the 1999 EAC Treaty?
2.   What are the implications of flexible regional economic integration for regional integration in the EAC and in Africa?

The first question seeks to provide a deeper understanding of variable geometry and its history in the EAC. This necessitates a theoretical evaluation of flexible regional economic integration, which is then placed in the context of the bloc. This is done in two stages. The first step, covering the next two chapters, is a review of the literature on regional economic integration and flexible regional economic integration. This is then juxtaposed with the history of the EAC, paying heed to the events and factors that rendered flexibility inevitable. Chapters four and five focus on this historical approach.

The second question is geared at determining how flexible regional economic integration affects the process of regional economic integration, both in the EAC and on the continental plane. At the EAC level, this is done by reviewing the closer cooperation between Kenya, Rwanda and Uganda and how this has affected trade patterns, relations between EAC states, and relations between the EAC and third parties. The continental level focuses on the incremental approach to integration to study how, if at all, this has facilitated the establishment of the AfCFTA.

Answering these questions reveals the link between the EAC's variable geometry and the AfCFTA's incremental approach. This link is circular: the EAC's flexibility is at the same time affected by and has an effect on the pace of continent-wide economic integration in Africa. While the link may be circular, the approach to studying it is linear, seeking to establish the causes and effects of the matters considered. The path followed, both by the historical chapters and the theoretical ones, is aimed at revealing the relationship between the EAC's variable geometry and the pace and progress of regional economic integration in Africa.

The research leading up to this book was mainly doctrinal, focusing on the review of laws and policies, and evaluating some of the negotiating context that led to the adoption of the Treaties and Protocols in their current form. Although to a lesser extent, some sociological, empirical and comparative methods are used to assess the history of variable geometry in the EAC and the impact it has had on the integration process. Given the nature of this study, multiple methods were relied on to make it comprehensive. This is so in part because it is informed by multiple disciplines outside law, especially history, politics and economics. The methods were selected for their potential to answer the main research question and the two sub-questions, and to meeting the objectives of this study.

IV. SIGNIFICANCE

One might wonder why another book on regional economic integration is relevant today. Regional economic integration in Africa is ripe for new research, especially with the establishment of the AfCFTA. As the current wave of regional economic integration in Africa and beyond increasingly relies on various forms of flexibility, further examination is imperative. With the process of regional cooperation increasingly codified and formalistic, there appears to be a shift towards the recognition of a vast array of imbalances. In the past, these imbalances have been addressed by largely informal, diplomatic, political, and occasionally, 'soft law' solutions. Today, especially in Africa, the formalised use of flexibility in regional economic agreements is a growing trend.

This book contributes to knowledge in several ways. First, it opens up a new dimension of understanding about regional economic integration in Africa, specifically by highlighting the creation and use of existing blocs to aggregate the gains of integration. Second, it is an evaluation of the success of flexibility in economic integration by telling the stories of the integration process at the EAC and AfCFTA levels. It relies on a diverse range of data sources, including interviews with people closely involved in the process of integration, from the inception of the EAC and the subsequent negotiations, to the implementation of the resultant treaties in the highest echelons of the business community. Third, it is an aggregation of existing literature on both regional economic integration and flexible regional economic integration. While it is a study in law, it relies heavily on politics, economics and history to weave together a more complete theory of economic integration that is based on the African experience. As such, and as a final point of importance, it returns pan-Africanism to the forecourt of studies on and about Africa, especially in a more formalised context.

There is still a near dearth of current literature on regional economic integration in Africa. The book takes a fresh perspective on the long-term role of pan-Africanism in African integration, considering the different schools of thought within pan-Africanist theory and how these interact when faced with often opposing ideals on integration and nationalism.[29]

---

[29] Chapter 2, section III and ch 7, section I study the evolution of integration in Africa in light of the different schools of pan-Africanist thought.

Further justification is to be found in the attitudes of African states towards the West, especially their former colonial masters. While this is symptomatic of a growing inward-looking trend – 'America first' and 'Brexit', for example – the position of African states is unique. When the rhetoric towards the West is considered on a broad range of matters, it is clear that African states feel like they have been placed in a position where being on the defensive is necessary for their survival. The threats and attempts to withdraw from the Rome Statute of the International Criminal Court on the grounds that it unfairly targets Africans is the leading example of this attitude. Further illustration of this dissatisfaction can be found in the refusal by some African states to sign Economic Partnership Agreements with the European Union (EU), and stalemates in negotiations at the World Trade Organisation. This book considers how a return to pan-Africanist ideals would strengthen the position of African states in asserting their positions on these matters. As chapter seven demonstrates, African states have become aware of the need to work in concert in order to achieve their goals, as demonstrated by the establishment of the AfCFTA.

It is hoped that this book will be an enlightening resource for scholars interested in regional economic integration in Africa, and to legal theorists studying flexible regional economic integration. It is, by virtue of the issues involved, interdisciplinary, combining historical analysis, political and economic theories with some traditional doctrinal material. It provides new takes on the interactions between pan-Africanist theory and international law, and seeks to assert the validity of African international law as it codifies pan-Africanist ideologies. In this regard, it is a contribution to third world approaches to international law, a constantly growing movement in the study of international law. In studying the treaty-making process in Africa, it highlights the issues considered in the establishment of regional economic blocs on the continent.

Beyond African integration, this book briefly considers the use of flexibility in the EU and in Mercado Común del Sur (MERCOSUR). In chapter three, these two blocs are studied for their different approaches to flexibility, highlighting similarities and differences between their use of flexibility and the African experience. This process is taken a step further in chapter eight, where the limited use of flexibility in multilateral trade is evaluated. This wider study of flexibility lays essential ground for the reform of the WTO, especially in light of contemporary conceptualisations of public international law.

V. OVERVIEW

This book comprises nine chapters. This first chapter has provided a contextual foundation, introducing the EAC and flexible integration, and setting out the approach taken. Chapter two turns to theory to explain the political and economic bases of regional economic integration. It considers some definitions and theories of economic integration, and studies integration from an African perspective. Chapter three reviews flexible regional economic integration, starting with an expansion of the EAC definition of variable geometry (the preferred nomenclature for flexible regional economic integration in African integration efforts). The fourth chapter is a detailed introduction to the EAC, evaluating the history of the EAC from 1917 to 2017, and considering the outlook for the bloc at the time of writing.

Having established the theoretical bases for regional economic integration and flexibility, chapters five and six take a closer look at the history of flexible regional economic integration in the specific context of the EAC. Chapter five traces the history of the principle in the EAC Treaty, evaluating this against the place of the principle in the African context, while chapter six takes a turn for the slightly more practical, studying the attempts by EAC states to apply flexible regional economic integration in the region.

Chapter seven is a study of Africa's latest and most audacious attempt at regional integration, the AfCFTA. Following the pattern of previous chapters, it considers the history of regional economic integration in Africa, starting at independence, when pan-Africanism reigned supreme, to the present-day, when trade is a new focus for African states. Chapter eight shifts the focus to the multilateral trading system, evaluating why a flexible approach to trade liberalisation has been avoided, and posing the question of whether it would provide an alternative to the slow development of law under the WTO.

Chapter nine contains a summary of the findings, conclusions and recommendations raised in the book. It also proposes areas for future study, covering questions that may have not been answered, either because they were outside the scope of this book, or because they were emerging issues at the time of its completion.

2

Integration Theory

EGIONAL ECONOMIC INTEGRATION is varied in classification and theory. This is mainly because the literature on the subject is a melange of economics, politics, and law. The reasons, methods and benefits of integration (whether economic, political or legal) often cut across subject areas. The complexity is compounded even further by the path regional integration generally takes – economists propose it, politicians negotiate it, and lawyers draft the agreements on which integration is to be based. It is difficult to evaluate the relative importance of political and economic considerations, partly because the relationship is not quantifiable, and partly because a degree of interdependence exists between these factors. This latter reason only further highlights the blurred lines that delimit integration theory.[1] As such, each of the disciplines involved has attempted, over the years, to propose theories of integration. Legal writers, however, have not been as prolific in this venture, and so most of the theories are postulated by scholars of economics and politics.

This chapter attempts to reduce the grey areas in integration theory, by considering the process from a non-trade, closed economy state to a single market between states. The first section deals with regional economic integration as distinguished from other forms of cooperation between nations. This section also deals with the place of regional integration in the multilateral trading system. The second section revisits integration theory, focusing on both the economic and political theories. It is a summary of why and how nations integrate their economies, and discusses the challenges involved in the postulation of new integration theories, especially from a legal perspective. The third and final section focuses on the theories of integration that are unique to the African experience, attempting to explain the relatively low success of regional integration on the continent.

I. DECIPHERING REGIONAL ECONOMIC INTEGRATION

The most straightforward definition of regional economic integration is offered by David Henderson, as the tendency for the economic significance of political

---

[1] B Balassa, 'The Theory of Economic Integration: An Introduction' in *The Theory of Economic Integration* (London, Routledge, 2012, 1st published 1961) 7.

boundaries to diminish.[2] Integration is an effort by states to erase constraints to trade between them, usually by the exchange of trade preferences beyond those extended to states that are not part of the integration. This typically takes on two dimensions. 'Economic integration' can refer to a *process* by which economies become more closely integrated, or the *end* – the *result or culmination* of such a process – that is, a situation in which integration is complete, so that political boundaries no longer possess economic significance.[3] From the political perspective, integration is the process whereby political actors in several distinct national settings are persuaded to shift loyalties, expectations and political activities to a new centre, whose institutions possess or demand jurisdiction over the pre-existing national states.[4]

Writing much earlier, Balassa highlights the complexity involved in defining regional economic integration:

> In everyday usage the word "integration" denotes the bringing together of parts into a whole. In the economic literature, the term "economic integration" does not have such a clear-cut meaning. Some authors include social integration in the concept, others subsume different forms of international cooperation under this heading, and the argument has also been advanced that the mere existence of trade relations between independent national economies is a sign of integration. We propose to define economic integration as a process and as a state of affairs. Regarded as a process, it encompasses measures designed to abolish discrimination between economic units belonging to different national states; viewed as a state of affairs, it can be represented by the absence of various forms of discrimination between national economies.[5]

Beyond the dual nature of the term 'integration', economic integration can take several forms that represent varying degrees of integration. In a free trade area, tariffs and quantitative restrictions between the participating countries are abolished, but each country retains its own tariffs against non-members. A customs union takes this a step further, by introducing a common external tariff on trade with non-member countries. A common market has the features of the first two, and adds the suppression of restrictions on commodity and factor movements with some degree of harmonisation of national economic policies, in order to remove discrimination that was due to disparities in these policies. The final degree is total economic integration, marked by the unification of monetary, fiscal, social and countercyclical policies and the establishment of a supranational authority whose decisions are binding for the member states.[6]

---

[2] D Henderson, 'International Economic Integration: Progress, Prospects and Implications, International Affairs' (1992) 68(4) *International Affairs* 633–653, 634.

[3] ibid.

[4] E Haas, *The Uniting of Europe* (1958, Stanford, Stanford University Press, 1958) 16.

[5] Balassa, 'The Theory of Economic Integration' (n 1) 1.

[6] ibid 2. See also General Agreement on Tariffs and Trade (GATT) Art XXIV:8 (discussed below) for WTO definitions of a free trade area and a customs union.

Regional economic integration can also refer to the externalisation of responsibility for policy and decisions, or, as Richard Sinott calls it, internationalised governance.[7] Internationalised governance can mean two things. The first is where a regional institutional body (European Commission, for example) has supremacy over domestic political systems, as defined in terms of the 'authoritative allocation of values'. Under the second meaning, states accept some minimal institutionalised constraints on their behaviour, through institutions for the management of interdependence.[8] This understanding of regional integration implies a spectrum, with the weakest form comprising a mixture of state and regional authority, while the strongest form is a fully-fledged international government system or political union.

A further layer of complexity encountered in the definition of regional economic integration is to be found in its constant evolution. In the past, the term 'regional trade agreements' was used to refer to the economic integration efforts between adjacent countries or countries in the same geographic region. In recent years, however, the countries involved in economic integration efforts are often countries or groups of countries from different regions.[9] Preferential trade agreements (PTAs) are increasingly common between countries and territories that do not have geographical proximity. Examples include the Economic Partnership Agreements between the European Union (EU) and countries in the African, Caribbean and Pacific regions (ACP countries), the United States (US) – Colombia Trade Promotion Agreement, and the India – MERCOSUR[10] Preferential Trade Agreement. According to the World Trade Organisation (WTO):

> One half of the PTAs currently in force are not strictly 'regional'. The advent of cross-regional PTAs has been particularly pronounced in the last decade. The trend towards a broader geographical scope of PTAs is even more pronounced for those PTAs that are currently under negotiation or have recently been signed (but are not yet in force). Practically all of these are of the cross-regional type.[11]

The WTO provides for regional integration in Article XXIV of the General Agreement on Tariffs and Trade (GATT). Indeed, the importance of RTAs in multilateral trade continues to grow, with 568 RTAs in force or notified to the WTO.[12] By 2011, half of world trade occurred among parties to regional trade

---

[7] R Sinnot, *Integration Theory, Subsidiarity and the Internationalisation of Issues: The Implication for Legitimacy*, 1994, EUI Working Paper RSC No. 94/13.

[8] ibid 4.

[9] P Van den Bossche and W Zdouc, *The Law and Policy of the World Trade Organisation – Text, Cases and Materials* 4 edn (Cambridge, Cambridge University Press, 2017) 671–672.

[10] Mercado Común del Sur (Southern Common Market).

[11] The WTO, *World Trade Report 2011, The WTO and Preferential Trade Agreements: From Co-existence to Coherence*, 2011, WTO, 6.

[12] The WTO's Regional Trade Agreements Information System (RTA-IS), available at http://rtais.wto.org/UI/charts.aspx (updated 6 July 2021).

agreements, although not necessarily on preferential terms.[13] The importance of RTAs cannot be overstated, with the average WTO Member being party to 13 regional trade agreements,[14] while all WTO Members are party to at least one RTA.[15] The obvious attraction of RTAs is in the offer of more favourable treatment in trade matters that members of the RTA provide each other. On the face of it, this runs contrary to the non-discrimination principles on which the WTO is founded,[16] and while this may be the case, it is not against the WTO's aspirations, as illustrated by the arguments in favour of regional integration below.[17]

Indeed, regional economic integration is an exception to the Most Favoured Nation (MFN) and national treatment requirements provided for by Articles I and III of GATT respectively. MFN treatment requires contracting parties to accord any advantage, favour, privilege or immunity to like products originating in or destined to all contracting parties immediately and unconditionally, while national treatment requires that all imported products be accorded no less favourable treatment than like domestic products.

Article XXIV:4 of GATT recognises the desirability of increasing freedom of trade by the development, through voluntary agreements, of closer integration between the economies of the countries that are party to such agreements. It further recognises that the purpose of a customs union or of a free-trade area should be to facilitate trade between the constituent territories. As such, the right to the formation of customs unions or free trade areas is protected by GATT, which goes on to define the two in Paragraph 8 of Article XXIV as follows:

(a) A customs union shall be understood to mean the substitution of a single customs territory for two or more customs territories, so that

    i. Duties and other restrictive regulations of commerce (except, where necessary, those permitted under Articles XI, XII, XIII, XIV, XV and XX) are eliminated with respect to substantially all the trade between the constituent territories of the union or at least with respect to substantially all the trade in the products originating in such territories, and,

    ii. Subject to the provisions of paragraph 9, substantially the same duties and other regulations of commerce are applied by each of the members of the union to the trade of territories not included in the union.

(b) A free-trade area shall be understood to mean a group of two or more customs territories in which the duties and other restrictive regulations of commerce (except, where necessary, those permitted under Articles XI, XII, XIII, XIV, and XX) are eliminated in substantially all the trade between the constituent territories in products originating in such territories.

---

[13] The WTO, (n 11) 72.
[14] ibid.
[15] Van den Bossche and Zdouc, *The Law and Policy* (n 9) 674.
[16] The Preambles to both the General Agreement on Tariffs and Trade, and the Marrakesh Agreement Establishing the World Trade Organisation.
[17] Section II.B of this chapter.

These provisions indicate the minimum expected requirements for a regional trade bloc. A free trade area usually is the starting point for the formation of a regional bloc, though this has, in practice, been more often called (and implemented as) a preferential trade area (PTA). Countries, usually in close proximity to each other and with some similarities (such as economic, historical, or political factors) agree to exchange trade preferences beyond what they have committed to in GATT, which is how it is defined in Article XXIV:8(b) of GATT. One of the older free trade areas is the European Free Trade Association (EFTA),[18] which came into force on 3 May 1960.[19]

The second stage typically is the customs union as defined by Article XXIV:8(a) of GATT and is the first step towards the erasure of national borders for purposes of trade. At this stage, members of a regional bloc eliminate duties and other restrictive regulations applicable to *substantially all trade* between themselves, and in addition adopt a common external trade policy, most commonly signified by the application of a common external tariff. The EU's predecessor, the European Economic Community (EEC),[20] is one of the oldest customs unions, having come into force in 1958.

The third stage, and at which point some regional blocs culminate, is the common market. This is essentially a customs union in which the borders between its members have been erased, for purposes of trade, and the factors of production as well as products move, unhindered, from one member's territory state to another in an internal market, common to all participating countries. The EAC Treaty defines it as the integration of the Partner States' markets into a single market in which there is free movement of capital, labour, goods and services.[21] The EAC Common Market Protocol provides for the free movement of goods, persons, labour, services and capital as well as the rights of establishment and residence.[22] The EU is currently the most advanced common market, bringing together its 27 Member States.

II. A BRIEF REVISITING OF INTEGRATION THEORIES

Theories of regional integration have evolved over the years and can be placed into two main categorisations: theories that explain *why* nations integrate,

---

[18] The Convention Establishing the European Free Trade Association was first signed on 4 January 1960.

[19] The WTO's RTA-IS, at http://rtais.wto.org/UI/CRShowRTAIDCard.aspx?rtaid=148 (accessed 16 January 2018).

[20] The Treaty Establishing the European Economic Community was signed in Rome on 25 March 1957.

[21] Article 1(1) of the EAC Treaty.

[22] Article 2(4) of the Protocol on the Establishment of the East African Common Market, herein called 'the EAC Common Market Protocol.'

and theories that explain *how* nations integrate. The majority of these theories are based on economics and politics, and the branch of economic analysis that deals formally with regional international economic integration is of quite recent origin. The core of the subject is the theory of customs unions, which is commonly regarded as having taken shape with the publication of Jacob Viner's study[23] in 1950.[24]

This section considers integration theories in four stages. The first stage summarises the classical justifications for trade based on David Ricardo's two-country model, giving a brief synopsis of the journey from the liberalisation of closed economies to regional integration. The second stage considers both the economic and political reasons for regional integration, while the third stage highlights some of the methods of regional economic integration. The fourth and final stage will summarise the effects of integration alluded to by Robson, Viner and other theorists.

A. From Autarky to Single Markets

Most of the justifications for integration are a direct result of theoretical economics. Building on Ricardian Economics[25] and the Heckscher-Ohlin model,[26] they extend the basis of trade to highlight the benefits of further erasure of trade barriers. In *The Principles of Political Economy and Taxation*, first published in 1817, David Ricardo proposed the theory of comparative advantage:

> Trade between two countries can benefit both countries if each country exports the goods in which it has a comparative advantage.[27]

A country has comparative advantage in producing a good if the opportunity cost of producing that good in terms of other goods is lower in that country than it is in other countries.[28] A representation of this theory can be made using two countries, A and B, producing two goods, potatoes and cars. If country A is a more agricultural country, it will be more efficient at producing potatoes, while B, more industrialised, will be more efficient in the production of cars. Without any trade between the two countries, it could be possible for both countries to produce both goods, but A would be inefficient in the production of cars, while

[23] J Viner, *The Customs Union Issue* (London, Stevens & Sons, 1950).

[24] P Robson, *The Economics of International Integration* 4th edn (London, Routledge, 1998) 7.

[25] D Ricardo, *The Principles of Political Economy and Taxation* (P Sraffa ed, Cambridge, Cambridge University Press, 1951).

[26] EF Heckscher and B Ohlin, *Heckscher-Ohlin Trade Theory* (trans and ed, H Flam and MJ Flanders, Cambridge, Mass, MIT Press, 1991).

[27] PR Krugman, M Obstfeld and MJ Melitz, *International Economics: Theory and Policy* 10th edn (Essex, Pearson, 2015) 58.

[28] ibid.

B would be inefficient in the production of potatoes. Before trade, the statistics for both countries would be represented by the table below:

Table 2.1 Production of Potatoes and Cars in A and B

	Potatoes (tonnes)	Cars (units)
A	80	20
B	30	60
Total	110	80

Table 2.1 shows that before applying the theory of comparative advantage, country A can only produce 20 cars for every 80 tonnes of potatoes it produces, while country B produces 60 cars for every 30 tonnes of potatoes.

Under Ricardian economics, if country A and B traded with each other and focused on the production of only those products in which they are more efficient, the production of potatoes in A would increase by 80 tonnes and B would produce 60 more cars. Country A produces 4 tonnes of potatoes for each car it produces, so giving up the production of 20 cars would yield an extra 80 tonnes of potatoes. Conversely, country B produces two cars for each tonne of potatoes it produces. If it gave up its production of potatoes, it would produce an extra 60 cars. This would leave the production between the two countries as represented in the table below:

Table 2.2 Comparative Advantage Production of Potatoes and Cars in A and B

	Potatoes (tonnes)	Cars
A	160	0
B	0	120
Total	160	120

By producing under the theory of comparative advantage, overall production of both potatoes and cars has doubled, and the excess potatoes produced in A can be traded in exchange for the excess cars produced in B. Such a situation takes advantage of economies of large-scale production, and creates economies that are more efficient. If a third country, C existed, then A and B could trade whatever they do not consume for whatever C produces, and so on.

While the Ricardian model on which the above example is based assumes a single factor of production (labour), Eli Heckscher and Bertil Ohlin proposed a theory that emphasises the interplay between the proportions in which different factors of production are available in different countries and the proportions in which they are used in producing different goods.[29] The Heckscher-Ohlin model extends the theory of comparative advantage by showing that countries produce based on what factors of production abound within their territories. In the

---

[29] ibid 116.

example above, two factors of production can be assumed: labour and capital. Both A and B would have fixed distributions of labour and capital, with A being more labour abundant, and B more capital abundant. Assuming that potatoes are labour intensive and cars require more capital, it would be more efficient for A to maximise the use of labour (in which it is abundant) in its production of potatoes, while B maximises the use of capital in its production of cars. Aside from the efficiency benefits, such a situation would yield higher earnings for the factors in each country when trade occurs.

Both the Ricardian and the Heckscher-Ohlin models show that production under comparative advantage with trade as the goal has great benefits for both trade partners. Admittedly, while these two theories provide the fundamental explanation for cross border trade, countless other theories have been advanced to extend or vary them. Integration theories are part of this extension. This body of theory investigates whether some geographically discriminatory change in trade barriers is of benefit to those countries that are party to the cooperation.[30]

World trade today operates on a system of tariffs and other barriers that restrict free trade. Integration theories therefore study how, by extending preferences under preferential trade agreements, states seek to liberalise their trade even further. As Balassa puts it, 'economic integration ... serves to avoid discrimination caused by trade-and-payments restrictions and increased state intervention, and it is designed to mitigate cyclical fluctuations and to increase the growth of national income'.[31]

The trade restrictions Balassa refers to are mainly in the form of tariffs and quotas. A tariff is a tax levied when a good is imported,[32] while a quota is a limitation on the quantity of imports.[33] The more important objective of tariffs is to protect the operations of domestic industries that compete with imports, and their secondary function is to raise revenues for the government.[34] Under the multilateral trading system, states may regulate their trade by the use of tariffs and quotas,[35] and since the coming into force of GATT under the WTO, states may not impose higher tariffs or new quotas except under specific exceptions in the treaty. One of those exceptions, discussed in section I above, is for purposes of extending preferences under regional trade arrangements.

B. Why Integrate?

The motives of regional economic integration are a mixture of economics and politics. Political motives may prompt the first step in economic integration, but

[30] JR Markusen, JR Melvin, WH Kaempfer and KA Maskus, *International Trade: Theory and Evidence* (New York, McGraw Hill, 1995) 313.

[31] Balassa, 'The Theory of Economic Integration' (n 1) 6.

[32] Krugman, Obstfeld and Melitz, *International Economics* (n 27) 238.

[33] ibid 239.

[34] Markusen, Melvin, Kaempfer and Maskus, *International Trade* (n 30) 245–246.

[35] Articles I and XI of the General Agreement on Trade and Tariffs (GATT).

economic integration also reacts in the political sphere. Similarly, if the initial motives are economic, the need for political unity can arise at a later stage.[36] The best example of this is the EU, which, through economic integration and trade liberalisation between its Member States created an even closer union among the peoples of Europe to avoid the recurrence of war.[37]

From the economic perspective, considerations such as avoiding economic depression, maintaining full employment, regional development, regulation of cartels and monopolies, and so forth, require state intervention in economic life. Consequently, any attempts to integrate national economies would necessarily lead to harmonisation in various policy areas.[38] Of course, it can be argued that many of these considerations double as political motivations, since states are concerned with them for political reasons, sometimes even more than for economic reasons.

The ultimate objective of economic activity is an increase in welfare. Juxtaposing states with individuals, Balassa argues that the welfare of states can be measured in much the same way as the welfare of individuals is measured, and that economic integration redistributes income between countries.[39] Welfare effects of trade imply that the world is more efficient and thus, richer, because international trade allows nations to specialise in different industries and thus reap the gains from external economies as well as from comparative advantage.[40]

It is difficult to discuss the reasons for regional economic integration without touching on, however briefly, the circuitous relationships between the integrating actors and the rest of the world. The study of these relations (regional bloc vis-à-vis the rest of the world) is of immense importance in explaining integration, and, as Haas argues, one result of the process of integration will certainly be the question of how the degree of interdependence among the members of the organisation is influenced by changing interdependence patterns vis-à-vis non-members.[41] The relationships between the EAC Partner States are compared with relationships between the EAC and the rest of Africa in chapter five, and with relationships between the EAC Partner States and the process of continent-wide integration in chapter seven.[42]

A related argument in favour of integration is what can be referred to as *the stepping stone argument*. As Peter Van den Bossche and Werner Zdouc argue:

> At a regional level, it may be possible to achieve a degree of trade liberalisation that may be out of reach at the global level. It has been argued that trade liberalisation

[36] Balassa, 'The Theory of Economic Integration' (n 1) 7.
[37] Van den Bossche and Zdouc, *The Law and Policy* (n 9) 675.
[38] Balassa, 'The Theory of Economic Integration' (n 1) 9.
[39] ibid 12.
[40] Krugman, Obstfeld and Melitz, *International Economics* (n 27) 188.
[41] E Haas, 'Turbulent Fields and the Theory of Regional Integration' (1976) 30 *International Organisation* 173–212, 187.
[42] Chapter 5, section I and ch 7, section III respectively.

will occur more quickly if it is pursued within regional trading blocs, and that trade liberalisation achieved at a regional level may serve as a stepping-stone for trade liberalisation at the multilateral level at a later time. Also, regional trade liberalisation may create significant economic growth within the region concerned, which can, in turn, generate more trade with the rest of the world.[43]

This can be related to the African Economic Community (AEC), which has, as its integrative pillars, the EAC, the Common Market for East and Southern Africa (COMESA), the Economic Community of Central African States (ECCAS), and others. The African Union planned for these regional blocs to coordinate their integration with the ultimate goal of merging into the AEC.[44] It was anticipated that this Africa-wide integration would increase Africa's participation in global trade, thereby leading to a quicker realisation of liberalisation aims.

Haas summarises the reasons for integration into three sets of 'background factors' that drive integration. These are social structure, economic and industrial development, and ideological patterns. According to Haas, integration proceeds most rapidly and drastically when it responds to socio-economic demands emanating from an industrial-urban environment, and when it adapts to cries for increasing welfare and security born by the growth of a new type of society. On the other hand, countries dominated by a non-pluralistic social structure are poor candidates for participation in the integration process.[45] In collaboration with Philippe Schmitter, Haas adds other factors, which, if strong enough, will drive integration faster. These are the size and power of the units (states) joining in the economic union, the rate of transaction among the participants, governmental purposes, powers of the union, decision making style, and the adaptability of governments.[46] Where economic unions have scored highly on these factors – such as in the EEC and the EFTA over time – the chances of 'automatic politicisation' were better than in the economic unions that scored poorly – such as in the EAC (1966–1977) and the West Indian Federation.[47]

A connected justification for integration is that it can provide an alternative to slow or to no progress in multilateral liberalisation. This occurs by leveraging the progress made in RTA negotiations on unresolved issues in the WTO, which also has the advantage of increased compliance with WTO rules across the board. To quote the WTO's former Director-General, Roberto Azevêdo:

> In some areas, RTAs are going further than multilateral rules and adding new layers of rules among the parties, while in others they tend not to change the existing WTO

[43] Van den Bossche and Zdouc, *The Law and Policy* (n 9) 674.

[44] The African Union, *The Lagos Plan of Action*, and *the Abuja Treaty Establishing the African Economic Community*. These are discussed in detail in ch 7.

[45] EB Haas, 'International Integration: The European and the Universal Process' (1961) 15(4) *International Organisation* 366–392.

[46] EB Haas and PC Schmitter, 'Economics and Differential Patterns of Political Integration: Projections about Unity in Latin America' (1964) 18(4) *International Organisation*.

[47] F Laursen, *Theoretical Perspectives on Comparative Regional Integration*, in F Laursen (ed), Comparative Regional Integration (London, Ashgate, 2003) 3–28, 8.

disciplines. Interestingly, in the areas where RTAs are introducing new rules, there appear to be common approaches taken by members. We can see this, for example, in service rules, dispute settlement, and intellectual property rights. This provides some reassurance to the recurring fear that RTAs represent a fragmentation of the global trading system.[48]

This increased cooperation at regional level with the attendant perceived fragmentation is discussed in chapter eight. It has been, at the same time, one of the reasons the WTO has not adopted flexibility, and almost paradoxically, an example of a flexible approach to trade liberalisation in the multilateral trading system.[49]

The reasons for integration are, understandably, endless. Some are related to the reasons for flexible integration discussed in chapter three,[50] such as common heritage shared by integrating states, as well as efforts to counter differences in integrating states. In addition, the reasons for integration are closely linked to the method of integration that will be applied by integrating partners, as discussed below. Some reasons are peculiar to the African story of integration, and these are dealt with in section III.A of this chapter.

This section has shown that the reasons for integration range from economic justifications to political motives. The next section briefly explores how countries go about the process of integration, focusing on Haas' theories of integration, and relates them to relevant examples from history.

C. How We Integrate

As discussed below,[51] theories on how regions integrate are difficult to postulate for several reasons, not least because of the diverse nature of the blocs. Each bloc follows a different path to integration, even where – as in the case of many African blocs – the members are the same. For example, all Partner States of the EAC were founding members of COMESA,[52] and yet the two blocs have had remarkably different paths and depths of integration. This section studies some writings on the integration process, relating these theories to the East African experience.

---

[48] Opening Remarks by the WTO Director General at the launch of Regional Trade Agreements and the Multilateral Trading System, on 29 September 2016, available at www.wto.org/english/news_e/spra_e/spra138_e.htm (accessed 18 January2018).

[49] See ch 8, section II.D.

[50] Chapter 3, section IV.

[51] Section II.E of this chapter.

[52] South Sudan is not a member of COMESA, but it seceded from Sudan, which is a member of COMESA.

In considering how nations integrate their economies, it is important to bear in mind the distinction between integration and cooperation. According to Balassa:

> Whereas cooperation includes actions aimed at lessening discrimination, the process of economic integration comprises measures that entail the suppression of some forms of discrimination. For example, international agreements on trade policies belong to the area of international cooperation, while the removal of trade barriers is an act of economic integration.[53]

Balassa went on to suggest two methods of integration: the 'liberalist' and the 'dirigist' ideals. Liberalism regarded regional integration as a return to the free trade ideals of the pre-First World War period within the area in question and anticipated the relegation of national economic policy to its pre-1914 dimensions.[54] Under this model, integration simply meant the abolition of impediments to commodity movements, so that the only mutually acceptable rule for close economic cooperation was the rule of the free market.[55] Wilhelm Röpke[56] suggested that European integration was nothing else than an attempt to remedy the disintegration of the post-1914 period, which destroyed the previous integration of national economies. Balassa was quick to criticise this approach, calling it a relic from the past whose application to present-day economic life appeared to be rather anachronistic.[57]

Under Balassa's dirigist model, integration could only be achieved through state trading and through the coordination of national economic plans without the lifting of trade barriers.[58] This method discards the use of market methods and relies solely on administrative, non-market means akin to André Philip's directed economy. Philip suggested that there was no alternative to a directed economy, since the market could not be extended by liberalising, but only by organising.[59] An extreme version of this view would be to have all aspects of the economy organised or directed, and while this is practically impossible today, Balassa proposed Maurice Byé's more practical 'stepping-up' approach.[60]

Byé's model is in response to Michael A Heilperin's proposition for a hybrid between the liberal and dirigist approach. According to Heilperin, free trade

[53] Balassa, 'The Theory of Economic Integration' (n 1) 2.

[54] ibid 7.

[55] ibid 8.

[56] W Röpke, 'Integration und Disintegration der Internationalen Wirtschaft', in W Röpke (ed), *Wirtschaftsfragen der Freien Welt* (Frankfurt, Erherd Festschrift, 1957) 500.

[57] Balassa, 'The Theory of Economic Integration' (n 1) 8.

[58] ibid.

[59] A Philip, 'Social Aspects of European Economic Cooperation' [1957] *International Labour Review* 255.

[60] M Byé, 'Free Trade and Social Welfare, Comments on Mr. Heilperin's Article' [1958] *International Labour Review* 38–47.

conforms to the nature of things and to the distribution of resources and 'men'[61] on the globe, while obstacles to trade are man-made.[62] He argued that the burden of proving that these obstacles were beneficial rests with those who either introduce them or desire the maintenance of already existing barriers to trade or indeed their further growth. Heilperin clearly admits that liberalism is advantageous but so is some level of protection and organisation, although for the latter, he argues that it can only be supported in exceptional circumstances, such as national defence and infant industry protection in the short term.[63] He appears to advocate for a cautious or accommodative liberalism; where integration is left to market forces but with some state intervention when need arises.

Haas discusses generalisations made in theorising on integration at different levels, but his views on integration in Least Developing Countries (LDCs) are the most important for the present discussion. According to him, integration in Africa has been largely symbolic and characterised by joint policymaking with economic objectives, which does not follow the European pattern. Actor expectations are prematurely politicised, preventing incremental bargaining on relatively non-controversial, shared objectives.[64] Although he was writing in 1970, this generalisation holds true, both for integration efforts at the time, and for today. For example, in the 1960s efforts to integrate the EAC, Uganda and Tanzania's unmet expectations were quickly blamed on colonial decisions, which it was claimed were skewed in favour of Kenya. In the current move to integrate the EAC, failure to implement the freedom of movement aspirations of the EAC Common Market Protocol have led Kenya, Rwanda and Uganda to have more open, joint policies on immigration, to the exclusion of Burundi and Tanzania. This recurring theme can also be explained by Haas' second generalisation: that bargaining with reciprocal benefits, especially where payoffs have to be deferred, is all but impossible because of the limits on resources. Since issues cannot be kept easily separated, national differences in size and power become divisive.[65]

Haas alludes to the importance of political coherence for integration in LDCs. The absence of pluralism makes the formation of voluntary groups on a regional basis difficult. Ideological ties between leaders, where they exist, are helpful to integration; ideological cleavages are most divisive and cannot be overcome by shared economic aims.[66] As has been the case in the EAC (Tanzania, a socialist republic vs. Kenya and Uganda, more capitalist countries), where the

---

[61] Heilperin uses the gender specific term, 'men', to refer to human beings. While this writer prefers the use of gender neutral language in such contexts, Heilperin's language is retained for this section.

[62] MA Heilperin, 'Free Trade and Social Welfare: Some Marginal Comments on the "Ohlin Report"' (1957) 75 *International Labour Review* 173, 178.

[63] ibid.

[64] Haas, *The Study of Regional Integration* (n 41) 618.

[65] ibid.

[66] ibid 619.

leaders of the different units in a bloc have divergent goals, regional integration between their countries is difficult to pursue.

Haas' final generalisation rings true for the EAC, especially in light of Burundi's and South Sudan's internal political turmoil. He argues that countries that are poorly integrated internally make poor partners in a regional integration process because of the reluctance of leaders to further undermine their control at home. This generalisation can extend to cover divisions within the leadership of integrating countries, with the result that there is no unified policy at the regional level that can be pursued by the leaders of the individual countries.

i. Haas' 'Pre-theories of Regional Integration'

Haas discusses three major 'pre-theories' of regional integration. These are federalism, the communications approach and neo-functionalism.[67] In a later publication,[68] he introduces the theory of disjointed incrementalism as the prevalent model in the EU. These are discussed briefly in light of the EAC's and the African integration process.

a. Federalism

Federalists are concerned with the primary importance of institutions and institution building, hence their efforts are devoted to the writing of constitutions and to research on the actual history of such federal entities as the US, Switzerland and (West) Germany. This would appear to be the path followed by the EAC in its integration process so far.[69] Further, federalists are preoccupied with the merits of rival methods of representation and elections and devote much attention to the proper division of powers between the federal, the 'national' and the local authorities. This has been quite common in the EAC, where regional replications of national administrative bodies (eg East African Court of Justice, East African Legislative Assembly, EAC Customs Authority, etc) are common. In this model, the terminal condition of the process of integration is the achievement of a federal union among the units being studied (nation states).

Haas' federalism has a dual nature: it can be used to unite hitherto separate jurisdictions, but it can also be applied to breaking up overly centralised national governments. In other words, federalism seeks simultaneously to meet the need for more effective governmental action in some domains

---

[67] ibid 622–630.

[68] Haas, *Turbulent Fields and the Theory of Regional Integration* (n 41).

[69] An interview with Abubaker Mohammad Moki, Commissioner Policy Development and Capacity Building – Office of the President, in Kampala (May 2016) proposed that the EAC way was 'Systems Theory': where systems and institutions are established in the hope that the public/market can take advantage of them. The literature covered so far does not identify systems theory.

(through centralisation) and the democratic postulate of local control and local autonomy (through decentralisation). The EAC integration process panders more to the former in that the ultimate goal of the integration process is to form a political federation.[70] In some ways, however, the second aspect is also present in the EAC. The EAC's principles of variable geometry and asymmetry[71] envision the need for Partner States to retain their autonomy and the liberty to implement integration programmes at their own pace.

b. The Communications Approach

This theory suggests (but does not assert or prove) that an intensive pattern of communication between national units will result in a closer community among the units if loads and capabilities remain in balance. While Haas does not define 'loads' or 'capabilities', it is possible to relate these to the East African experience in both past and present integration attempts.[72] For the present purpose, it is sufficient to define loads as the burden borne by individual integrating states, specifically in terms of the costs of trade and associated activities. Capabilities are similar to 'objective capacity' dealt with in chapter three, and include what can realistically be achieved or implemented by an integrating state.[73]

The communications approach proposes that 'transactions' – which Haas does not define, but can be interpreted from their context to mean any range of dealings from trade to cooperation on policy – are the basis for closer cooperation between states, which, where borders are shared, will lead to regional integration between the transacting states. Accordingly, 'if the rate of transaction is such and so, under conditions of balanced loads and capabilities, then elite responsiveness increases. If elite responsiveness increases, then a security community will arise.'[74]

This theory's terminal condition is a security community – whether it is of the amalgamated or pluralistic variety. The model can be associated with related factors that favour integration, including trust, friendship, complementarity and responsiveness, as it is believed that, in some form, they are essential to the survival of a new bloc. In addition, these aspects are strengthened by repetitive effort (ie transactions) – as opposed to smaller, one-time transactions – between states. By this measure, for example, Uganda is more likely to integrate with Kenya, one of its largest (by share of international trade) and longest standing

---

[70] Preamble of the Amended Treaty for the Establishment of the East African Community.

[71] Articles 1 and 7(1)(h) of the EAC Treaty, where the principle of asymmetry is defined as the principle which addresses variances in the implementation of measures in an economic integration process for purposes of achieving a common objective.

[72] Chapter 4 discusses the reasons for the collapse of the EAC in 1966 and 1967, including the relatively uneven cost borne by Tanzania and Uganda.

[73] Chapter 3, section IV.A.

[74] Haas, *The Study of Regional Integration* (n 41) 626.

trade partners, than it is to integrate with the Democratic Republic of Congo (DRC), its neighbour to the west.[75]

The communications approach, however, seems to be less developed than the federalist approach discussed above and the neo-functionalist approach discussed below. As such, it seeks more to explain (retroactively) than to predict relationships.

c. Neo-Functionalism

Proponents of neo-functionalism rely on the primacy of incremental decision-making over grand designs. They argue that most political actors are incapable of long-range purposive behaviour because they stumble from one set of decisions to the next as a result of not having been able to foresee many of the implications and consequences of the earlier decisions.[76] This approach is consistently phenomenological, avoiding normative assertions and systemic generalisations, favouring instead the instrumental motives of actors. It looks for the adaptability of elites in line with specialisation of roles, and takes self-interest for granted.

According to this theory, in the timeline of integration, ever more controversial (and thus, system transforming) policies emerge, starting from a common initial concern over substantively narrow but highly salient issues. Ultimately, a new central authority may emerge as an unintended consequence of incremental earlier steps.[77] The terminal condition here is a political community/political union – a concept that also subsumes a federal union but is less sweeping than a security community because it makes specific assumptions about central institutions and the progressive centralisation of decision-making among its members.

Haas is quick to offer criticism of the neo-functionalist model. The source of the neo-functional theory – the modern pluralistic industrial democratic polity – offers a rationale for linking the separate variables found in the neo-functional model in western Europe. Application to the third world has so far sufficed only to accurately predict difficulties and failures in regional integration. Meanwhile in the European case, some successful positive prediction has been achieved. While this is true, it is also difficult to predict the path of integration, especially in Africa, due to the diversity of paths followed and the aims of the different integration efforts. For example, Haas' neo-functionalism predictions are based mainly on economic reasons for integration, while in Africa, the economic

---

[75] According to the World Bank (http://wits.worldbank.org/CountrySnapshot/en/UGA/textview), in 2015, Ugandan exports to Kenya were worth US$427 million (18.84% of total export trade), while exports to the DRC were worth US$153 million (6.73% of total export trade).

[76] Haas, *The Study of Regional Integration* (n 41) 627.

[77] ibid.

reasons for integration are often secondary to other bases of integration, such as pan-African political concerns and regional security.[78]

The Inter-governmental Authority on Development (IGAD) is a classic example of this latter dimension, as it is mainly aimed at achieving peace, prosperity and regional integration in the Horn of Africa Region.[79] It has members that are already in other blocs together, such as Kenya, South Sudan and Uganda, which are all in the EAC, but also members that barely trade with each other, such as Eritrea and Ethiopia, both of which had closed shared borders until 2018. IGAD was created in 1996 to succeed the Intergovernmental Authority on Drought and Development (IGADD), which had been founded in 1986 to combat drought in the region.[80]

d. Disjointed Incrementalism

This model describes decision-making under conditions of uncertainty, where bargaining participants have partly convergent and partly opposing interests. It is a 'rational' second-best strategy under these constraints, which is valued as a process by certain analysts and actors because it is participatory and consensual, and is accepted by decision makers as a reality, good or bad.[81] While this reads like a varied definition of flexible integration, it was a favoured integration strategy in the early days of the European Union (when it was still the EEC) and of the EAC. According to Haas, the objective remains constant, though tactics and means of achieving this objective may vary in line with actor disappointments or satisfaction with benefits obtained. This is remarkably similar to the variable geometry method of flexible integration discussed in chapter three of this book.[82] As Chapters 5 and 7 illustrate, disjointed incrementalism is the path that has been followed by the AfCFTA in its integration, by building on the success of existing regional groups.[83]

Haas favoured disjointed incrementalism because it allowed for changes in the capabilities of the Member States. When the objective seemed attainable without the EEC – because governments were able to get what they wanted without further integration – disintegration would set in.[84] Incrementalism, then, is a rationality hanging on the choice of means considered appropriate by the group for attaining a constant basic objective. Haas proposed improving this model,

---

[78] See section III below, and ch 7 for detailed discussions of the reasons for integration in Africa.
[79] IGAD includes Djibouti, Eritrea, Ethiopia, Kenya, Somalia, South Sudan, Sudan and Uganda. (IGAD, *About Us*, at https://igad.int/about-us (accessed 5 January 2019)).
[80] ibid.
[81] Haas, *Turbulent Fields and the Theory of Regional Integration* (n 41) 183.
[82] Chapter 3, section III.A.ii.
[83] Chapter 5, section I, and ch 7, section I.B.
[84] In *Turbulent Fields and the Theory of Regional Integration* (n 41) Haas argues that states integrate for the purpose of achieving what they cannot achieve at a domestic level, such as environmental goals where the environmental aspects cut across borders and cannot be dealt with by individual states.

through rational-analytic decision-making and fragmented issue linkage, both of which are similar to flexible integration.

D. The Effects of Integration

Regional economic integration has effects on the integrating states and their economies. These include allocation effects (trade creation and trade diversion), international specialisation, the exploitation of economies of scale, terms of trade, the productivity of economic factors, profit margins, the rate of economic growth, and the distribution of income. This section considers those effects, mainly from an economics perspective. In keeping with most of the literature on the effects of integration, allocation effects and international specialisation will be dealt with in greater detail than the other effects, since they are the most significant of the effects.

i. *Resource Allocation and International Specialisation: Trade Creation and Trade Diversion*

The first effect studied by most classical economists is the relationship between regional integration, resource allocation and international specialisation. The basic theory analyses the effects of customs unions on resource allocation, specialisation and welfare at individual Member State level, at group level, and at world level.[85] These effects are dependent on the level of tariffs imposed by the individual states before they form a customs union. Where the prospective member countries initially enjoyed identical tariff rates on all commodities, and the tariffs are not redundant, no trade effects would follow from the introduction of the customs union if tariffs remained unchanged. For a customs union to have allocation effects, it is necessary that the tariff rates of prospective members should differ for at least some products, unless some of the tariffs are ineffective. The resulting harmonisation of tariffs gives rise to the allocation effects of the customs union.[86]

Allocation effects are present in two phenomena associated with economic integration. These are trade creation and trade diversion. According to Jacob Viner, trade creation is an effect in which trade between partner countries expands in accordance with international comparative advantage (and would have occurred under multilateral liberalisation as well). Conversely, with trade diversion, trade between countries expands as a result of the preferential treatment given to imports from within the region as compared to those from the rest of the world. Put another way, trade creation is the substitution of imports of

---

[85] Robson, *The Economics of International Integration* (n 24) 18.
[86] ibid 18–19.

lower cost goods produced by a country's partner for its own domestic products, while trade diversion is the shift in imports from the least cost exporter to the more expensive product from the nation's partners.[87] It is important to explore these two in further detail.

Trade creation has two aspects. The first is the reduction or elimination of the domestic production of goods that are identical to those produced abroad, since these goods are instead imported from the partner country. Peter Robson calls this the production effect. The second, which he calls the consumption effect, is the increased consumption of partner-country substitutes for domestic goods that formerly satisfied the need at a higher cost.[88]

Trade diversion, like trade creation, has two aspects. The first is an increase in the cost of the goods previously imported from abroad due to the shift from foreign to Partner States. The second is a loss of consumer's surplus resulting from the substitution of higher cost partner goods for lower cost foreign goods of a different description.[89]

Trade creation and trade diversion are useful measures of whether a customs union is beneficial. Both can be empirically measured, and in an ideal union, trade creation should be higher than trade diversion. A union that is on balance trade creating is regarded as beneficial to welfare, whereas a trade diverting union is regarded as detrimental.[90] It is difficult to give the ideal conditions for this optimal union because each one has varying circumstances that affect its allocation effects, but Robson summarises some generalisations:

- the larger the economic area of the customs union, and the more numerous the countries of which it is composed, the greater will be the scope of trade creation as opposed to trade diversion;

- the relative effects can be related to the height of the average tariff level before and after the union. If the post-union level is lower, the union is more likely to be trade creating. Similarly, if it is higher, trade diversion effects are more likely;

- trade creation is more likely where the member states are more competitive in the sense that the range of products produced by higher cost industries in the different parts of the customs union is similar. Likewise, the smaller the overlap, the smaller the possibilities of reallocation will be; and

- trade creation is more likely where the differences in unit costs of protected industries of the same kinds in different parts of the union are greater, since these will determine the allocation gains to be derived from free trade among the members.[91]

---

[87] TN Srinivasan, J Whalley and I Wooton, 'Measuring the Effects of Regionalism on Trade and Welfare', in K Anderson and R Blackhurst (eds), *Regional Integration and the Global Trading System* (New York, St. Martin's Press, 1993) 52–79, 54.

[88] Robson, *The Economics of International Integration* (n 24) 19.

[89] ibid.

[90] ibid 20.

[91] ibid 27.

From these generalisations, trade creation is more likely to be observed in the EU, a bloc currently composed of 27 Member States, than in the five-member EAC, which is more likely to be a trade diverting bloc. This flows directly from the generalisations. First, the EU is a much larger bloc, not just in terms of membership, but also in terms of the size of the economy and trade volumes across the region. Second, a rise in the average tariff after integration will most commonly lead to trade diversion, while a falling average tariff will lead to trade creation. In the EAC, the average tariff remained largely unchanged, falling from 12.9 per cent in 2006[92] to 12.7 per cent in 2012.[93] These two years are significant because although the EAC became a customs union in 2005, the customs union only became effective after a five-year transition period, which ended in 2010.[94] While it is conceded that correlation does not necessarily mean causation, total intra-regional trade for the EAC grew from US$1,617.1 million in 2006[95] to US$5,470.7 in 2012.[96] Of course, there could be other factors responsible for this growth beyond the 0.2 per cent drop in the average tariff but it can be argued as one of the factors for increased intra-regional trade in the EAC.

Robson's third generalisation is that trade creation would be more likely where the range of products produced by higher cost industries in the different parts of the customs union is similar. This is more likely in highly industrialised economies, such as those that make up much of the EU, and less likely in the less industrialised economies that make up the EAC. The final generalisation requires larger unit cost differences for competing products produced in different members of the customs union. While this is true for the EAC, it is not clear whether these differences have led to trade creation or trade diversion, although the statistics show a rise in intra-regional trade that can be associated with the customs union.

ii. The Exploitation of Economies of Scale

Economies of scale explain the phenomenon by which production is more efficient when it takes place on a larger scale.[97] This can be illustrated by a comparison of comparative advantage (explored in section II.A above) and reality. As already noted, comparative advantage is based on the assumption of constant returns to scale, ie that if inputs to an industry are doubled, industry output will double as well. In practice, however, where there are economies

---

[92] World Trade Organisation, *EAC Trade Policy Review, Report by the Secretariat*, 20 September 2006, WT/TPR/S/171, p 19.

[93] World Trade Organisation, *EAC Trade Policy Review, Report by the Secretariat*, 17 October 2012, WT/TPR/S/271, p 19.

[94] Article 11 of the EAC-CU Protocol.

[95] The EAC Secretariat, *The East African Community Trade Report 2006*, p 15.

[96] ibid, p 30.

[97] Krugman et al, *International Economics* (n 27) 178.

of scale, doubling the inputs to an industry will more than double the industry's production.[98] Applying the comparative advantage assumption of constant returns to scale to the example in section II.A, we can assume that if it takes one unit of labour to produce a tonne of potatoes in Country A, then doubling the labour will result in the production of two tonnes of potatoes. However, with increasing returns to scale, the output of labour in the production of potatoes in Country A would follow the trend in the table below:

Table 2.3 Labour Productivity for Potatoes in Country A

Output (tonnes of potatoes)	Labour Input	Average Labour Input
20	10	0.5
40	15	0.375
60	20	0.333
80	25	0.313
100	30	0.3

From the table above, each extra unit of labour results in a greater increase in potato production. Indeed, doubling the labour from 10 units to 20 results in a threefold increase in output of potatoes. It can also be seen from the declining average labour input that as production increases, less labour is required to produce each tonne of potatoes. These effects signify the presence of economies of large-scale production, which is a direct result of the specialisation that comes with international trade and resource allocation in a customs union. Each country specialises in producing a limited range of products, which enables it to produce these goods more efficiently than if it tried to produce everything for itself. These specialised economies then trade with each other to be able to consume the full range of goods.[99] This theory assumes a perfectly competitive framework in which homogeneous products are produced by firms that lack market power and incur few or no transaction costs.[100]

iii. Terms of Trade

Terms of trade refer to the ratio of the price of a country's exports to the price of its imports.[101] Put another way, 'terms of trade' is the cost at which countries exchange their products in international trade. If a country or group of countries gets more for what it sells (exports) than it pays for what it buys

---

[98] ibid.
[99] ibid 179.
[100] Robson, *The Economics of International Integration* (n 24) 82, and section II.A above.
[101] Krugman et al, *International Economics* (n 27) 151.

(imports), then its terms of trade have improved.[102] In general, terms of trade are assumed to not be affected by the creation of a customs union.[103] In the real world, however, terms of trade will change both among the countries within the union and between member and non-member countries. Peter Robson explains the relationship between integration and terms of trade:

> If the formation of a customs union does not affect the demand for imports from the rest of the world, the union's terms of trade will be unaffected ... Otherwise, there will be a tendency for the union's terms of trade with the rest of the world to improve. This effect will operate to reduce the loss that any trade diversion imposes, and it may suffice to eliminate it altogether if the fall in the price of the imported product is sufficient.[104]

While the effect of the creation of a free trade area is less clear,[105] the creation of a customs union results in improved terms of trade since the members of a customs union may be able to exploit their influence on those terms more effectively than if they imposed tariffs separately. Other things being equal, the greater the economic area of the tariff-levying unit, the more likely an improvement in its terms of trade with the outside world. In addition, the larger the customs union, the greater its bargaining power is likely to be, which will result in improved terms of trade.[106] A rise in the terms of trade increases a country's welfare, while a decline in the terms of trade reduces its welfare.[107]

iv. The 'Other' Effects: Post Vinerian Literature

Regional economic integration has further implications for the integrating region that are generally given less treatment in the literature. Amr Sadek Hosny reviews economic and political literature on theories of economic integration to summarise some of these effects.[108] They include the production and consumption effects of integration, welfare effects, 'secondary' effects, the effect of the size of tariff reduction, terms of trade effects, and the effect of integration between competitive vs. complementary countries. Much of the literature he cites is critical of Viner's more limited view which assumes limited products and limited countries, and does not account for several other factors that would

---

[102] AV Deardorff, *What do We (and Others) Mean by "The Terms of Trade"?*, Gerald R. Ford School of Public Policy, The University of Michigan, Discussion Paper No. 651, 23 May 2016, p 1.

[103] M Mikić, *International Trade* (New York, St. Martin's Press, 1998) 454 and Robson, *The Economics of International Integration* (n 24) 39.

[104] Robson, *The Economics of International Integration* (n 24) 39–40.

[105] ibid 40.

[106] ibid 40–41.

[107] Krugman et al, *International Economics* (n 27) 156.

[108] AS Hosny, 'Theories of Economic Integration: A Survey of the Economic and Political Literature' (2013) 2(5) *International Journal of Economy, Management and Social Sciences* 133–155.

affect the process of integration in a customs union. For example, citing R G Lipsey,[109] he argues that Viner's portrayal of trade creation as good and trade diversion as bad is an incorrect position, as economic welfare includes both production and consumption effects. He proposes a new theory:

> When a customs union is formed, relative prices in the domestic market of member countries change as a result of the reduction in tariff barriers between them. These price changes have two effects. A production effect as illustrated by Viner, and a consumption effect where union members will obviously increase their consumption of each other's products, while reducing consumption from countries outside the union.[110]

This theory differs from Viner's by rejecting the assumption that consumption effects are independent of the relative price changes caused by a customs union. Even if world production is fixed, there will still be some changes in world consumption due to the relative change in prices.

Hosny considers further effects of integration proposed by other authors since Viner. Citing J E Meade[111] and Ralph Hawtrey,[112] he argues that additional welfare may be gained if the secondary effects on complements and substitute goods are considered. This school of thought suggests that the repercussions a tariff reduction on a single commodity would have on all the quantities of all the products traded internationally must be studied in order to assess the actual effect of this reduction on the economic welfare of the country.[113]

Hosny proposes that the welfare effects of a customs union are dependent on the size of the tariff reduction. A small reduction in tariffs will raise welfare, while a large reduction may raise or lower it.[114] He bases this on, among others, Jaime De Melo et al's argument that partial preferences can yield a better outcome than a 100 per cent preference.[115]

Most of these 'other' effects are still relatively new, with some not being developed beyond their postulators. This book instead focuses on what has been accepted as integration theories, especially because they are relevant to the EAC experience. They have been useful in informing the direction, and evaluating the progress, of the bloc's integration.

---

[109] RG Lipsey, 'The Theory of Customs Unions: Trade Diversion and Welfare', (1957) 24 *Economica* 40–46.

[110] Hosny, Theories of Economic Integration (108) 136.

[111] JE Meade, *The Theory of Customs Unions* (Amsterdam, North Holland, 1995) 67–82.

[112] R Hawtrey, 'Review of 'The Theory of Customs Unions' by J.E. Meade' (1956) 66(262) *The Economic Journal* 337–339.

[113] Hosny, Theories of Economic Integration (108).

[114] ibid.

[115] J De Melo, M Panagariya, and D Rodrik, 'The new Regionalism: A Country Perspective', ch 6 in J De Melo and A Panagariya (eds), *New Dimensions in Regional Integration* (Cambridge, Centre for Economic Policy Research, 1993) 171.

The next section considers the challenges involved in arriving at a harmonised theory of integration, in spite of the fertile ground laid by Viner and other economists.

E. The Complexity of Theorising

These integration theories have received a fair bit of criticism from Haas and other authors. The federal approach has been falsified in the sense that none of its assertions/predictions have proven to be true. The neo-functional and communications theories have neither been falsified nor have they demonstrated positive predictive prowess outside western Europe; they have only been better in predicting failures. They have been accused of neglecting 'high politics', especially in the form of hiding such obviously important matters as international power and prestige, war and peace, arms and alliances under such mundane labels as 'interaction', 'task expansion', or 'welfare maximisation'. And even where some authors have stressed the unique qualities of high politics, they only provide critical qualifiers to both of these theories, without advancing a theory of their own.[116]

This last criticism reignites the chicken and egg debate of whether politics or economics drives regional integration. Pro-politics scholars hold that all political decisions are either important or routine, and that propositions seeking to relate political activity to economic or social objectives err intrinsically by assuming that human conduct in both spheres is identical. The devotees of high politics are thus forced to conclude that while common markets may flourish because of some people's grubby and greedy minds, such mundane arrangements will never lead to political union because that status demands that the pride and fury associated with nationalism be eliminated first. For Haas, whether 'politics' is more important than 'economics' is an empirical question, not a dichotomy given by nature.[117]

Identifying a specific theory with which to explain the process of integration is more complex than the preceding section would have us believe, mainly because integration itself is not linear. Sometimes, integration happens along multiple planes, with, in some cases, activities being achieved (*fulfilment*), abandoned (*retraction*) or even reassigned (*extension*).[118] The best example for this

---

[116] Haas, *The Study of Regional Integration* (n 41) 629.
[117] ibid 630.
[118] L Lindberg and S Scheingold, *Europe's Would-Be Polity: Patterns of Change in the European Community* (New Jersey, Prentice-Hall, 1970) suggest three possible outcomes of integration. Fulfilment of a postulated task on the part of practices and/or institutions created for integrative purposes; the retraction of such a task (ie disintegration); and the extension of such a task into spheres of action not previously anticipated by the actors.

is the EU, which grew out of three organisations (the European Coal and Steel Community, the EEC and EURATOM), each of which went through various stages of fulfilment, retraction and extension. Integration along each of these paths may have followed a different model, and this is true for the EAC too.

One major challenge presents itself in the constantly evolving nature of regional integration. 'End states' are a moving target, so that even where the ultimate goal is laid down in the constituting treaty – as the EAC has done – by the time that goal is reached, the theory defining that target has changed. For example, the EAC has decided to follow a conventional path to integration (preferential trade area, customs union, common market, monetary union and eventually, political federation). However, accepted practice for what constitutes each of those stages continues to evolve.[119] This is not helped by the fact that the EAC is implementing both its Customs Union and Common Market Protocols at the same time, which further blurs the lines that would define what the bloc is today. Haas proposes a shift from using end states as a measure, to measuring system transformation leading toward centralisation. This way, we would specify separate dimensions or conditions which would constitute a higher degree of integration as compared to a previous point in time.

III. PAN-AFRICANISM, INTEGRATION THEORY AND THE AFRICAN EXPERIENCE

Pan-Africanism remains a common thread throughout this book, and this chapter would be incomplete without a study of the African experience of integration, especially in light of pan-Africanist ideals. As defined earlier, pan-Africanism is based on a cooperative movement among peoples of African origin to unite their efforts in the struggle to liberate Africa and its 'scattered and suffering' people.[120] It is the belief in a shared heritage among Black Africans, both in Africa and in the diaspora, and aims to unify Black people wherever they may be. It is the perceived need to mobilise all peoples of African descent against racism and colonialism, and is perhaps one of the most enduring responses to the legacy of European slavery and imperialism.[121] As chapter seven reveals, earlier forms of pan-Africanism were geared towards achieving independence for African states.[122] These definitions are therefore based on that aim: uniting

---

[119] Haas (*The Study of Regional Integration* (n 41) 631) explains that the verbally defined single terminal conditions with which we have worked in the past – political community, security community, political union, federal union (etc) are inadequate because they foreclose real-life developmental possibilities.

[120] M Williams, 'The Pan-African Movement', in M Azevedo (ed), *Africana Studies: A Survey of Africa and the African Diaspora* (Durham, Carolina Academic Press, 2005) 175.

[121] T M'bayo, 'W.E.B. Du Bois, Marcus Garvey, and Pan-Africanism in Liberia, 1919–1924' (2004) 66(1) *Historian* 19–44, 19.

[122] Chapter 7, section I.A.

Africans all over the world to push for the independence of the states that were still, at that time, under colonial rule.

More recently, however, this has changed, with continental unification being the main goal of pan-Africanism. Since all African states are now independent, the focus for the push for unity has changed from the liberation struggles of the 1950s and 60s, to more collaborative efforts geared at development and securing markets for African products. This shift in pan-Africanism's focus has led to a rethinking of the goals behind continental unification, and although Kwame Nkrumah's dream of a United States of Africa[123] may have been shelved, efforts to bring the states together have recently increased. The most significant step in this direction was the transformation of the Organisation of African Unity (OAU)[124] into the African Union (AU).[125] The main difference between the two is that while the OAU was established mainly 'to rid the continent of the remaining vestiges of colonisation and apartheid', the AU exists to create 'an integrated, prosperous and peaceful Africa, driven by its own citizens and representing a dynamic force in the global arena'.[126]

Pan-Africanism, therefore, is the political philosophy behind the current effort to achieve political unity in Africa through the instrumentality of the AU.[127] According to the AU,

> Pan-Africanism is an ideology and movement that encourages the solidarity of Africans worldwide. It is based on the belief that unity is vital to economic, social and political progress and aims to 'unify and uplift' people of African descent. The ideology asserts that the fates of all African peoples and countries are intertwined. At its core, pan-Africanism is a belief that African peoples, both on the continent and in the Diaspora, share not merely a common history, but a common destiny.[128]

This definition of pan-Africanism presented by the AU reveals several things about both pan-Africanism itself and the new push for unification. First, pan-Africanism today remains true to its roots of 'solidarity of Africans worldwide'. This is no different from the early days of pan-Africanism, during which all Africans and people of African descent were considered to have a common heritage and a shared future. Second, the main goals of this unity have changed. While in the past, they were mainly aimed at securing the independence of Africans and African states, the AU views this unity as essential for economic,

---

[123] Discussed in ch 1.

[124] The OAU was established on 25 May 1963 by the signature of the OAU Charter in Addis Ababa, Ethiopia.

[125] The AU was established by the Constitutive Act of the African Union, signed on 11 July 2000 in Lome, Togo.

[126] African Union, *AU in a Nutshell*, available at https://au.int/en/history/oau-and-au (accessed 9 January 2019).

[127] S Okhonmina, 'The African Union: Pan-Africanist Aspirations and the Challenge of African Unity' (2009) 3(4) *Journal of Pan African Studies* 85–100, 88.

[128] African Union, *Echo*, 2013, p 1.

social and political development. This shift is particularly important because, as discussed in chapter seven, early pan-Africanism did not pay a lot of attention to economic and other forms of development, leaving these to the states to handle internally. Eventually, this led the states to focus on internal policies of development, neglecting regional and indeed continent-wide cooperation.

The third thing of note is the reference to the connected history and future of all Africans and African countries. This is a preservation of classical pan-Africanism, which to paraphrase Julius Nyerere, informs Africans all over the continent, without a word being spoken between them, that in relation to the European – or any other race – they are one.[129] The final thing is also based on earlier forms of pan-Africanism, and this is that it aims to be inclusive of Africans in Africa as well as people of African descent in the diaspora. This last point deserves some further consideration, as it goes to the root of any understanding of pan-Africanism.

There are two leading schools of thought on the origins of pan-Africanism, the Afrocentric interpretation and the Eurocentric perspective. The Afrocentric view is that pan-Africanism is rooted in Africa, and can be traced as far back in time as the era before Christ. The historical struggle by African peoples against foreign/external aggression, exploitation, occupation, domination and so forth did not begin with European contact with, or incursion into, Africa in the fifteenth century.[130] As far back as 1783 BC, African peoples in ancient Kemet (present-day Egypt) fought against foreign invaders and conquerors like the Hyksos ('Shepherd Kings'), and this went on through various resistances. Others included the Assyrians (Syrians) in 666 BC, Persians (Iranians) in 552 and 343 BC, and the world's first Europeans, the Greeks, under Alexander the Great in 332 BC. Similar conflicts are recorded until the Arabs arrived in 642 AD, and the French, under Napoleon Bonaparte, on 19 May 1798.[131]

This historical telling reveals that African struggles against foreign occupation predate colonialism, and that the Egyptian unification of the Upper and Lower Nile into one nation to fight external aggressors in 3200 BC was an act of pan-African nationalism. It formed one country under one rule to be able to resist foreign aggression and invasion, inter alia.[132] This view is in direct opposition to the Eurocentric view of pan-Africanism, whose name is itself an oxymoron.

The Eurocentric view is that pan-Africanism only started in response to the European slave trade, and some proponents of this perspective assert that pan-Africanism did not even start in Africa. For example, Walter Rodney argued that

[129] J Nyerere, *Africa's Place in the World*, in *Symposium on Africa* (Massachusetts, Wellesley College, 1960).
[130] K Nantambu, 'Pan-Africanism Versus Pan-African Nationalism' (1998) 28(5) *Journal of Black Studies* 561–574, 567.
[131] ibid 568.
[132] ibid.

Pan-African sentiments were born in the Caribbean because it was the first area of the world to which Africans were taken to labour as slaves. It is in that context that the necessity to define oneself as an African, if one came from the African continent, arose. Prior to that, it was historically irrelevant as an African in Africa would self-identify in terms of their particular ethnic group or clan or family group.[133] Ali Mazrui appears to agree with this view, by attempting to divide pan-Africanism into swathes based on where it is expressed. According to him, Sub-Saharan pan-Africanism limits itself to the unity of Black people or Black countries south of the Sahara, excluding the Arab states and Africans in the diaspora, while Trans-Saharan pan-Africanism extends solidarity to only those across the Sahara, regarding the great desert as a symbolic bridge rather than a great divide. Mazrui also adds to these two, the layer of Trans-Atlantic pan-Africanism, which limits itself to the Black diaspora and Black people on the African continent to the exclusion of the Arabs of North Africa and Black people with non-African origins, such as the West Indies and Brazil.[134]

Another branch of this school of thought suggests that pan-Africanism was racially inspired based on race relations between Black people in the diaspora and (most often) Europeans and white Americans. Thus, pan-Africanism was a racially conscious movement born outside of Africa.[135] Julius Nyerere's definition above appears to fall in this category as it proposes that the pan-African movement was born as a reaction to racism.

As might be expected, the Afrocentric school is critical of the Eurocentric view. Kwame Nantambu argues that Mazrui's microanalysis perpetuates the European divide-and-conquer manoeuvre by disintegrating the pan-African movement.[136] This criticism makes the argument that the Eurocentric view renders some Africans un-African by ascribing pan-Africanism to particular parts of the continent, especially sub-Saharan Africa. Sub-Saharan pan-Africanism, for example, expressly excludes Africans in North Africa and the diaspora, and this is an argument that is difficult to support for reasons Nantambu espouses:

> The pan-African struggle should not limit itself to any geographically dispersed or dislocated African peoples or their descendants. To do so is to play into the hands of the coloniser, thus enhancing the coloniser's continued control and exploitation. African specific geographic dispersal came about by the design, not the accident of slavery.[137]

---

[133] W Rodney, *Pan-Africanism with Special Reference to the Caribbean,* Lecture Given at Howard University, Washington DC, September 1975.

[134] AA Mazrui, *Africa's International Relations: The Diplomacy of Dependency and Change* (Colorado, Westview, Boulder, 1977) 68–69.

[135] JN Karioki, 'Tanzania and the Resurrection of Pan-Africanism' (1974) 4(4) *Review of Black Political Economy* 2–22, 2–3.

[136] Nantambu, 'Pan-Africanism' (n 130) 563.

[137] ibid.

An even greater criticism, however, is the fact the Eurocentric perspective erases the precolonial history of Africa, thereby doing the exact thing pan-Africanism exists to counter – ie granting primacy over African history and destiny to foreigners. To quote Nantambu again:

> The pan-African movement was not born as a reaction to racialism. If we were to accept such a dogmatic conclusion, then we would be using a Eurocentric, ahistorical and disjunctive analysis of our absolute African struggle. We would logically be succumbing to the traditional micro-approach that pan-Africanism began in 1900 when Henry Sylvester Williams had the parochial conviction that the "problems of Black folk in England were largely based on racism".[138]

How then, does the tussle between Afrocentric and Eurocentric perspectives fit within the AU's definition of pan-Africanism above? It boils down to who pan-Africanism serves. In the 1960s, pan-Africanism was aimed at the liberation of Black people, both on the continent in the form of the independence of states, and in the diaspora in the form of the civil rights movement in the US and other places.[139]

Today, as shown from the transformation from the OAU to the AU, pan-Africanism seeks to serve a development agenda that benefits Africans in Africa. This does not necessarily disregard Africans in the diaspora or Black people elsewhere, but it is no longer a liberation movement aimed at securing freedom from European colonisers, and is instead an economic and political push to achieve self-reliance. Chapter seven discusses this path in more detail, showing how integration in Africa started out on the basis of liberation spurred on by pan-Africanism, and evolved to focus more specifically on economic integration than the achievement of continent-wide political aims.[140]

At independence, most African countries lacked large internal markets, human, social, technical or material capital, or the physical or institutional infrastructure for industrialisation, even though they had an abundance of raw materials. Consequently, they were unable to capture any comparative advantage they might have had.[141] For example, the average GDP per capita (currently US$) for Sub-Saharan Africa in 1960 stood at US$118.6[142] compared to the European Union at US$876.5 the same year.[143] Needless to say, regional integration did not solve the small market challenge, though it is possible to argue that a small

---

[138] ibid 564–565.

[139] I Potekhin, *Pan-Africanism and the Struggle of the Two Ideologies* (South African Communist Party, 1964, republished by South African History Online) available at www.sahistory.org.za/archive/pan-africanism-and-the-struggle-of-two-ideologies (accessed 9 January 2019).

[140] Chapter 7, section I.

[141] K Kimbugwe, N Perdikis et al, *Economic Development Through Regional Trade: A Role for the New East African Community?* (New York, Palgrave Macmillan, 2012) 36.

[142] World Bank Data Bank, http://data.worldbank.org/indicator/NY.GDP.MKTP.CD?locations=ZG (accessed 11 October 2016).

[143] ibid.

market at independence (and indeed, today), was not able to absorb whatever intra-regional trade was generated by regional integration.

It is important to consider the motivations and paths towards integration common across the African continent. This is so because it provides context for the history and process of integration in the EAC, which is a recurrent theme in this research. As chapter four shows,[144] integration in Africa predates independence. The earliest form of the EAC dates back to 1917, and the Southern African Customs Union (SACU) has its origins in 1889.[145] This section considers the writings of scholars of regional integration in Africa, specifically on why they have had limited relative success when compared with RTAs in other regions.[146]

A. Reasons for Integration in Africa

Integration in Africa is driven by similar economic and political reasons as in other regions. This section will therefore avoid a repetition of the more general justifications for integration, and summarise those peculiar to African regional blocs.

Regionalism on the African continent has always had a strong political motive. The Pan-Africanist ideals of most African RTAs are an expression of continental identity and coherence, which distinguish the region's integration from other regions in the developing world. The resurgence of regionalism emerges both from within (internal dimension) and from external agents (especially the EU and the US) interested in African development.[147] As Oduor Ong'wen puts it,

> The internal impetus for integration of African economies is driven by the realisation that 'the continent has, over the centuries, suffered wanton exploitation of its natural, material, and financial resources at the hands of imperialist forces.[148]

Internal motivation to integrate is driven by the expected benefits of a more efficient use of capital, labour and natural resources. There is also a desire for the development of regional African markets instead of the high transaction, political and economic costs incurred so as to gain access to markets in Europe and North America. Further internal motivation is due to the reduced

---

[144] Chapter 4 deals with, among others, the history of the East African Community.

[145] Southern African Customs Union (SACU), *History of SACU*, SACU Website, at www.sacu.int/show.php?id=394 (accessed 29 January 2018).

[146] Sections II.B and III.A of this chapter discuss the reasons for integration, with the latter discussing reasons specific to Africa, while section II.C refers to examples of RTAs in Africa in the discussion how integration is pursued.

[147] Kimbugwe et al, *Economic Development* (n 141) 38.

[148] O Ong'wen, 'The Political Economy of Regional Trade Agreements in Africa' 7(6) *SEATINI Bulletin*.

overall transaction costs following the removal of barriers to trade and, for African industry, an exposure to regional competition in preparation for global competition.[149] On the other hand, external interests are pushing for regional integration in Africa as part of the search for larger markets to trade with, and to secure a source of raw materials by dealing with a larger regional entity offering uniform policies and procedures, in an increasingly globalised world.[150]

It would seem that the main motivating factor for integration in Africa is the need to stimulate economic development. For example, the Preamble to the EAC Treaty repeatedly states the need to strengthen economic and other ties for the fast, balanced and sustainable development of the Partner States. The reduction or elimination of barriers to intra-African trade, although not in itself sufficient, remains a necessary precondition for the accelerated economic development of African countries.[151] As Ong'wen states above, African integration is driven by a desire for states – and indeed regions – to aggregate their capacities and pursue development goals jointly. A detailed discussion of how integration leads to development has been conducted in section II of this chapter, and need not be repeated here.

The next section attempts to explain why integration in Africa has remained relatively unsuccessful, especially in achieving the development goals that seem to so keenly inspire cooperation between states.

B. The Slow Pace of Integration in Africa

In spite of at least eight regional blocs notified to the WTO,[152] integration in Africa has been much slower than, and not as deep as, it has been in other regions. It is arguable that this is due in large part to the fact that much of Africa remains less developed, and therefore struggles with the requisite capacity to meet integration obligations and targets. This is, however, only part of the story. The challenges to integration in Africa are summarised in this paragraph by Ombeni N Mwasha:

> Regional economic integration in Africa … faces some challenges including overlapping memberships due to the multiplicity of its economic communities. In reality, geographical proximity, cultural, historical and ideological similarities, competitive or complementary economic linkages, and a common language among the Partner

---

[149] Kimbugwe et al, *Economic Development* (n 141) 38.

[150] ibid.

[151] A Hazlewood, 'Problems of Integration Among African States', in A Hazlewood (ed), *African Integration and Disintegration: Case Studies in Economic and Political Union* (Oxford, Oxford University Press, 1967) 4.

[152] WTO RTAIS, http://rtais.wto.org/UI/PublicAllRTAList.aspx (accessed 5 September 2018.

States are among the desirable conditions for effective economic integration. The similarity and smallness of the African countries together with the competition between each other in the global market for the same agricultural products are among the reasons responsible for the past lack of success in the economic integration on the continent.[153]

This quote reveals several issues with integration in Africa, which should be discussed in some detail. One major challenge to integration in Africa is the simultaneous membership of many states in multiple regional blocs. Overlapping membership occurs when one country subscribes to multiple RTAs, making it difficult for the Member States to implement competing strategies.[154] This causes complications and inconsistencies due to conflicting obligations and divided loyalty,[155] discourages commitment to any of the organisations, and appears to be peculiar to Africa.[156]

In the EAC, for example, Tanzania is also a member of the Southern African Development Council (SADC), while Burundi, Kenya, Rwanda and Uganda are members of COMESA. In addition to trade blocs, states will be party to regional treaties of a different nature, so that in the EAC, Kenya, Uganda and South Sudan are members of the Inter-Governmental Agency for Development (IGAD),[157] while all EAC Partner States are also members of the Nile Basin Initiative (NBI).[158] Similarly, all EAC Partner States are members of the Tripartite Free Trade Area for Africa (TFTA), which combines the EAC, SADC and COMESA, and like all African states, all EAC Partner States are members of the African Economic Community (AEC/Abuja Treaty).[159] All six states have signed the AfCFTA Treaty, although Burundi, South Sudan and Tanzania have

---

[153] NM Ombeni, 'The Benefits of Regional Economic Integration for Developing Countries in Africa: A Case of East African Community (EAC)', (2008) 11:1 *Korea Review of International Studies* 69–92, 70.

[154] ibid 72.

[155] M Iyoha, *Enhancing Africa's Trade: From Marginalization to an Export-Led Approach to Development*, African Development Bank, Economic Research Working Paper No 77 (August 2005), p 5.

[156] E Osagie, *African Economic Integration: Lessons from Outside Africa, in The Challenges of African Economic Integration*, Selected papers for the 1992 Annual Conference of the Nigerian Economic Society, Ibadan.

[157] Discussed in section II.C.i, and n 77 above.

[158] NBI includes Burundi, the Democratic Republic of Congo, Egypt, Ethiopia, Kenya, Rwanda, South Sudan, The Sudan, Tanzania and Uganda. It is aimed at sustainable and equitable development of the River Nile Basin. It provides a forum for consultation and coordination among the Nile Basin States for the sustainable development of the shared Nile Basin water and related resources (NBI, *Who We Are*, available at www.nilebasin.org/index.php/nbi/who-we-are (accessed 5 January 2019)).

[159] In March 2018, the African Union members signed and began the ratification of the African Continental Free Trade Area, which is a culmination of the AEC and the Abuja Treaty. Further details of this bloc and its history are discussed in chs 5 and 7.

not ratified it by the time of writing. Represented graphically, this spaghetti bowl is shown in the image below:

Figure 2.1 EAC Spaghetti Bowl of Overlapping Treaty Memberships

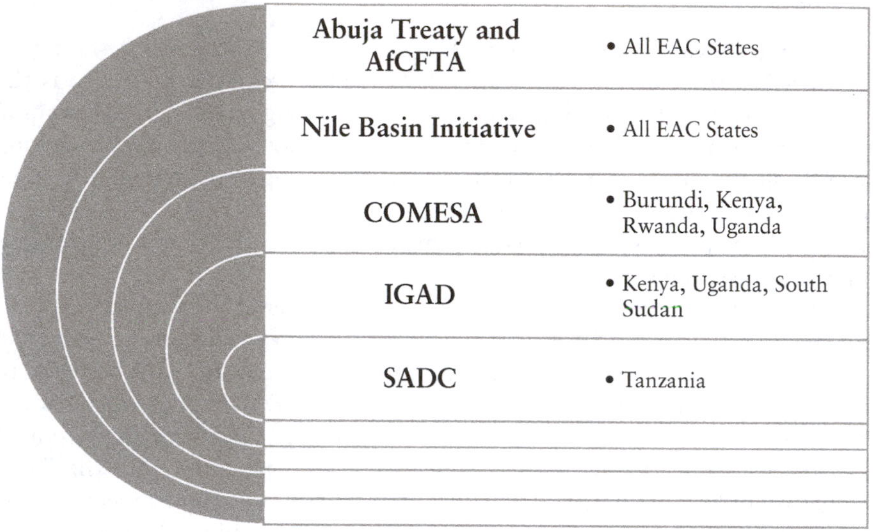

Abuja Treaty and AfCFTA	• All EAC States
Nile Basin Initiative	• All EAC States
COMESA	• Burundi, Kenya, Rwanda, Uganda
IGAD	• Kenya, Uganda, South Sudan
SADC	• Tanzania

When a Partner State subscribes to multiple treaties/RTAs, it becomes difficult for it to fulfil its obligations to any one treaty, especially where there is a potential clash in the aims of those treaties. For example, the NBI, while not a trade bloc, is geared towards the sustainable development and preservation of the River Nile Basin.[160] Arguably, conservation commitments to the NBI could run contrary to the industrialisation objectives of the EAC, which would leave all EAC Partner States with conflicting loyalties. This is, of course, compounded by the fact that these are just two out of five treaties to which all Partner States are party, and even then, there is at least one other treaty imposing obligations on the states. Another good example would be the conflict in obligations that Tanzania faces when it comes to trade. As discussed in chapter six,[161] Tanzania has displayed trepidation with the success of the EAC, since that success would threaten Tanzania's position in SADC. As a result, Tanzania remains aloof as far as its commitment to a speedy EAC integration is concerned. Integration, therefore, is likely to slow down as states grapple with their multiple obligations under the overlapping treaties.

---

[160] Nile Basin Initiative – *Who We Are*, NBI Website at www.nilebasin.org/index.php/nbi/who-we-are (accessed on 30 January 2018).

[161] Chapter 6, section II.C.i, and GO Omenya, *Coalition of the Willing as a Pathway to African Future Integration: Some Reflections on East Africa Regional Integration*, Paper Presented at the 14th CODESRIA General Assembly, 8–15 June 2015, Dakar, Senegal.

RTAs in Africa have been criticised for having less than optimal conditions for integration. While most blocs satisfy the need for geographical proximity, many lack cultural, historical and ideological similarities, do not have competitive or complementary economic linkages, and rarely have a common language. The sub-optimal conditions for integration are compounded by the similarity and smallness of integrating countries, which translates into lower opportunities for mutually beneficial trade. Africa's regional arrangements have the lowest levels of recorded intra-regional trade of all such integration schemes in the world, with shares of intra-regional exports typically below 5 per cent in African RTAs.[162] With the exclusion of the so-called 'big brother economies' (Kenya in Eastern Africa, Nigeria in Western Africa and South Africa in Southern Africa[163]), few countries have the capacity to significantly take advantage of regional trade agreements. In an ideal world, these three economies would benefit from an RTA between them if they had common borders and largely similar legal and commercial systems.

Integration in Africa has also been hampered by the absence of an internally generated unity. Writing about earlier integration efforts, Arthur Hazlewood described the 'illusory' nature of African unity:

> It was a unity imposed from outside for the administrative convenience of the colonial power – it was a unity of Europe in Africa, reflecting the hegemony of the metropolitan country over its various colonies. It was not to be expected that, with the removal of Europe from the scene, the unity would necessarily continue.[164]

This is an important observation for the integration of Africa, especially when related to Ombeni Mwasha's desirable conditions above, and to pan-Africanism. While Hazlewood refers to the unity between nations, it is arguable that similar unity did not properly exist in the states established through colonialism. Hazlewood describes it as 'odd that the "national" boundaries established by the colonial powers have proved so much more durable than the inter-territorial links established by the same powers'.[165] This endurance appears odd because before colonialism, most of the continent was administered without formal borders, with each administrative unit (mainly tribes and kingdoms) existing in traditionally – and often mutually – recognised delineations. The introduction of national borders in the late nineteenth and early twentieth centuries did not have any real regard for existing structures, with the result that tribes would often end up on both sides of national borders.

---

[162] Iyoha, *Enhancing Africa's Trade* (n 155) 6.

[163] International Monetary Fund, *IMF Data Mapper – GDP by Current Prices*, at www.imf.org/external/datamapper/NGDPD@WEO/OEMDC/ADVEC/WEOWORLD/AFQ (accessed 30 January 2018).

[164] Hazlewood, 'Problems of Integration' (n 151) 3.

[165] ibid.

From the pan-African perspective, the failure of externally-imposed unity between nations provides some justification for the pan-Africanist movement itself. This is so mainly because, as has been argued in section III, pan-Africanism seeks to foster internal cohesion between African peoples, based on shared values and a common heritage. A unity imposed by colonial powers would not achieve this for two reasons. First, it was a unity that sought to create new units based on the coloniser's values. Second, given the diversity of colonial masters that different regions of Africa had, continent-wide unity would be difficult, if not impossible, to foster.

According to Hazlewood, if the economic characteristics of the countries of Africa are examined in the light of these various criteria for a beneficial customs union, it would appear that the formation of customs unions in Africa was irrelevant, if not positively harmful. African countries may be competitive in the sense that many of them produce the same range of primary products, but their existing economic structures are hardly complementary. The removal of barriers between them would not have any great redistributive effect on production by lower-cost supplies from other members of the union. The generally low level of industrialisation rules out major adjustments of this kind.

In addition, external trade is not small in relation to domestic trade. On the contrary, exports and imports are both large in relation to the national income in the monetary sector of most countries. Finally, only a small proportion of the external trade of the countries of Africa is with other African countries.[166] For example, in 2017, Africa's intraregional imports were valued at US$62,488 million, which, when compared with the continent's imports from the rest of the world at US$491,999 million, account for only 12.7 per cent of Africa's imports.[167]

Another glaring difficulty limiting regional integration in Africa, on which both Ombeni Mwasha and Arthur Hazlewood agree, is the small size of the integrating nations and economies. The countries of tropical Africa are at a low level of industrial development, are highly dependent on foreign trade, and trade little between themselves. While some cover a large area, superficial area is not a significant determinant of economic size; population size is more important.[168] This smallness of numbers is accompanied by extremely low levels of income – on average US$1,484 per person each year (2020 estimates).[169] This, in turn, translates into a small market for manufactures in most countries.

---

[166] ibid 6.
[167] International Trade Centre (ITC), *Trade Map*, available at www.trademap.org/Bilateral_TS.aspx?nvpm=1||7||7|TOTAL|||2|1|1|2|1|1|1|1 (accessed 1 October 2018).
[168] Hazlewood, 'Problems of Integration' (n 151) 9.
[169] World Bank, *World Bank National Accounts Data*, available at https://data.worldbank.org/indicator/NY.GDP.PCAP.CD?locations=ZG.

In the 1960s, the cash market of most African countries individually was about the same size as that of a moderately-sized European town.[170] This trend remains true today, as shown by the comparison between the entire African continent and China. Africa's population in 2021 was estimated to be 1.37 billion,[171] about 70 million less than China's 1.44 billion inhabitants.[172] The GDP per capita for China in 2020 was US$10,500,[173] seven times the African income. Where a small total national income is distributed over a large geographical area, and where the market is geographically fragmented, the effective size of the market is even smaller than is indicated by the country-wide statistics.[174] Following Viner, a small country will reduce its welfare by joining a 'small' bloc that cannot supply a greater volume of imports to the small country, except at higher intra-bloc prices. In this case, the welfare of the trading bloc is reduced.[175] This is often the case with blocs in Africa, with small states coming together in the hope of taking advantage of economic synergies, but since none of their economies is developed enough to make the union profitable, the effort is ineffective and quite often, abandoned.

Integration in Africa is greatly hampered by the poor state of physical and other infrastructure in much of the continent. Integration is not simply a matter of lowering tariffs, although tariffs are a major – but not the sole – impediment to intraregional trade in Africa. For example, the removal of tariffs between Kenya and Ethiopia would not add significantly to the market for industrial products produced in either country, nor would it add significantly to their attractiveness to investors. The reason is that there is virtually no means of surface transport between the two countries. Tariff concessions will be irrelevant until the projected road[176] is completed.[177] Even when the road is open to traffic, the cost of transport between Kenya and Ethiopia might remain extremely high because of the distances to be covered, as well as relative insecurity in parts of northern Kenya. It would, therefore, require a high external tariff for a customs union to shift the advantage in favour of inter-territorial trade.[178]

---

[170] ECA, *Approaches to African Economic Integration: Towards Cooperation in Economic Planning and an African Common Market*, 7 May 1963.

[171] World Population Review, *Africa Population 2018*, available at http://worldpopulationreview.com/continents/africa-population/.

[172] World Population Review, *China Population 2018*, available at http://worldpopulationreview.com/countries/china-population/.

[173] World Bank, *World Bank National Accounts Data*, available at https://data.worldbank.org/indicator/NY.GDP.PCAP.CD?locations=CN&view=chart.

[174] A Hazlewood, 'Problems of Integration' (n 151) 9.

[175] DA DeRosa, *Regional Integration Arrangements: Static Economic Theory, Quantitative Findings and Policy Guidelines*, Policy Research Working Paper No. WPS2007, 1998.

[176] The project is described as 'in progress' on the LAPSSETT website, www.lapsset.go.ke/projects/highways/.

[177] Hazlewood was writing in 1967, but by 2018, this road was only partially complete. It has been subsumed in the Lamu Port-South Sudan-Ethiopia Transport (LAPSSET) Corridor. This is discussed in some detail in ch 6, section III.B.

[178] Hazlewood, 'Problems of Integration' (n 151) 10.

Closely related to this last argument is the significantly low level of intra-union trade in African customs unions. This has been attributed, albeit circuitously, to the small size of African economies, small markets, and low purchasing power in these states. Given the appropriate investments in infrastructure, the widening of potential markets which would result from a freeing of intra-African trade could play a vital part in the industrialisation of the continent. Not that these two measures would in themselves be enough; they are necessary but not sufficient conditions for industrialisation.[179] Such industrialisation would stimulate growth of regional trade in Africa, especially if policies are aimed at producing for wider markets instead of the more common import substitution approach. Import substitution directed towards national markets will be a far less successful and more costly process than if it were directed to the market of a group of states.[180]

Even with industrialisation, intra-regional trade will remain low, and consequently, so will the success of customs unions in Africa. The preference created by a customs union is of great importance in switching demand to intra-union trade, but is not the only aspect of a customs union which needs to be taken into account. The absence of this preference is not the only effect of the absence of a union. The existence of tariffs between the countries of Africa is also an indication of nationally-oriented development policies, or rather, of development policies which take no account of the plans of neighbouring countries. Under these circumstances, the development of intra-African trade is not just a matter of competing in a neighbouring market with the products of outside, industrially-developed countries, but of having to compete with the national industry of the neighbour, an industry its government is determined to protect. These are not circumstances in which intra-African trade and intra-African specialisation are likely to develop.[181]

Another challenge making regional integration in Africa more complex, especially at customs union level, is the fact that many countries are landlocked, and must get their imports through the ports of neighbouring countries. In such a union there will have to be arrangements for the allocation of customs revenue to the inland country. No problem arises with respect to imports consigned direct to the inland country, but many of its imports will probably be re-consigned from the country into which they are originally imported. Unless customs posts are to be maintained between the members of the union – which would defeat the purpose of a customs union – arrangements will have to be devised for the recording or estimation of the value of these transfers of imported goods, and for the payment of the customs revenue to the country of final consumption. These arrangements are liable always to be a matter of controversy, with

---

[179] ibid 11.
[180] ibid.
[181] ibid 11–12.

the inland country believing it does not receive its fair share of revenue from customs duties.[182] As discussed in chapter four, such controversies were at the heart of the collapse of the EAC in 1977.[183]

From the history of integration in Africa, a common threat to integration is the disequilibrium effect of trade blocs. As was the case with the EAC in the early 1960s and again in the 1970s, regional market mechanisms tend to favour one – usually the larger – economy over the others.[184] Where market forces are allowed to freely operate within a tariff-free market area, the benefits are likely to be unequally distributed between the associated states. Some countries might even lose from integration, although the area, taken as a whole, clearly benefits. The losing states will not voluntarily adhere to such a union, and even states which are only relative losers, gaining less than others, may come (probably mistakenly) to believe that they would be absolute gainers from separation.[185] The recent exit of the UK from the European Union is perhaps the best illustration of this belief.

In a regulated economic union, measures are introduced to correct the inequalities that develop within a laisser-faire union. The difficulty with regulated integration is that it requires even further surrender of autonomy in the field of economic policy.[186] This, however, is not the only challenge to a regulated union. As was the case with the EAC's second attempt at integration from 1967–1977, such regulation is often confusing and complex to establish, and usually leaves businesses in Member States unclear as to how to trade.[187]

The disequilibrium effect also leads to another challenge: the tendency for the polarisation of development in some members of the union. Development will tend to take place mainly in the countries which, for one reason or another, are the most attractive for industrial investment. The clustering of industry will generally be associated with and reinforced by disequalising movements of capital and labour. The cumulative causation, which is an important feature of the development process, reinforces and increases the divergences between the relatively advanced and relatively backward members of the customs union.[188] This effect was one of the causes of the EAC's first collapse in the mid-1960s, with Kenya attracting more development and benefiting more from regional trade than Tanzania and Uganda. A union in which the benefits are unequally distributed is unlikely to survive for long. The weaker countries will come to believe (even if wrongly) that it would be better for them to go it alone. This is why

---

[182] ibid 14.
[183] Chapter 4, section II.D.
[184] Chapter 4, section II.D deals in detail with the reasons for the EAC's collapse in the post-independence period.
[185] Hazlewood, 'Problems of Integration' (n 151) 14.
[186] ibid.
[187] Chapter 4, section II.D.
[188] Hazlewood, 'Problems of Integration' (n 151) 15.

it is unrealistic to emphasise the benefits to be gained in the aggregate from a common market, while neglecting the question of their distribution. Beyond a certain point, the actual existence of the gains may depend on their tolerable distribution.[189]

IV. SUMMARY: THEORIES, REALITIES AND THE ENSUING FRUSTRATION

This chapter has been an attempt to look at the theories that drive regional economic integration, with some focus on why efforts at integration in Africa have not been as successful as hoped. From the literature and the African experience, the realities on the continent make it difficult to achieve the same goals as other, especially more developed regions. This frustration remains even where pan-Africanism has driven integration, as discussed in chapter seven.[190] Where some success is registered, the rate of success is slow, even when compared with regions that paralleled Africa in the past, such as Asia and Latin America. This, of course, would easily lead to the belief that regional economic integration in Africa is futile. This is not necessarily the case, as can be illustrated from some of the more successful blocs on the continent, especially SADC and more recently, the EAC. The successes of the latter are considered in chapter four of this book. The next chapter considers flexible integration from a mostly theoretical perspective, attempting to explain why it exists, and the different forms it takes.

[189] ibid.
[190] Chapter 7, section I.A.

3

Flexible Regional Economic Integration

THIS CHAPTER IS a review of decades of literature on flexible regional economic integration. It has five main sections, with the first two sections dealing with relevant definitions, and taking a detailed look at the EAC's definition of its version of flexible regional economic integration – variable geometry. The third section takes the definitions a step further in considering how flexible regional economic integration has been applied in various integration projects, looking at theory and giving examples of this application. This section also focuses on the application of flexible regional economic integration in Africa, and considers literature on its use in the European Union (EU) and other blocs. The fourth and fifth sections respectively consider justifications and criticisms of flexible integration in its different forms.

I. A DEFINITION OF FLEXIBLE REGIONAL INTEGRATION

The literature on flexible regional economic integration is as varied in definitions and descriptions as there are authors. In fact, the main challenge with arriving at a satisfactory definition is the diversity of literature and the variations in which it has been applied. To quote Alexander Stubb, who calls it 'differentiated integration':

> The debate about *differentiated* integration – i.e. the general mode of integration strategies which try to reconcile heterogeneity within the European Union – is characterised by an excess of terminology which can give even the most experienced specialist of European integration a severe case of semantic indigestion. Two-speed, multi-speed, step-by-step, strengthened solidarity, graduated integration, hard core, variable integration, concentric circles, two-tier, multi-tier, multi-track, two-track, 'swing-wing', circles of solidarity, variable speed, imperial circles, pick-and-choose, overlapping circles, structural variability, opt-in, opt-out, opt-down, bits-and-pieces, ad libitum integration, multi-level, two-level, restrained differentiation, flying geese, magnetic fields, hub-and-spoke and many circles are a few examples of the rhetoric in English.[1]

---

[1] A C-G. Stubb, 'A Categorisation of Differentiated Integration' (1996) 34(2) *Journal of Common Market Studies*.

This quote is a representation of the dilemma of definition that surrounds flexible regional economic integration. While the East African Community (EAC) has adopted the nomenclature of 'variable geometry' for the flexibility prescribed in the EAC Treaty, the literature reveals that there are as many names for this flexibility as there have been attempts to apply it. However, even with this diversity, some core attributes remain, which can reasonably be used interchangeably with the term variable geometry. The main factor common to all the names and definitions of flexible regional economic integration encountered in this study is the element of flexibility, denoting an expectation of non-uniformity in the implementation of treaty provisions.

This section takes, as a starting point, the definition of variable geometry as used in the EAC Treaty, and considers its components in light of existing literature. Article 1 of the Amended Treaty for the Establishment of the East African Community defines variable geometry in some detail:

> The principle of variable geometry means *the principle of flexibility which allows for progression in cooperation among a subgroup of members in a larger integration scheme in a variety of areas and at different speeds.*[2] (emphasis added)

Article 7(1)(e) of the Treaty, which provides for the application of the principle, has a slightly different wording:

> The principles that shall govern the practical achievement of the objectives of the Community shall include … *the principle of variable geometry which allows for progression in co-operation among groups within the Community for wider integration schemes in various fields and at different speeds.* (emphasis added)

This variation in wording and its effect are investigated in chapter five, which considers the history of flexible regional economic integration in the EAC Treaty.[3]

Several implications can be deduced from this definition, and these are considered below.

A. A Principle of Flexibility

The first thing to note about the EAC definition of variable geometry is that it is a principle of flexibility. The term 'flexibility' in trade law circles has become synonymous with 'special and differential treatment'. In their most basic form, flexibility provisions in the World Trade Organisation (WTO) rules provide extra time for developing countries to fulfil their obligations, and are designed to increase their trading opportunities through greater market access. They also

---

[2] Article 1(1) of the EAC Treaty (the interpretation Article).
[3] Chapter 5, section I.

require WTO members to safeguard the interests of developing countries when adopting some domestic measures and altogether provide various means of helping developing countries (benefit more from trade).[4] This flexibility allows developing countries to have less burdensome obligations than their developed counterparts. On this basis, Part IV of GATT was designed on the basis of non-reciprocity, which arguably is a variant of variable geometry.

Under Paragraph 3(b), Article XXVIII bis of the General Agreement on Tariffs and Trade (GATT), tariff negotiations are to be conducted on a basis which takes account of the needs of less-developed countries for a more flexible use of tariff protection to assist their economic development and the special needs of these countries to maintain tariffs for revenue purposes. It is on the basis of such flexibility that special and differential treatment provisions exist in the WTO, whether as non-reciprocity in tariff elimination,[5] or as longer periods for adjusting legal regimes on intellectual property.[6]

While this may be true with regard to the flexibility available to developing nations in most – if not all – WTO agreements, the flexibility in the EAC definition of variable geometry is unique since it applies laterally between states of similar or almost similar levels of development. It is nonetheless beneficial to borrow from the WTO application of 'flexibility' and 'special and differential treatment' to explain the flexibility in the EAC's variable geometry.

In regional economic integration, flexibility is more diverse than it is in the WTO context. It is the differentiated (instead of uniform) treatment among members of the same region, in terms of time, issue areas and members.[7] Of course, the flexibility does depend on the level of political will and capacity to implement measures agreed upon by the parties, and can take on several forms. Alexander Stubb categorises these into three types. The first would be multi-speed integration. Here, the pursuit of common objectives is driven by a core group of Member States which are both able and willing to pursue some policy areas further, the underlying assumption being that others will follow later. The second type is variable geometry, which admits to unattainable differences within the integrative structure by allowing permanent or irreversible separation between a core of countries and lesser developed integrative units. The third, and extreme opposite of multi-speed integration, is à la carte, a differentiated integration whereby respective Member States are able to pick-and-choose, as

---

[4] S Lester, B Mercurio and A Davies, *World Trade Law: Text Materials and Commentary* (Oxford, Hart Publishing, 2012) 822.

[5] Article XXXVI(8) of GATT.

[6] Article 65(2) of the WTO Agreement on Trade Related Aspects of Intellectual Property (The TRIPS Agreement).

[7] M Filadoro, *Flexibility in the EU External Relations With Other Regions: The Cases of MERCOSUR, CAN, EFTA, ENP, Western Balkans and ACP*, unpublished, available at www.ies.be/files/Filadoro-A2.pdf (accessed 18 March 2016) 5.

from a menu, in which policy area they would like to participate, whilst at the same time maintaining a minimum number of common objectives.[8]

In all three approaches above, integration remains the goal, with the modification that in all three, it does not happen at the same rate for all members. Stubb's first model implies that multi-speed integration envisions a common end, albeit that the Partner States (as is the case in the EAC[9]) have agreed to achieve integration goals at different speeds. Stubb's variable geometry is narrower than the EAC definition, since it focuses only on the scope of integration as determined by the differences each Partner State faces at a domestic level. The à la carte model seems to be almost anti-integration, since partners would choose what areas/subject matter they would like to open up to integration.[10] Again, as seen in section I.E below, the EAC definition envisions this, and it is fair to propose that Kenya, Rwanda and Uganda chose more areas than Burundi and Tanzania did.[11]

In evaluating flexible regional economic integration in Africa, the EAC's use of variable geometry is compared with the literature's portrayal of flexibility. As chapters five, six and seven show, the EAC's and indeed Africa's variable geometry is mostly an accurate representation of what is predicted by the authors reviewed in this chapter.

B. Progression in Cooperation

The second implication of the EAC's variable geometry is that it allows or indeed facilitates *progression in cooperation*. This strongly suggests that the aim of the principle is to prevent stalling in the integration process where some member states would be willing to progress and others not willing, or unable to. While it is a positive statement, it can be interpreted as having a negative implication: 'to prevent impediments to integration that would otherwise arise out of a single undertaking'. As will be seen later,[12] flexible regional economic integration (specifically in the EAC) exists precisely for that purpose – to deepen cooperation in spite of differences between the Member States that would otherwise slow down the process of integration.

It has been argued, in the EU context,[13] that variable geometry's starting point is the admission that there will inevitably be substantial differences

---

[8] Stubb, 'A Categorisation of Differentiated Integration' (n 1).

[9] Discussed in section I.F below.

[10] Sir Stephen Wall (Chair) et al, *Flexibility and the Future of the European Union,* Federal Trust Report on Flexible Integration in the European Union, October 2005, p 9.

[11] South Sudan was not a member of the EAC by the time Kenya, Rwanda and Uganda started pursuing closer cooperation.

[12] Section IV below, ch 5, section II, and ch 6, section II.C.

[13] Wall et al, *Flexibility and the Future of the European Union* (n 10).

between the integrative capacities and desires of 25 or more Member States. It would be surprising if even in the long term, these capacities and desires can fully converge. Variable geometry therefore offers new possibilities as a general strategy in negotiations leading to greater integration, a notion that points to its utilisation to foster progress in cooperation.[14]

In the EAC, progression in cooperation can be along several planes. For example, Kenya, Rwanda and Uganda attempted this by the creation of the Northern Corridor Integration Projects (NCIP), which is charged with several areas of cooperation, including infrastructure, immigration, regulation, land ownership and fast tracking political federation.[15] Chapter six of this book evaluates them in greater detail, but it is important to note at this point that this closer cooperation is a direct result of the variable geometry adopted by Article 7(1)(e) of the EAC Treaty.

C. A Subgroup of Members

The EAC's model of variable geometry allows for cooperation *among a subgroup of members*. This is, along with flexibility, one thing on which most, if not all, of the literature agrees – that variable geometry (by whichever name) allows a subset of a larger group to cooperate more than the whole group. The subgroup in the EAC that is most closely studied by this research is made up of Kenya, Rwanda and Uganda.

In the EU context, this concept refers to a situation in which some countries may integrate more (or faster) than others.[16] As a strategy, it allows negotiations of one or more particular issues to lead to an agreement that is not binding on all the parties. This is a preferable alternative to strategies that require *all* parties to be bound by *all* of the terms agreed in a complex many-country, many-issue negotiation.[17] While the EAC is not a many-country setting, there are many diversities that necessitated the inclusion of variable geometry and its eventual application.

The multiform nature of flexible integration has been categorised on the basis of two axes of differentiation: the scope of the enhanced cooperation, and the treaty base of the flexible arrangement.[18] Under the first scope, 'ad hoc groups' made up of a limited group of Member States try to implement

---

[14] P Lloyd, 'The Variable Geometry Approach to International Economic Integration' (2009) 1(1) *International Journal of Business and Development Studies* 51–66, 64.

[15] NCIP website, www.nciprojects.org (accessed 9 November 2015).

[16] R Leal-Arcas, 'The Fragmentation of International Trade Law: Is Now the Time for Variable Geometry?' (2011) 12(2) *The Journal of World Investment and Trade* 145–195, 177.

[17] Lloyd, 'The Variable Geometry Approach' (n 14) 52.

[18] F Dehousse, W Coussens and G Grevi, *Integrating Europe: Multiple Speeds – One Direction?* EPC Working Paper No. 9, April 2004.

a programme of action, comprehending a whole set of measures, in one specific domain. This subgroup can be taken a step further, with the subgroup forming an 'avant-garde' with a fixed composition that proceeds in different areas at the same time. This study tests whether the subgroup of Kenya, Rwanda and Uganda have constituted themselves into a 'first mover' club that hopes to spur faster integration, and whether this has been successful.[19]

Arguably, this introduces the idea that the flexible integration can be along the lines of participation rather than subject matter. As Stubb's variable geometry demonstrates, differentiated integration can take place due to country-specific differences. Chapter six considers the differences that led the NCIP to rise to the exclusion of Burundi and Tanzania, specifically by considering the historical (legal, economic and political) factors that led to the selection of those members of the subgroup. It also argues (in agreement with a lot of the literature) that flexible integration happens along two planes: implementation (of subject matter) and participation (of Member States).

D. A Larger Integration Scheme

In order to allow for a differential or variable speed of obligations among negotiating parties, there must be more than two negotiating parties.[20] In the context of the EAC's definition, variable geometry is only possible where some members of the bloc are 'hived off' and pursue closer cooperation between themselves to the exclusion of other members in the group. This aspect is an extension of the foregoing discussion on subgroups, and is exemplified by initiatives such as the Schengen Agreement, Eurozone, and the NCIP, which in their creation do not distinguish themselves from the regional grouping in which they are created. This would seek, at least in theory, to preserve the unity of the bloc, because the differentiated integration is only allowed to exist temporarily. The goals and objectives of integration in a multi-speed arena are set jointly at community level to prevent undermining solidarity and the community system.[21]

Similar arguments have been made in favour of the other methods of flexible regional economic integration, including the seemingly exclusive 'avant-garde' subgroup. The general line of argument is that these subgroups create a leadership trail, with their deeper integration gradually spreading to the other members that may not have started out at the same level of integration. In multi-speed differentiation, the 'slower' states eventually catch up with the 'faster' states, since the ultimate goals of the integration scheme remain the same.

---

[19] Chapter 6, section III.
[20] Lloyd, 'The Variable Geometry Approach' (n 14) 52.
[21] Stubb, 'A Categorisation of Differentiated Integration' (n 1).

This book proposes that variable geometry in the EAC will result in a disintegrated bloc, with Kenya, Rwanda and Uganda being more deeply integrated among themselves than with Burundi, Tanzania and possibly South Sudan.[22] On the continental level, the use of flexible integration (through disjointed incrementalism, discussed in chapter two)[23] has had a more positive result, although as chapter seven demonstrates, the results have been slow, and the method has been abandoned in favour of a single agreement that allows for variable geometry instead.[24] This view is, arguably, contrary to what most of the literature proposes, except with regard to à la carte integration, which has been described as a denial of future integration.[25]

E. A Variety of Areas

The EAC Treaty allows variable geometry to be pursued in a variety of areas. On a wider scale, this definition implies that there is no restriction on the implementation of variable geometry in the EAC. Since it is a principle in the constitutive treaty (as opposed, for example to the EAC Customs Union Protocol), it can be applied in virtually any area covered by any of the agreements of the EAC. If anything, Article 7 of the EAC Treaty (on operational principles of the EAC) is an integral part of the EAC Common Market Protocol.[26]

In the words of Frederick M Abbott, all subject matter is not created equal.[27] Variable geometry consists of a new variety of flexible agenda-setting coalitions between individual Member States in specific policy areas.[28] The EU is increasingly characterised by 'pairs or groups of member states seeking to project particular policy or political preferences within the EU system'[29] and these coalitions do not necessarily need to include Germany or France to influence opinion, although more often than not they will be included in some capacity. Nicole Koenig refers to internal differentiation, where rules cease to apply uniformly to all EU Member States because some of them opt out from a given policy area or integration project.[30]

---

[22] Chapter 6, section III.B.

[23] Chapter 2, section II.C.

[24] Chapter 7, section II.A.

[25] Wall et al, *Flexibility and the Future of the European Union* (n 10) 9.

[26] Article 3(1) of the EAC Common Market Protocol.

[27] FM Abbott, 'Toward a New Era of Objective Assessment in the Field of TRIPS and Variable Geometry for the Preservation of Multilateralism' (2005) 8(1) *Journal of International Economic Law* 77, 98.

[28] W Wallace, 'Exercising Power and Influence in the EU: The Roles of Member States', in S Bulmer and C Lequesne (eds), *The Member States of the European Union*, 2nd edn (Oxford, Oxford University Press, 2005).

[29] ibid 29.

[30] N Koenig, *A differentiated View of Differentiated Integration*, Policy Paper 140, Jacques BelorInstitut, Berlin, 23 July 2015.

Flexible regional economic integration will be applied to allow the members of a regional bloc to pay more attention to certain policy interests over others. Indeed, flexibility arises out of two main variances: the intrinsic differences between states, and the differences in policy interests in a regional grouping. The ability to pick and choose areas in which to further cooperation, as has been done in the EAC, the EU and elsewhere, is a core characteristic of flexible integration and, increasingly, regional integration. Flexible integration enables blocs to achieve multiple objectives at the same time, and, as in the case of the EAC, to ride on trade as a means to achieving other areas of closer cooperation.

F. Different Speeds

The final main deduction from the EAC definition of variable geometry is that it allows for different speeds of integration on matters of cooperation. This calls to mind Stubb's 'multi-speed integration' and Lloyd's and other authors' 'two-speed Europe'. The 'different speed' aspect of flexibility gives the member states flexibility in terms of the time in which they can pursue integration goals. Integration should be driven forward by sub-groups of Member States, allowing those who are initially unable or unwilling to participate to remain outside the adoption of a new policy area or the development of an existing field of integration for the time being.[31]

It can be argued that this gives the Member States even further flexibility on whichever matters they decide to prioritise. In the EAC, for example, there might be a greater emphasis on infrastructure and immigration between Kenya, Rwanda and Uganda, and a lesser emphasis on, for example, military cooperation. Chapter six considers, among other things, whether a slow pace of implementation of integration plans was a factor that led Kenya, Rwanda and Uganda to pursue a fast-tracked cooperation. Indeed, as the first name of the NCIP – the Tripartite Initiative for Fast Tracking East African Integration (TIFTEAI) – suggests, this appears to be the case.[32]

II. STREAMLINING DEFINITION: FLEXIBLE REGIONAL ECONOMIC INTEGRATION

The six implications from the EAC definition reveal that the framers of the EAC Treaty, and indeed other treaties for economic integration in Africa, anticipated challenges to the integration process, which they hoped to counter using variable

---

[31] Wall et al, *Flexibility and the Future of the European Union* (n 10).

[32] Chapter 6, section II tracks the milestones along the NCIP's creation, including the different names that were used to describe it during its evolution.

geometry. This deliberately worded definition allows parties to not only pick and choose areas for deeper cooperation but to do so even when some parties would rather not. And even when such areas are selected, parties need not implement cooperation at similar speeds, as permitted by the Agreement.

The general position seems to be that variable geometry is only one of the methods of flexible regional economic integration. However, closer observation of the EAC definition suggests that the drafters of the Treaty sought to incorporate multiple aspects of flexible integration in the treaty (especially multi-speed and à la carte integration). This, of course, goes back to the dilemma of definition and nomenclature alluded to earlier. 'Flexible integration', as an abstract idea, is generally appreciated and perhaps, understood. There are, however, still differences of interpretation when it comes to the fine print – the varying theories and mechanisms by which the flexible integration is pursued. The next section of this chapter studies the most prevalent ones.

What, then, is an acceptable definition of 'flexible regional economic integration'? I propose a definition that relies heavily on the East African definition of variable geometry. While it is admitted that variable geometry is only one of the methods of flexible regional economic integration in use today, the East African definition appears to have fallen victim to the challenge of nomenclature mentioned early in this chapter. This argument is advanced on the basis of how inclusive the definition is, covering more than just what is covered by the accepted definition of variable geometry as discussed in section III.A.ii below. In order to transpose the EAC definition of variable geometry to cover wider aspects of flexible regional economic integration, this study must resort to Roscoe Pound's 'case-knife' analogy.

Roscoe Pound tells the story of Tom Sawyer and Huck Finn, who are determined to rescue their friend Jim by digging under the cabin where he was confined. Tom had read that the *right way* to dig, no matter how foolish it sounded, was to use a case-knife. When they fail after hours using a case-knife, Tom drops the knife and asks for a 'case-knife', at which point Huck hands him a pickaxe. Tom receives it and goes about his work without saying a word.[33]

In addition to defining flexible regional economic integration using the EAC's definition of variable geometry, I contend that flexible regional economic integration is not just a principle of integration as it has been used in the EAC and other treaties for economic integration in Africa. Rather, flexible regional economic integration is in fact a method of integration. As chapter seven shows, by pursuing an incremental approach to integration, the Africa Continental Free Trade Area (AfCFTA) has used a method of flexible regional economic integration to pursue continent-wide economic integration.

---

[33] R Pound, 'Law in Books and Law in Context' (1910) 44 *American Law Review* 12, 19.

I therefore propose the following definition:

> Flexible regional economic integration is a method of preferential trade in which parties to an agreement are allowed to implement treaty provisions at different speeds and in smaller groups in order to facilitate continued integration.

This definition takes account of the various aspects of flexible regional economic integration discussed in this chapter, and does not restrict itself to a particular method. It covers the three main variables of integration that can be affected by flexibility provisions – speed/time of implementation, scope of integration, and subject matter. Like the EAC definition, it keeps the ultimate goal – integration – at its core, admitting that this flexibility might be necessary to allow continued integration.

III. THE APPLICATION OF FLEXIBLE REGIONAL ECONOMIC INTEGRATION

So far, it is clear that flexible regional economic integration involves the non-uniform implementation of treaties in pursuit of regional economic integration. The next question to ask is how this differentiated application of treaties is pursued. This section looks at the application of flexible regional economic integration in the EAC and other regional blocs in Africa and beyond.

A. Flexible Integration: A Broad Spectrum

The diversity of flexible regional economic integration is a common thread throughout this chapter. While it presents challenges for definition and conceptualisation, it is a reflection of how dynamic the application of flexible integration can be. Nicole Koenig writes about 'fifty shades of differentiation', while Alexander Stubb, Sir Stephen Wall, Mario Filadoro and other authors propose a classification of flexible integration that ranks the methods of applying flexibility according to how likely they are to facilitate deeper (and eventually, wider) integration. Following the Stubb classification, this chapter explores three broad categories to rank the different methods of flexible integration, namely multi-speed, variable geometry, and à la carte. These are dealt with briefly below in accordance with the variables to which their flexibility relates, from the most integrationist to the least integrationist. This classification is selected because it fits neatly with the proposed definition in the previous section.

i. *Time as a Variable: Multi-Speed Integration*

Multi-speed integration is a form of differentiated integration according to which the pursuit of common objectives is driven by a core group of Member States that are both able and willing to pursue some policy areas further, the underlying assumption being that others will follow later.[34] It involves the implementation of policies, initially by those Member States immediately capable of doing so, and the subsequent implementation by the other Member States without that initial capacity as soon as they have it; thus differentiating among Member States is a temporary and unfortunate necessity.[35] Under this model, the main variable is time, while the policies and actions pursued remain the same. The outlook here is positive in that although the differences are admitted, the Member States maintain the same objectives that will be reached by all members in due time.

In the EAC, the most outstanding examples of multi-speed integration include the accession of Burundi and Rwanda, which were given a longer time to adapt to the common market requirements, and the varied transitional provisions on the elimination of internal tariffs under the EAC Customs Union Protocol. Article 11 of the EAC Customs Union Protocol created a longer transition period for the elimination of tariffs for some goods from Kenya to Uganda and Tanzania. In both cases, the ultimate goal remained the same, and was in fact achieved, although it was reached at different rates for different members.

While the reasons for flexible regional economic integration are discussed at length below,[36] it should be noted that multi-speed integration evolved mainly to accommodate countries that may have lacked the capacity to implement integration goals at the same rate as the rest of the bloc. The other reason would be the need to account for inequalities in the enjoyment of integration benefits, especially those caused by unbalanced or unequal economic development. Chapter five assesses some of the capacity differences existing in the EAC, as well as the unequal development of the Partner States, and how these affect their ability to integrate at the same rate.[37] It argues that part of the reason for the rise of the NCIP was the differing capacities of the Partner States to meet their treaty obligations.

There is reason to remain critical of multi-speed integration. For example, under this model, states with capacity implement regionally agreed policies, followed by a subsequent implementation by the states that did not initially have that capacity. Questions, however, remain. What are the implications if the other members of the bloc do not develop the capacity, or acquire the capacity, but do not implement the policies to 'catch up' with the states that did so earlier? The EAC Treaty is silent on this matter, and this leaves room for 'slower' states to eternally drag their feet.

One possible effect of flexible regional economic integration is that it could lead to a 'disintegrated integration,' and as chapter six shows, this appears to

---

[34] Stubb, 'A Categorisation of Differentiated Integration' (n 1) 287.
[35] Filadoro, *Flexibility in the EU* (n 7).
[36] Section IV of this chapter.
[37] Chapter 5, section II.B, and ch 6, section II.C.

be the case in the EAC, especially with regard to Burundi.[38] Chapter four also discusses the crumbling relations in the EAC, with part of the blame being on Burundi's continued incapacity to participate in integration projects.[39] Undoubtedly, a question can be asked as to whether flexible regional economic integration should be applied with no limits, so that lines, especially in terms of time, should be drawn to ensure that the 'slower' states do keep up with their treaty obligations.

ii. Scope as a Variable: Variable Geometry

Unlike multi-speed integration, variable geometry admits to unattainable differences within the integrative structure by allowing permanent or irreversible separation between a core of countries and lesser-developed integrative units.[40] It assumes that certain Member States are incapable of adopting certain policies for long periods of time (and maybe forever), and thus the integration is reorganised into divisions[41] – usually those who can separate from those who cannot. The most common variables in this model are scope and space, ie different depths of integration for different countries. Variable geometry institutionalises diversity more than multi-speed does, and is considered less ambitious since political, cultural and economic diversity makes an ambitious set of common objectives both unrealistic and unattainable. Gradually, it encourages the organisation of the bloc around a multitude of integrative units.

Since variable geometry is an opt-in agreement devised by a proper subset of a larger group of countries, its benefits are restricted to the subset of countries. Therefore, countries outside the 'club' only enjoy a 'lesser' integration with those members that are part of the club, as seen in both the Schengen Agreement and the NCIP. In all these cases, the benefits of deeper integration are restricted to the members that participate in that deeper integration. In spite of this, the members engaging in this form of differentiated integration do not purport to depart from the auspices of the bloc. This could involve the use of overlapping agreements, where one agreement containing 'core' provisions to which all parties subscribe, coexists with separate agreements in which more advanced obligations are assumed by subsets of the members of the 'core' agreement that are in a position to do so.[42] This appears to be the most prevalent approach taken by the EU.

Variable geometry can be applied in cases where multiple regional groupings are merging to form one larger group. Two contemporary examples dealt

---

[38] Chapter 6, section III.B.

[39] Chapter 4, section IV.

[40] Stubb, 'A Categorisation of Differentiated Integration' (n 1).

[41] Filadoro, *Flexibility in the EU* (n 7).

[42] R Scollay, *Prospects for Linking PTAs in the Asia-Pacific Region*, in the Pacific Economic Cooperation Council (PECC)/ABAC Joint Study on FTAAP, 2007.

with in chapter seven of this study are the Tripartite Free Trade Area for Africa (TFTA)[43] and the AfCFTA. The TFTA combines the Common Market for East and Southern Africa (COMESA), the EAC, and the Southern African Development Community (SADC). The AfCFTA started out on the basis of existing regional blocs in Africa, but as chapter seven shows, this has since been disregarded in favour of a more ambitious, continent-wide initiative. Similarly, plans have also been afoot for years in the Asia-Pacific Economic Cooperation (APEC) to merge multiple regional groupings under the proposed Free Trade Area of the Asia-Pacific (FTAAP).[44]

As Robert Scollay proposes:

> If convergence is viewed as the creation of a single agreement through the amalgamation or expansion of existing agreements, the neatest solution is the establishment of a single set of provisions to which all members of the new, larger agreement subscribe. This requires either full acceptance by all parties of the provisions of one of the pre-existing agreements, or agreement by all parties to a modified set of provisions acceptable to all. A possible variant is the adoption of a "variable geometry", or "tiered" approach, with provisions divided into a common "core" set of provisions adopted by all parties, and a further set of provisions from which some members may be allowed to wholly or partly opt out. The conditions under which opting out is permitted might also be the subject of agreement among the parties.[45]

Chapter six considers the similarities and differences in the EAC that led to the existence of the two camps (NCIP states vs. Burundi and Tanzania). It shows that even within the NCIP, there are still differences that can only be accommodated by tailoring the variable geometry the three countries have decided to implement. These are brought to light to show how such differences affect the course of integration efforts, especially in few-country, many-issue settings.[46]

iii. Subject Matter as a Variable: à la Carte Integration

À la carte integration is a differentiated integration whereby respective Member States are able to pick-and-choose, as from a menu, in which policy area they would like to participate, whilst at the same time maintaining a minimum number of common objectives. In this model, the variable is the subject matter or area of cooperation. Countries choose their most suitable policy area of participation and leave those they consider undesirable or non-beneficial. All Member States would be part of a core common trading zone only and then be allowed to choose the subject areas (such as social policy, monetary policy or

---

[43] Article 6(b) of the Agreement Establishing a Tripartite Free Trade Area Among COMESA, EAC and SADC adopts variable geometry as a principle governing the Agreement.

[44] Scollay, *Prospects for Linking PTAs* (n 42).

[45] ibid.

[46] A modification of Peter Lloyd's 'many-country, many-issue' negotiation setting.

defence policy) in which they wished to be represented. It has been argued that this approach is a denial of future integration rather than a model of further and deeper integration, as it would allow each Member State considerable latitude to pick and choose the policy areas in which it wants to participate.[47]

À la carte integration is predicated on a political will. It focuses on the expression of choices to participate or not, and can accept patterns of differentiation as permanent, such as in the case of an opt-out.[48] In the EU, this is most prominent in the European Monetary Union, where the UK and Denmark elected not to participate in the common currency. The EAC definition clearly envisions à la carte integration by allowing 'cooperation in various fields'. Indeed, by adopting the East African Tourist Visa, which allows tourists to visit any of the three countries on a single visa, Kenya, Rwanda and Uganda have approached the table and deepened their integration on movement of persons, while Burundi and Tanzania have stayed away.

The EAC has modified à la carte integration to accommodate varying political wills and aspirations, taking account of the differences in the political, legal and economic histories of the EAC Partner States. This could explain both the existence of variable geometry in the EAC treaty, and why such an all-encompassing definition was adopted by the bloc.

B. Flexible Integration in Africa

This section introduces the use of flexible regional economic integration in Africa in light of the three variables discussed in the previous section: time, scope and subject matter. Chapters five, six and seven are detailed studies of the use of flexible regional economic integration in various forms in the EAC and continent-wide integration efforts, and therefore only a brief note is necessary at this stage.

James Gathii has evaluated the application of flexible integration in African integration efforts, identifying three methods of its implementation on the continent. In the first method, states are permitted the flexibility and autonomy to pursue policy changes at slower paces, rather than based on a fixed schedule applicable to all parties.[49] This is a variant of the multi-speed integration discussed above, and the EAC has adopted a variation of this model on two fronts. The immediate implication of Article 7(1)(e) of the EAC Treaty is that states can speed up the pace of integration between a subgroup if it is considered beneficial to the goals of integration. This is what Kenya, Rwanda and

---

[47] Wall et al, *Flexibility and the Future of the European Union* (n 10).
[48] Filadoro, *Flexibility in the EU* (n 7).
[49] JT Gathii, *African Regional Trade Agreements as Legal Regimes* (New York, Cambridge University Press, 2011) 35.

Uganda attempted by pursuing integration projects to the exclusion of Burundi and Tanzania. The second implication is that states can opt out of integration projects until they are ready to undertake them. It can be argued that in taking a back seat, this is what Burundi and Tanzania have done.

Gathii's second method seeks to minimise distributional losses by creating opportunities such as compensation for losses arising from implementation of region-wide liberalisation commitments, by the equitable distribution of the institutions and organisations of regional integration in order to avoid concentration in any one member. While it is not immediately apparent, this method is based on the second variable – scope. Pursuing equitable distribution is due to the need to accommodate states' differing capacities and political will, mostly geared towards a reduction of the adverse effects of regional integration. This model has been applied by the EAC before. As recounted in chapter four, during the first common market uniting Kenya, Tanzania and Uganda (1917–1965), Kenya enjoyed many advantages that caused tension in the Community as it was perceived to be developing at the expense of its counterparts. To remedy this, adjustments were made to the distribution of duties and to the location of institutions in the region. The remedies led Kenya to host the headquarters of the transport systems (air and rail), while Tanzania hosted the headquarters of the bloc, and Uganda hosted the East African Development Bank.

In the third method, preferences are employed in industrial allocation among members in a bloc, along with preferences in the allocation of credit and investments from regional banks. Again, this method has been applied by the EAC in the past. In order to further remedy the unequal development in the region, the EAC apportioned different industries to be pursued almost exclusively (if not entirely) by specific countries. Uganda would have its coffee, textile and melamine ware industries protected, so that they could produce for the region. Tanzania went on to focus on sisal production, while Kenya continued to industrialise, especially based on processed agricultural products. More recently, however, a modified version of this method has been applied by the NCIP states, with the main difference being the voluntary nature of participation. Under the NCIP, for example, Kenya, Rwanda and Uganda collaborated on the tourist visa discussed above, and attempted to cooperate in the construction of a standard gauge railway across the three states. These and other areas of deeper cooperation are reviewed in chapter six of this book.

While Gathii's first method of flexible integration rhymes with Stubb's and other authors' multi-speed integration, the latter two appear to be unique to African efforts, or at least hybrids between African approaches and Stubb's methods. The first is more straightforward as it clearly relates to variations in implementation that are related to time. The second, although it is arguably based on scope, has a less direct connection to Stubb's variable geometry. This is mainly because it approaches the scope element from the perspective of the effect of integration in a 'middle-ground' method that seeks to allow integration to progress in spite of the negative effects. On the contrary, Stubb's approach seeks to eliminate all possibility of those effects, by giving states the opportunity to gradually deepen integration as their capacity improves.

Gathii's third method is a hybrid of African approaches and Stubb's à la carte method of flexible regional economic integration. The EAC definition of variable geometry allows the selection of subject matter (a variety of areas) in which Partner States may deepen integration or withdraw from it. In the 1917–1966 EAC, this was based on decisions made by the colonial government,[50] and the second version of the EAC attempted to pursue similar industrial allocations in order to mitigate the adverse effects of integration. This 'compensatory approach' to flexibility remains present today in the EAC and even in AfCFTA, mainly in the form of lists of sensitive goods which continue to receive protection from regional liberalisation.

C. Beyond Africa: Flexibility in the EU and MERCOSUR

While flexible regional economic integration is a unique feature of integration in Africa, it is not unique to the African continent. Its diverse nature is a testament to its varied origins, and although it may not always be expressly provided for in treaties as has been the case in Africa, it is increasingly used across the globe. This section considers the use of flexibility in two other regions of the world – the (EU) and Mercado Común del Sur (MERCOSUR). These two blocs enrich this chapter in specific ways. The EU is, admittedly, larger (27 members), and has more developed nations, but will provide valuable lessons on flexibility for two main reasons. In the first place, it was one of the first blocs to use flexible integration, and therefore has a lot of experience to learn from. Second, it has been largely successful and has made efforts to adjust its course where its successes have not been as stellar. MERCOSUR is a relatively small bloc (five members,[51] only one less than the EAC) and is made up of one high income, and a mix of low income and middle-income countries. This provides a closer proximity to the EAC in terms of size and market quality, since the EAC is made up of low income and lower middle-income countries (LMICs).

This section highlights similarities and differences on theoretical, historical, political and even philosophical bases for flexibility where it exists. Admittedly, each instance and form of flexible integration covered here can be the subject of an entire volume, and this chapter does not purport to cover any of these exhaustively. It cannot provide a detailed history of flexible regional economic integration in the regions covered here, except as necessary to explore why it has not caught on or why it works the way it does.

---

[50] Chapter 4, section I.

[51] Venezuela is currently suspended, but remains a state party. MERCOSUR also has 7 additional 'Associated States': Bolivia (acceding), Chile, Colombia, Ecuador, Guyana, Peru and Surinam.

i. The European Union: The Face of Modern Flexibility?

It is tempting to argue that the EU is inadvertently the face of flexible regional economic integration today. The almost a la carte nature of the Common Agricultural Policy, the Schengen Area and indeed the Eurozone are just some of the prominent examples of the EU's flexibility. While some of these have been called 'non-EC forms of cooperation in the framework of the EU', this idea that not all rules apply to all Member States is a form of variable geometry.[52] A useful starting point would be, as has been done for the African and East African contexts, to define the EU understanding of flexible regional economic integration. Naturally, this is hampered by the semantic indigestion Alexander Stubb attributes to an excess of terminology.[53] Fortunately, the Treaty on European Union (TEU) offers a good starting point for the study of flexibility in the EU.

a. The Nature of Flexible Integration in the EU

The most prominent forms of flexibility in the EU are opt-outs, parallel treaties, and enhanced cooperation. Opt-outs are fairly regular, such as with Denmark (and the UK – when it was still a member) choosing to remain outside the Eurozone. This is similar to the variable geometry described variously in this book. Parallel treaties are reminiscent of Africa's multiple memberships, and have been used to pursue closer cooperation in Europe outside the EU framework. One prominent example is the European Fiscal Compact[54] signed by all EU members except the UK and the Czech Republic. The Compact was agreed as an alternative after the UK vetoed a treaty change designed to impose stricter budgetary discipline on EU Member States and lay the ground for a fiscal union.

Enhanced cooperation is another approach, and is provided for in the Treaty of Amsterdam:

> Member States which wish to establish enhanced cooperation between themselves within the framework of the Union's non-exclusive competences may make use of its institutions and exercise those competences by applying the relevant arrangements laid down in this Article and Article 326 to 334 Treaty on the Functioning of the European Union.

> Enhanced cooperation shall aim to further the objectives of the Union, protect its interests and reinforce its integration process. Such cooperation shall be open at any time to all Member States, in accordance with Article 328 of the Treaty on the Functioning of the European Union.[55]

---

[52] See J Usher, 'Variable Geometry or Concentric Circles: Patterns for the European Union' (1997) 46 *International Competition Law Quarterly* 243.

[53] Stubb, 'A Categorisation of Differentiated Integration' (n 1). See also section I above.

[54] Treaty on Stability, Coordination and Governance in the Economic and Monetary Union.

[55] Article 20(1) Treaty on European Union (TEU).

The framing of this provision is important for several reasons. First, it reveals the elective nature of enhanced cooperation. Much like the EAC and AfCFTA's variable geometry, it accommodates the varying abilities and political wills of the bloc's members. Second, it creates limits for the use of enhanced cooperation. By restricting it to the framework of the EU's non-exclusive competences,[56] it is specifying that some aspects of cooperation are not available for flexibility. As proposed in chapter nine, this is an important consideration that African integration efforts have appeared to overlook. Third, it allows for enhanced cooperation to take place within the Union's frameworks and use the Union's institutions. As shown in chapter six,[57] the lack of institutional structure and the risks associated with duplication of structures and institutions was a principle cause of the failure of the NCIP. Fourth, it specifies that enhanced cooperation must further the objectives of the Union, protect its interests and reinforce its integration process. This prevents the aforementioned duplication, but more importantly, avoids the disparity predicted in this chapter, where some states are more integrated inter se than others.[58] And finally, by requiring compliance with Articles 326–334 of the Treaty on the Functioning of the European Union (TFEU), the use of and procedure for enhanced cooperation are regulated. This avoids the ad-hoc approach adopted by the NCIP.

Enhanced cooperation is not, by any means, a blank cheque that EU members can resort to whenever differences arise:

> The decision authorising enhanced cooperation shall be adopted by the Council as a last resort, when it has established that the objectives of such cooperation cannot be attained within a reasonable period by the Union as a whole, and provided that at least nine Member States participate in it … (emphasis added).[59]

This safeguard is conspicuously absent from flexibility provisions in the EAC, TFTA and AfCFTA treaties. As a result, any number of states can – even if only in theory – cooperate more closely on any matters of the bloc to the exclusion of the others, even if no actual stalemate has been reached. The effects of this are illustrated in detail in chapter six. The final paragraph of Article 20 TEU codifies what should otherwise be axiomatic:

> Acts adopted in the framework of enhanced cooperation shall bind only participating Member States. They shall not be regarded as part of the *acquis* which has to be accepted by candidate States for accession to the Union.[60]

---

[56] Under Arts 4 and 5 TEU, the Union acts based on competences conferred by the states, and after conferral, EU law takes precedence over national laws. Where such competence is exclusively vested in the Union, national law is subsidiary to Union law. See ch 5 of D Chalmers, G Davies and G Monti, *European Union Law, Cases and Materials*, 2nd edn (Cambridge, Cambridge University Press, 2010).
[57] Chapter 6, section III.B.
[58] Section V below.
[59] Article 20(2) TEU.
[60] Article 20(4) TEU.

The express provision for this limitation appears unnecessary in light of *pacta sunt servanda*. However, in contexts as complex as regional integration, whether purely economic or, as in the EU, also political, it is prudent to make the extent and applicability of laws as clear as possible.

Even with such robust provisions, the EU's enhanced cooperation has not been applied in practice,[61] with parallel agreements and institutions being preferred instead. Some of these later get brought within the ambit of the EU, with the effect that there is some differentiated integration. In addition to the Fiscal Compact, the operation of the Schengen area – a result of the Schengen Conventions of 1985 and 1990 – was effectively outside the EU framework and integrated by the use of a Protocol.[62] This approach has been replicated in the 2005 Prüm Convention, signed between Austria, Belgium, France, Germany, Luxembourg, the Netherlands and Spain. In 2008, it was made part of EU Law binding all Member States.[63]

Two principle questions arise out of this trend. One major critique of African integration efforts in this and other literature is the existence of multiple agreements to which African states are party, with the result that such multiple memberships slow down integration. How is this different from the EU approach to integration? Considering the disjointed incrementalism adopted by African integration under the MULPOCs, this criticism can appear unwarranted, especially when different agreements deal with different issues. In the EAC context, for example, three Partner States are members of the Inter-Governmental Authority on Development (IGAD), whose main aim is the pursuit of peace in Eastern Africa.[64] Arguably, this would be similar to a parallel agreement in the EU context, which does not attract as much criticism. One reason for this might be the fact that the parallel agreements in the EU are geared at closer integration between the members and are based on fundamental EU ideals. This could explain why it is relatively easy for these to be integrated into the EU framework, sometimes binding on all Members, at a later date.

The second question is partly answered in section V below: why has the EU had limited use of flexible regional economic integration? It is not necessary to repeat the reasons here, but a summary of some of the reasons unique to the EU experience, especially more recently, is inescapable.

---

[61] See Chalmers et al, *European Union Law* (n 56) 114, and M O'Brien, 'Company Taxation, State Aid and Fundamental Freedoms: Is the Next Step Enhanced Cooperation?' (2005) 30 *European Law Review* 209.

[62] Protocol on the Schengen Acquis Integrated Into the Framework of the European Union.

[63] Council Decision 2008/615/JHA on the stepping up of cross-border cooperation, particularly in combating terrorism and cross-border crime.

[64] See ch 2, sections II.C and III.C.

b. Opposition to Flexibility

The political and relatively broader societal support for European integration is fairly self-evident. From the outside, therefore, the EU appears to prefer an all-or-nothing approach, with the result that flexible integration would be an impediment rather than aid. This might explain the preference for more inclusive parallel agreements over enhanced cooperation. Given that it is becoming customary for these to be integrated into EU frameworks, they are a more reliable approach to achieving group objectives in the face of minority opposition. This view is subject to the criticism that frequent recourse to international treaties is less transparent and inclusive, and could reduce the incentive to seek consensus among the EU-27. If the larger states regularly negotiate parallel treaties to circumvent their smaller opponents, it could boost Eurosceptics who argue that the EU is undemocratic because the big member-states dictate the rules.[65]

More recently, there have been attempts at flexible integration, including proposals by the European Commission to use coalitions of the willing in specific policy areas.[66] These were perceived as attempts to side-line Eastern and Central European members, reinvigorating debates between Eastern and Western European states that had appeared to have diminished.[67] Further challenge presents itself on the changing shape of the Union, with both enlargements and departures taking place. Candidate countries are wary of flexibility, especially with the risk that transitional status could become a permanent feature, thereby locking them out of the full benefits of the union. On the other hand, Brexit appeared like an attempt to invent a bespoke status for a former Member State,[68] especially given the challenges presented by the Irish border. More recently, moves by Switzerland to enjoy a looser relationship with the Union have led to the suggestion that piecemeal disintegration is possible.[69]

The support for flexibility in the EU is likely to follow the swing of a pendulum for the foreseeable future. It is not a new concept to the bloc, but is viewed with suspicion by the 'smaller' states, while the 'bigger' states wield it as an alternative to consensus. The factors unique to the EU combine with the fear of fragmentation and the implementation challenges explored in Chapter three to limit, for now, the use of flexibility in the bloc.

---

[65] See A Gostyńska-Jakubowska and C Odendahl, *A Flexible EU: A New Beginning or the Beginning of the End?* CER Insight, 18 May 2017.

[66] See European Commission, *White Paper on the Future of Europe: Reflections and Scenarios for the EU27 by 2025*, 1 March 2017.

[67] P Vimont, *Flexibility is not Europe's Miracle Solution*, Carnegie Europe, 26 June 2018, available at https://carnegieeurope.eu/2018/06/26/flexibility-is-not-europe-s-miracle-solution-pub-76681.

[68] ibid.

[69] S Gänzle, T Hofelich and U Wunderlich, *Why the EU's System of Flexible Integration Will Likely Accommodate Switzerland's Special Requests*, LSE, 9 June 2021, available at https://blogs.lse.ac.uk/europpblog/2021/06/09/why-the-eus-system-of-flexible-integration-will-likely-accommodate-switzerlands-special-requests/.

ii. MERCOSUR: Home of Uncodified Flexibility?

There has been limited use of flexibility in the Southern Common Market (MERCOSUR) since its inception in 1991. The constituting treaty does not provide for such flexibility, and although it has been argued that the Trade Liberalisation Program established multi-speed liberalisation, this differentiated application of rules was in fact compensatory to Uruguay and Paraguay.[70] When a common external tariff was adopted between the integrating states, it was based on Brazil's more protectionist tariffs, with the result that Paraguay and Uruguay suffered trade diversion.[71] This is akin to the varied allocations under the East African Development Bank discussed in chapter four.[72]

While there is little literature on the subject, it is reasonable to conclude that there is some flexibility in the bloc. It is mostly ad hoc, based on prevailing circumstances and, as with the EU, dominated by parallel arrangements. To quote Bouzas et al:

> The 'imperfections' that pervade MERCOSUR common trade policies are numerous. There is a large number of exemptions (many of which are discretional), there are bilateral agreements that grant different treatment to the same goods imported from the same origin, and there is nothing else to 'free circulation' (as revealed in the subsistence of origin requirements and internal borders).[73]

Bouzas et al attribute this state of play to size and development asymmetries, which have been established as ideal conditions for the existence of flexible regional economic integration.[74] In addition to the flexible approaches adopted, MERCOSUR prefers intergovernmental cooperation to the supranational integration adopted by the EAC and the EU.[75] This suggests that the bloc is not perceived as independent from the states, with the result that Member States remain at the pinnacle of decision making. Under this approach, all important decisions are based on consensus among the Member States, and differentiation helps to create a rebalancing mechanism for smaller countries to defend their interests against regional powers.[76]

This notion of subsidiarity is explored in some detail in chapter eight,[77] but it warrants brief mention here to explain the low uptake of flexibility in

---

[70] B Gaens, B Venturi and A Ayuso, *Differentiation in ASEAN, ECOWAS and MERCOSUR, A Comparative Analysis*, EUIDEA Policy Paper No. 6, August 2020, p 12.

[71] For a detailed discussion on trade effects, see ch 2, section II.D.

[72] Chapter 4, section II.B.

[73] R Bouzas, P Da Motta Veiga and R Torrent, *In-Depth Analysis of MERCOSUR Integration, its Prospectives* (sic) *and the Effects Thereof on the Market Access of EU Goods, Services and Investment*, Observatory of Globalisation (University of Barcelona), November 2002, p 150.

[74] See section IV.A below.

[75] Gaens et al, *Differentiation in ASEAN* (n 70) 13.

[76] ibid.

[77] Chapter 8, section II.C.

MERCOSUR. The EAC, AfCFTA and the EU all envision a supranational status for the regional bodies, with laws, institutions and structures that function independent of, and indeed in precedence of national laws, institutions and structures.[78] These allow for a separation between the blocs and their members, so that the members can undertake cooperative projects outside the purview of the blocs. While this has not happened yet in the AfCFTA, the NCIP was an attempt in the EAC, and this section has highlighted some successful ventures of this nature in the EU. Flexibility, therefore, requires a separation between the bloc and its members in order to be effective. Chapter eight explores how this would work in the multilateral context, with a proposition that might point to a rethink of our perception of international economic law and indeed, public international law.

IV. ARGUMENTS IN FAVOUR OF FLEXIBLE INTEGRATION

This section reviews the arguments in favour of flexible regional economic integration as given by the various authors. It considers these arguments both at the regional level and at the multilateral level. The reasons for flexible integration in this section are discussed along two main themes: causes – ie factors that have led to its existence, and benefits – ie the advantages that have been enjoyed by applying flexible integration. This approach is useful because the reasons for flexible integration are gleaned mostly from experiences prior to its application, while the benefits are from experiences that follow. This approach therefore allows for an evaluation of the reasons against the experiences after the application. As might be expected, the two are not always related, and in fact, the reasons weighed against the benefits might appear to have promised more than they have delivered. This will be reflected in the criticisms of flexible integration, most of which only become manifest after the application of the differentiation.

A. Reasons for the Existence of Flexible Integration

The main argument for flexible integration in Africa is that it is useful for adjusting the costs and benefits of integration. Indeed, variable geometry in Africa arises out of the need to counter the unequal benefits that accrue from integration, which is primarily focused on trade liberalisation.[79] There is some inequality among African nations based on asymmetric economic benefits of trade integration, and unequal networks of power, information and knowledge. It therefore makes sense to 'compensate' countries that suffer losses from

---

[78] For an illustration of this in the EAC, see ch 4, section III.B, and for AfCFTA, see ch 7.
[79] Gathii, *African Regional Trade Agreements* (n 49) 37.

liberalisation commitments, though this compensation is itself a challenge. This disparity usually is due to technological and economic dominance of the 'big brother' countries, a position enjoyed by Kenya in the EAC.[80]

Colonial history is also likely to affect the imbalance between integrating nations. By the second iteration of the EAC in 1967, Kenya had a bigger share of the employees of the EAC institutions, many of whom were located in Kenya, as well as the largest share of the customs revenue. This was a vestige of the first attempt at integration by the colonial governments, and the 1967 Treaty attempted to correct this in several ways. The headquarters of the Community and its Tribunal were shifted to Arusha (Tanzania), the EAC Bank and the East African Posts and Telecommunications Corporation moved their headquarters to Kampala (Uganda), while the headquarters of the East African Harbours Corporation were moved to Dar-es-Salaam (Tanzania). The East African Railways Corporation and the East African Airways Corporation headquarters were left in Nairobi (Kenya).[81]

Further justification for flexible integration can be found in the role played by the private sector, especially transnational corporations (TNCs). Regional cooperation pursued solely on the basis of commercial integration, ie reduction of intra-regional trade barriers and harmonisation of some other market-oriented policy instruments with or without a common external tariff, implies an increase in the bargaining power of TNCs.[82] This enables the TNCs to bargain with *each* government for the best conditions they can obtain.[83] In addition, while regional integration in the EU resulted in the merger of locally controlled firms, this has not been the case in Africa. This often results in local subsidiaries of foreign firms enjoying the protection of both regional and national tariff walls, leading to unequal gains in trade integration and does not result in the expected benefits of integration among poor economies that share the same characteristics. It was just such a failure that led to the ultimate disbandment of the EAC in 1977.[84]

One significant reason for the existence of flexible integration, especially in Africa, is the impact of insecurity and political instability in Member States of a regional economic bloc. In the EAC, the worst insecurity is experienced by Burundi and South Sudan, which even at the time of writing are going through periods of civil strife that leave many dead and more displaced. The most obvious effect of such instability is that such countries are precluded from useful participation in trade because the political and economic environment does not foster trade. Additional challenges arise out of the inability of these states to

---

[80] ibid.

[81] ibid 39.

[82] CV Vaitsos, 'Crisis in Regional Economic Cooperation (Integration) Among Developing Countries: A Survey' (1978) 6 *World Development* 719, 730.

[83] Gathii, *African Regional Trade Agreements* (n 49) 39–40.

[84] ibid, but also discussed in ch 4, section II.D.

implement regional agreements at par with their integrating counterparts. In both cases, where the political will at the regional level is in favour of integration, a flexible method will be necessary to accommodate struggling states, and arguably, this is part of the reasons the EAC adopted flexible integration.

Regional integration in Africa is quite often not purely for the purposes of trade liberalisation. Other considerations such as history, culture, security, the environment, shared resources and development form an integral part of the justifications for integration. While the EAC has attempted to pursue trade as the mainstay of its integration, a reading of the Preamble to the EAC Treaty and the objectives therein suggest that cooperation extends beyond trade, and has, indeed, political union as the ultimate goal.

In fact, for some regional groupings, trade is merely incidental to the integration process, and this is only made more complex by the membership of states in multiple regional groups. These factors result in the need for flexible integration, so that cooperation may move faster on some aspects than it does on others, although this can be a chicken and egg argument. For example, in the Common Market for Eastern and Southern Africa (COMESA), which was aimed at encouraging trade between members, the biggest benefit has been the easier movement of persons (most member countries allow visa-free access for COMESA member citizens), though this has not translated into increased trade in goods or even services. Even then, the movement of persons has not been useful for trade as it is only short-term movement that is facilitated. Flexible integration might explain this focus on movement of persons at the expense of other areas of cooperation, while it can also be argued that a focus on movement of persons ultimately led to the application of flexible integration in COMESA.

Flexible integration in the EU arose out of two factors. First, the realisation in the early 1990s that the Member States of the European Union were no longer able to achieve a consensus on the goals, scope and pace of their integration; and more recently, the expansion of the Union's membership to countries with widely differing levels of social and political development, differences so great as to form a substantial practical barrier to monolithic integration even when all possible participants might desire it.[85] These two factors show that as integration deepens and blocs expand, it is difficult to have all parties agreeing on all matters. For purposes of practicality, flexibility must be adopted in order for the bloc to both survive and advance.

When an integration effort involves relatively small economies all of which produce relatively small quantities of highly differentiated goods or services, then it is difficult to benefit from external markets by aggregating production. This is common with developing countries, whose external sectors often depend on one or a few commodities, minerals or services. These in turn determine their rate of exchange, the generation of savings (government savings), their relative

---

[85] Wall et al, *Flexibility and the Future of the European Union* (n 10).

inflation rates and the concomitant possibilities for development projects.[86] In the EAC, Kenya historically depended on tea, Uganda on coffee, and Tanzania on an assortment of minerals. This meant that when integration efforts were revived in the mid-1990s, there would be little for the countries to aggregate in order to exploit foreign markets.

This would give rise to two conundrums. First, adopting region-wide export policies would expose domestic producers to risk – an outcome governments would not want to contend with – and second, it would be difficult to decide which sector to favour over the others, since the three countries did not have one from which they could commonly benefit. The most logical solution would be to adopt policies which, while having a regional outlook, allowed the domestic economies of the Partner States to thrive, and flexible integration was, at the time, the most suitable way to achieve this balance.

Closely related to the foregoing, flexible integration can sometimes be applied because it is the only thing that makes economic or logical sense. For example, at the formation of the European Common Market, the Benelux import duty on plate glass was 16 per cent and the Italian tariff on the same commodity was 31 per cent, the arithmetical average would be approximately 24 per cent. However, since Benelux accounted for 31.3 per cent of the imports of the six Common Market countries, and Italy only 14.2 per cent, it was obvious that almost twice as many foreign exporters would suffer from a tariff increase in Benelux than would benefit from its decrease in Italy.[87] The most sensible thing to do then, rather than apply an arithmetic mean, would be to adjust the tariffs relative to the market share of the importing countries.

From a Member State perspective, differentiated integration can be seen as a function of the *objective capacity* and *subjective political will* to integrate.[88] Koenig offers no definition for either term, but I understand 'objective capacity' to refer to what can realistically be achieved or implemented by an integrating state, while 'subjective political will' relates to the willingness of the integrating states to implement or support region-wide policies. As chapter six shows, Kenya, Rwanda and Uganda had more political will towards integration than Burundi and Tanzania. Similarly, Burundi and eventually, South Sudan, are shown to have a lower objective capacity to implement integration goals. Both factors are intertwined in the weaving of the NCIP cords and the gravitation of Kenya, Rwanda and Uganda towards each other.

In the multilateral context, VanGrasstek and Sauvé argue in favour of flexible integration in the WTO on the basis of the members' scheduled commitments. They propose that GATT applies flexible integration in adopting specific tariff

---

[86] Vaitsos, 'Crisis in Regional Economic Cooperation' (n 82) 737.

[87] JJ Allen, 'The European Common Market and GATT – A Study in Compatibility' (1961) 26(3) *Law and Contemporary Problems* 559, 565.

[88] Koenig, *A differentiated View of Differentiated Integration* (n 30) 7 (emphasis added).

bindings that are negotiated country by country (as opposed to generic commitments that are uniform across the board). They identify two stages of variance arising out of scheduled commitments: the first is that scheduled commitments are inherently unequal, and the second is that even seemingly identical commitments may turn out to be unequal. While, internally, all countries may have laws that are consistent with GATT, they may indeed have radically different tariff or services schedules. While this is arguably not an overt adoption of flexible integration, the result is the same – different applications of the rules to different states.

B. Benefits of Flexible Integration

Arguably, the most glaring advantage of flexible integration is that it allows integration to proceed regardless of member differences. Further advantage is to be found in the existence of different models of flexibility to accommodate the varied differences. Where members of a bloc do not have the same capacity, they can adopt multi-speed flexibility; variable geometry where the goals/ political interests of integration are different; or the à la carte model where some members lack political will. For the future of the WTO, especially the Doha Round – should it be revived – variable geometry might be the most viable option, since non-participation in a particular agreement that a WTO member does not want, or like, might make other members more willing to accept an overall package.[89] This has been true for the most part in the EAC, although, as might be expected, the flexibility has resulted in some fragmentation with regard to the countries not participating in the NCIP.

Flexible integration is beneficial for its convenience. It is usually open to members of the bloc (as opposed to third parties), takes place within the bloc's institutional structure, and is subject to established rules and procedures.[90] This is true in most cases since, in the spirit of integration, blocs would rather keep all activity centrally administered, even though different members enjoy differing treatment depending on what policy areas they cooperate on and at what level. However, this is not necessarily true in the case of the EAC and NCIP. Chapter six shows that one of the main challenges the NCIP faced was a lack of structure, since it did not fully rely on EAC institutions for its administration.

Flexible integration allows integrating countries to preserve their sovereignty on sensitive policy areas. By its nature, flexible integration allows for cooperation in areas that are not considered to intrude on national sovereignty, so states

---

[89] Lloyd, 'The Variable Geometry Approach' (n 14) 62–63 and BM Hoekman and PC Mavroidis, 'WTO: 'à la carte' or 'menu du jour'? Assessing the Case for More Plurilateral Agreements' (2015) 26(2) *The European Journal of International Law* 319, 320.
[90] Koenig, *A differentiated View of Differentiated Integration* (n 30) 7.

are more willing to participate where there is the assurance that they will not be yielding their sovereignty to the regional or multilateral arena. The EU has seen countries refrain from participation where they did not feel comfortable yielding their sovereignty on some matters. The most notable of these are the UK on the Eurozone and Denmark electing to implement its own defence regime.

Regional integration in a much more organic sense is about the diffusion of strengths and weaknesses throughout the integral parts of a system and the enlargement of overall possibilities for achieving development where the whole exceeds and is qualitatively superior to the sum of its parts. On the basis of this goal, economic integration should not contemplate all-embracing schemes. Instead, it needs to concentrate sectorally or inter-sectorally on the functional fulfilment of specific goals and tasks. Under his model, integration is not valued as an end in itself, but rather the target is the achievement of specific integration goals.[91] This is true of many integration efforts worldwide, such as in the EAC where integration has been based on targets (preferential trade area, customs union, common market, and eventually, monetary union). Even then, each of these stages has been achieved by focusing on specific targets rather than a total integration of the bloc.

If the goal of economic integration is to aggregate production, as has been variously argued,[92] then integration needs to select and, in many cases, concentrate on areas where there are possibilities for a significant or massive expansion of the group's production frontier and in redressing the economic relations with the rest of the world.[93] In the EAC, attempts have been made to regionalise some sectors, but this has hitherto been unsuccessful. However, since the NCIP began, more progress has been made with the realisation of supranational[94] policies and activities, such as the EAC Tourist visa, which the region had failed to implement prior to the NCIP.

Flexible integration coalitions tend to be short-term and issue-focused. None of these constellations has aspired to establish itself as a permanent leadership axis and all of them have operated on a temporary and issue-related basis.[95] This is a reflection of the fact that in the larger and far more complex EU of 27 Member States, the establishment of a 'single core model as a motor of the EU' is unlikely.[96] While this may be a deeply held belief about flexible integration, it is not necessarily true. History has shown that flexibility has indeed endured

---

[91] Vaitsos, 'Crisis in Regional Economic Cooperation' (n 82) 736.

[92] Chapter 2, sections II.A and II.B study the reasons for integration, including the goals of integration.

[93] Vaitsos, 'Crisis in Regional Economic Cooperation' (n 82) 736.

[94] The word 'regional' is avoided here because these policies and actions are not truly regional, but only concern the NCIP.

[95] C Schweiger, 'Poland, Variable Geometry and the Enlarged European Union' (2014) 66(3) *Europe-Asia Studies* 394–420, 396–397.

[96] WE Patterson, 'Does Germany Still Have a European Vocation?' (2010) 19 *German Politics* 1.

and not only been a temporary measure. The UK and Denmark's abstention from the Eurozone, and the special and differential treatment afforded to least developed and developing countries in WTO treaties are just some examples of how flexibility has and can endure, hampering full integration rather than encouraging it.

V. CRITICISMS OF FLEXIBLE INTEGRATION

The critics of flexible integration place their arguments along two general themes: the fragmentation effects it has, and the complexities involved in the implementation of differentiated rules to different states.

The biggest fear expressed by sceptics of flexible integration is that it will result in the fragmentation of the integrating bloc, thereby defeating the purpose of integration.[97] For example, there is a fear that flexibility can create a host of small cooperation organisations of every kind and fragment markets and economic spaces.[98] It also presents the dilemma between flexibility and unity, with the risk that differentiation can spur further heterogeneity, undermine the fragile sense of a common identity and trigger tendencies of disintegration.[99] At the multilateral level, there is a danger of the bifurcation of the WTO membership, splitting 'insiders' from 'outsiders', and the risk of negotiating plurilateral agreements with the strategic objective of excluding others.[100] These arguments support the proposition that the implementation of flexible integration by the EAC will result in the disintegrated integration of the region. It is predicted that as a result of the NCIP, Kenya, Rwanda and Uganda will be deeply integrated amongst themselves, while Tanzania and Burundi remain members of the EAC, but not as deeply integrated and therefore not fully benefitting from the integration process.

Flexible integration can result in the marginalisation of some members, whether in a regional or multilateral setting. Variable geometry would give preference to certain issues above others, and thus to the interests of some members over others. In the multilateral context, the risk of the plurilateral approach is to marginalise WTO members, typically the weakest and poorest members of the WTO.[101] While this might seem like a fragmentation-related risk in bigger groupings, it is also largely true in the smaller blocs like the EAC. Over time, Burundi,

---

[97] Hoekman and Mavroidis, 'WTO: 'à la carte' or 'menu du jour'?' (n 89) 333–335.

[98] United Nations Economic Commission for Africa (UNECA), *On the General Scheme for Coordinating and Harmonising Integration Activities in Africa (A Critique of the Principle of Variable Geometry)*, Seventh Joint ECA/UNDP/African IGOs/UN Specialised Agencies Meeting, Addis Ababa, 23– 24 April 1993.

[99] Koenig, *A differentiated View of Differentiated Integration* (n 30) 7.

[100] Hoekman and Mavroidis, 'WTO: 'à la carte' or 'menu du jour'?' (n 89) 334.

[101] Leal-Arcas, 'The Fragmentation of International Trade Law' (n 16) 177–180.

the smallest economy in the bloc, has been side-lined in many Community initiatives, either because of its perceived capacity issues, or because its concerns have not been considered to be as significant as those of the bigger economies.[102]

The fragmentation argument extends to the operation of businesses in respective domestic jurisdictions. Since the content of preferential trade agreements[103] is idiosyncratic, they result in increasing fragmentation of the rules of the game for businesses engaged in international trade and generate substantial information costs for traders.[104] This point ties in with the implementation challenges discussed below, but can be demonstrated by an example from the tourism sector in the EAC.

Kenya, Rwanda and Uganda cooperate closely on tourism-related matters, and have opened up their borders and markets to each other in order to benefit better from economies of scale. Consequently, tourist operator vehicles from the three countries can operate across the borders of each of the three countries. Tanzania, on the other hand, has kept its tourism sector closed, so that tourist operator vehicles from the three countries (each of which share a border with Tanzania) are not allowed into Tanzania.[105] As a result, tour operators from NCIP states have to work with differing rules when dealing with Tanzania, and this translates into different operation costs and consequently, differentiated costs for travel packages that include trips to Tanzania. This affects Kenya the most since some tourist attractions (notably, Mt. Kilimanjaro and the Maasai Mara) are on both sides of the Kenya-Tanzania border.

Flexible integration is avoided in the multilateral arena because it exposes integrating parties to the risks of confusion and free-riding. The shift away from the à la carte approach was deliberate and an explicit objective of many of the negotiators, who sought to extend their disciplines negotiated in earlier rounds to all members of the WTO. Their argument was that the Tokyo Round Codes created unnecessary confusion concerning who had signed what and who was bound by which obligations and, more importantly, that it was necessary to address free-riding by non-signatories to the Codes (given that most of the Codes were applied on an MFN basis).[106] This contention, especially the latter

---

[102] Chapter 4, section IV shows that Burundi has boycotted EAC Summit meetings on grounds that its concerns have not been adequately met by the EAC.

[103] Hoekman and Mavroidis argue that preferential trade agreements, like plurilateral agreements are a form of flexible integration in the WTO since they allow 'clubs' to negotiate deals they otherwise would not be able to negotiate at the multilateral level.

[104] Hoekman and Mavroidis, 'WTO: 'à la carte' or 'menu du jour'?' (n 89) 320.

[105] In the EAC Common Market Schedule on Trade in Services, Burundi, Kenya, Rwanda, and Uganda all committed to eliminate market access and national treatment restrictions on tourism and travel related services, specifically on travel agencies and tour operator services, as well as tourist guides services. Tanzania opened up considerably less (only for tour operators on the mainland), retaining the right to charge higher licensing fees for foreign tour operators.

[106] Hoekman and Mavroidis, 'WTO: 'à la carte' or 'menu du jour'?' (n 89) 321.

argument, is important for this study because it concerns itself with the future of the EAC. In assessing the possible impacts of the NCIP on the future of the bloc, it will be important to consider whether Burundi and Tanzania can later join the integration projects undertaken by the NCIP, and how.

On implementation, differentiated integration raises several concerns. Questions arise as to whether existing institutions should be used for the 'special groups', as has been done in the Eurozone and Schengen area. In the EAC, this has caused some discomfort as the NCIP could not justify using EAC institutions for its affairs. In the EU context, for example, the use of existing institutions raises legitimacy issues due to the misfit between decision-makers and decision-takers, and it also raises questions as to why non-participant members should have a say in Eurozone matters in light of their countries' EMU opt outs. Establishing parallel governance structures is not a panacea either, since it can lead to costly duplication. Consequently, variable participation within a single treaty, and linkages between separate treaties raise the question of how far a single institutional structure may operate at all levels.[107] Chapter six explores the effect of variable geometry on the EAC's institutions, examining how the NCIP was administered, and whether this resulted in additional costs for the EAC, or indeed had any impact on the efficiency of its institutions.

VI. SUMMARY

The definition of flexible integration is as varied as the descriptions of the five blind men and an elephant – each author defines it according to their own experience or the experience of their context. This is therefore a great time to study it because the literature is gradually being consolidated and points of agreement being reached. As this chapter reveals, variable geometry is only one of many methods of flexible regional economic integration, but as the EAC shows, there is still no clear understanding of how each method works. The next part of this book tests the actions of the EAC and the NCIP against the theories as they have been written so far. This starts with the next chapter considering the history of the EAC, and chapter five showing the link between the EAC's variable geometry and Africa-wide efforts at economic integration.

---

[107] Usher, 'Variable Geometry or Concentric Circles' (n 52) 266.

4

An Introduction to the EAC

THE EAST AFRICAN Community (EAC) is the regional intergovernmental organisation of the Republics of Burundi, Kenya, Rwanda, South Sudan, Uganda, and the United Republic of Tanzania, with its headquarters in Arusha, Tanzania.[1] The Community, in its current form, is a third attempt at integration, and while this may be the most robust of all efforts so far, it is important to briefly consider some aspects of previous efforts. This is so in order to understand the dynamics and historical context that led to the EAC Treaty and the protocols, and especially why variable geometry was considered a valuable operational principle for the implementation of these instruments. This chapter details the history of the bloc in its three iterations, highlighting the factors that created an environment in which flexibility was necessary, and considers the Community's prospects for the future.

I. EARLY BEGINNINGS

While the history of political and economic integration in Africa pre-dates the colonial era,[2] the Customs Union of Kenya and Uganda was first established in 1917, and was expanded to include Tanzania in 1927.[3] The colonisation of Africa during the nineteenth century serves as the backdrop to most of Africa's current political and economic integration efforts. Particularly in British colonial Africa, protectorates (and colonies) were administered jointly in an attempt to lower administrative costs. As a result, colonial governments ushered in regionalism through free trade, common currencies and services.[4]

Before the Uganda Railway was constructed, linking the hinterland to the Kenyan port of Mombasa, goods headed to Uganda were moved by road through Tanganyika (German East Africa, at the time).[5] The German administration

---

[1] Overview of the EAC, EAC Website, http://eac.int/about/overview (last accessed 12 October 2016).

[2] K Kimbugwe, N Perdikis et al, *Economic Development Through Regional Trade: A Role for the New East African Community?* (New York, Palgrave Macmillan, 2012) 34.

[3] A Hazlewood, *Economic Integration: The East African Experience* (London, Heinemann Educational Books, 1975).

[4] J Nye, *Pan Africanism and East African Integration* (Oxford, Oxford University Press, 1966).

[5] Kenya and Uganda were a British Colony and Protectorate, respectively, while Tanzania was a German Colony until after the First World War.

regarded these as goods in transit and did not subject them to any duty. In addition, each of the three countries collected import duties at their own borders, though this trend changed when the railway line shifted the import route for Ugandan goods. Rather than import by road through Tanganyika, Uganda imported its goods through the Kenyan port of Mombasa. Initially, duties were collected at Mombasa, and Uganda received no part of them. In 1909, efforts were made to transfer revenue from Kenya to Uganda, though with little success. In 1917, the customs departments of Kenya and Uganda were amalgamated, and by this time, most of Uganda's imports were arriving through Mombasa, and Uganda's import duties were practically non-existent as they were all collected at Mombasa.[6]

The 1917 Agreement provided for free trade in local produce and imported goods, so the two territories had a common external tariff and free internal trade. In 1923, free trade in local produce was expanded to Tanzania, but duties were still chargeable on most re-exports to, and re-imports from, Tanzania. This was changed in 1927 with the creation of a full customs union between the three countries, and integration deepened over the years until the establishment of a common customs administration in 1949. By this time, there was free movement of capital, and substantially free movement of labour. The economic union was fostered by a common currency and the common administration of transport, communications and other infrastructure.[7]

The economic development of the three countries followed demonstrably varying patterns. Even though all three economies were based on export cash crops, Uganda relied on coffee and cotton; Tanganyika (Tanzania), on Sisal and coffee; while Kenya depended on tea, coffee and cotton, in addition to crops for domestic consumption. Kenya's industrial-scale agricultural sector had the competitive advantage in the region, given that the European settlers had easy access to capital and export markets.[8] These models grew out of patterns established by the colonial governments in the three countries, which in turn depended on what was perceived as marketable, especially in the colonial masters' home countries.

The story was, however, not always rosy. There were on and off conflicts on tariffs, and Kenya became quite protective of its agricultural producers. In 1932, Tanzania felt like it was depleting its revenue to protect the products of its neighbour. This stemmed mainly from the negative effects of the common tariff. In 1930, 'suspended duties' were introduced, to give some flexibility from the rigour of the common tariff. This tariff could be imposed by a territory in addition to the basic (regional) duty, but did not have to be applied by all.[9] It can

---

[6] Hazlewood, *Economic Integration* (n 3) 21–22.
[7] ibid 23.
[8] AT Mugomba, 'Regional Organisations and African Underdevelopment: The Collapse of the East African Community' (1978) 16(1) *Journal of Modern African Studies* 261–272, 265.
[9] ibid.

be argued that this was the earliest form of variable geometry in the region, since it was a flexibility introduced to remedy the costs of integration.

By the end of the 1950s, Tanganyika and Uganda felt increasingly dissatisfied with the operation of the common market and other institutions that linked them with Kenya.[10] As explained by Walter Elkan and Leslie Nulty:

> Between 1945 and the early 1960s, Tanganyika almost certainly developed more slowly than the rest of East Africa. Virtually no industrial development took place there as it did in Kenya; and ... there was no agricultural development comparable in scale to the expansion of coffee- and cotton-growing in Uganda. Sisal benefitted less than cotton and coffee from the favourable conditions in world markets for primary products in the 1940s and 1950s. In any case, it provided neither backward nor forward linkages to promote further development, and suffered from all the well-known disadvantages of an 'enclave' industry. Coffee-growing was confined to a few thousand farmers around Mount Kilimanjaro and the Bukoba area, while cotton-growing was similarly limited to a small area adjacent to Lake Victoria where there happened to be a coincidence of favourable natural conditions and the availability of transport.[11]

Similar sentiments existed concerning Uganda in the same period, though the disparity with Kenya was murkier and objectively less obvious. Uganda's gross national product (GNP) rose from £47.6 million to £110.8 million between 1950 and 1960, and Kenya's grew from £63.7 million to £175.3 million in the same period. However, in Kenya, the benefits of economic growth were largely confined to Europeans and Asians, while in Uganda the benefits of growth were more widely distributed.[12] Therefore, while Kenya as a country had better growth statistics than Uganda, Uganda had better actual development and income distribution than Kenya.

In real terms, Uganda was in a better off position since large numbers of African farmers, especially in Buganda and Eastern Uganda, enjoyed better improvements than their Kenyan counterparts. In fact, Uganda enjoyed considerably higher levels of African income than the other two countries, with Africans in Uganda claiming two-thirds of the country's monetary Gross Domestic Product (GDP), while in Tanganyika and Kenya, Africans only took half and one-third, respectively.[13]

However, even with the 'silver lining' presented by the distribution of income in Uganda, there were still real concerns brought on by the rise of the Kenyan economy. First, more and more businesses that were coming to East Africa, and intending to operate throughout the region, followed the precedent set by the

---

[10] W Elkan and L Nulty, 'Economic Links in East Africa from 1945 to Independence', in DA Low and A Smith (eds), *History of East Africa, Volume III*, (Oxford, Clarendon Press, 1976) 331–347, 334.

[11] ibid 334–335.

[12] ibid 335.

[13] P Robson and DA Lury, *The Economies of Africa* (London, George Allen and Unwin, 1969) 316–317.

large European and Asian export and import businesses and located their head offices in Nairobi. Second, in its natural and processed form, Kenya's agricultural produce found a growing market throughout East Africa. Third, Kenya was a preferred location for new manufacturing industries, especially if they were branches of overseas firms or if they were established by locally domiciled European businessmen. With the exception of a textile mill and an enamelware factory in Uganda, virtually all new industrial enterprises which hoped to serve the region came to be sited in Nairobi or elsewhere in Kenya.[14]

Some reasons for this trend have been proposed. First, Kenya had the advantage of the early start. There were external economies of scale to be gained from a location in which others had already begun and where they were in close proximity to the headquarters of the principal import houses with their detailed knowledge of the East African market. Second, Nairobi and its environs, with its large European and Asian population constituted the largest single concentration of purchasing power for manufactures in East Africa. Third, it had 'high level manpower' which was mostly European and Asian, though among Africans, Kikuyu and Kamba were regarded as displaying the greatest commercial and mechanical aptitudes in East Africa, and they were close at hand as well.[15] A fourth reason was that some of the industrialisation took the form of the processing or canning of Kenyan dairy produce, vegetables, and fruit. Since these products lose their weight and bulk during processing, and are more fragile in their unprocessed form, the location of processing was bound to be nearer the farm than the market if there was a conflict – and the farms were in Kenya.[16]

The causes of disparities extend beyond Kenya's value addition to agriculture. Kenya developed service and manufacturing sectors well in excess of what would normally be expected for an economy with its level of *per capita* income. This was for two reasons. First, the Kenyan economy provided services and processing facilities for the other two East African countries (in addition to supplying processed goods as reported by Elkan and Nulty). Second, the non-African community in Kenya represented an enclave with income levels not only much higher than the rest of the population, but also higher, in the case of the Europeans, than average levels of income in the UK. This section of society had a higher demand for services and imported commodities, generating incomes in commerce.[17] This precipitated growth for the Kenyan economy, which the Tanzanian and Ugandan economies could not keep up with.

---

[14] ibid 336.

[15] It can be argued that this was a direct result of the divide and rule method of colonialism applied across East Africa. In Uganda, the Baganda were identified as the more commercially savvy group, while others, such as the Bagisu of Eastern Uganda, were considered farmers (hence their early success in coffee farming). Similar trends can be identified with the Acholi and others from Northern Uganda being regarded as warriors, and therefore being suitable for military and police roles.

[16] Elkan and Nulty, 'Economic Links in East Africa' (n 10) 336.

[17] Robson and Low, *The Economies of Africa* (n 13) 317.

It became apparent that Tanganyika (Tanzania) and Uganda were not bene-fitting from the common market, since they benefitted more from trade with third parties. Tanganyika and Uganda only exported 5 per cent and 10 per cent of their total respective exports to the rest of East Africa, while they respectively imported 16 per cent and 17 per cent. Kenya, on the other hand, exported 31 per cent to the region, and only imported 6 per cent from the other two countries.[18] Naturally, Tanganyika and Uganda woke up to their unfavourable position as part of the bloc, and attitudes towards integration began to head south.

The economic tensions were not helped by growing political divergences towards independence. Kenya and Uganda abandoned the idea of a political federation, while in what would become Tanzania, Julius Nyerere went as far as proposing that Tanganyika should delay her independence so that an East African Federation could be established.[19] At independence, each country also began to further develop its own domestic agenda, resulting in more actively divergent development policies.[20] These political issues combined with pressure from domestic producers as the economic disparities grew to make the union more and more dysfunctional.

The final blow to the EAC came, ironically, in the form of the independence of the Member States. As discussed in chapter seven, integration efforts across the African continent were hampered by governments looking to consolidate their power and positions in their states, resulting in inward looking policies.[21] In the case of the EAC, these policies were not only inward looking, but were often in opposition with each other. This was compounded by the fact that prior to independence, the EAC was centrally administered by the colonial authority, which facilitated the smooth and coordinated operation of the bloc as a supra-national entity. With the departure of the British, this central power was whittled down, with the result that different countries became responsible for running different aspects of the bloc. As might be expected, this proved unfeasible, so in June 1961, it was agreed that it would be in the interest of all the territories for common services (communications, finance, commercial and industrial coordi-nation, social and research services) to be provided on an East African basis. The administration of those services was then placed under a new organisation, the East African Common Services Organisation (EACSO).[22]

The EACSO and other interim organisations[23] with similar mandates were only temporary, and did not achieve much in the efforts to save the EAC. The machinery for economic coordination provided by EACSO was weak,

---

[18] Elkan and Nulty, 'Economic Links in East Africa' (n 10) 341.

[19] Mugomba, 'Regional Organisations and African Underdevelopment' (n 8) 264.

[20] P Robson, *Economic Integration in Africa* (London, Allen and Unwin, 1968).

[21] Chapter 7, section I.A studies regional economic integration efforts in Africa, focusing on the reasons for the slow integration across the continent.

[22] Hazlewood, *Economic Integration* (n 3) 36–39.

[23] Such as the East African Common Services Authority (EACSA), the Common Services Organisation, and the East African Statistical Department.

and while the East African Statistical Department (EASD) produced statistics on a regional basis, the individual governments relied on their own statistical services to formulate their economic policies. The regional industrial licensing system was not used to promote balanced development, and only applied to a few industries.[24] Attempts at resolving the imbalances, such as the Kampala Agreement of 1964, did not create the harmony that was intended. If anything, they had adverse effects in some cases. For example, the Kampala Agreement allowed the application of quotas and 'suspended quotas', whereby exports from the surplus countries would be progressively reduced, and local production increased in the deficit countries according to the build-up of the productive capacity of the deficit country.[25] A quota on beer exports from Kenya to Tanzania was imposed, but it restricted trade by more than production in Tanzania was immediately able to substitute. A net shortfall in the supply of beer followed, and this resulted in a switch to imports from outside East Africa.[26]

Gradually, efforts to rescue the disintegrating bloc seemed as effective as treating a fracture with a piece of plaster. Relations worsened as imbalances increased, and things took an irreversible tumble with the decentralisation of currencies. The East African Shilling had been in use since 1920, even though no central regional bank had been established, and was abandoned in 1965.[27]

With all three states gaining independence from the British, an attempt was made to fill the aforementioned leadership void by pursuing federation. On the eve of Kenya's independence, the political leaders of the three countries declared:

> The East African High Commission and its successor, the Common Services Organisation, have taught us the value of links in the economic field ... An important factor in view of our determination to achieve Federation is the existence of shared currency, and a functioning East African Common Market .... We are convinced that the time has now come to create such a central political authority.[28]

In keeping with the law of unintended consequences, the focus on federation led to a neglect of the economic coordination available within the EACSO.[29] Like Oedipus of Thebes, the EAC met its destiny on its way to avoiding it.[30] With the Kampala Agreement damaging more than it remedied, and the federation failing

---

[24] Hazlewood, *Economic Integration* (n 3) 56–57.

[25] Paragraph 1(c) of the Agreement of Ministers of Kenya, Uganda, and Tanganyika on Redressing Trade Imbalance.

[26] Hazlewood, *Economic Integration* (n 3) 59.

[27] ibid 61–63.

[28] Declaration of Federation by the Governments of East Africa, 5 June 1963.

[29] Hazlewood, *Economic Integration* (n 3) 64.

[30] In the play by Sophocles, *Oedipus Tyrannos*, it is prophesied that the king, Laios, would die at the hands of his child, who would then marry the queen, Jokasta. In an attempt to prevent this, Laios sends off Oedipus to be killed, but his life is spared, and he ends up adopted by Polybus of Corinth. Later on, the prophecy is repeated to Oedipus, who, worried he will kill Polybus and marry his mother, flees from Korinth to avoid fulfilling the prophecy. On his flight, he kills a man who offends him, and goes on to find a beautiful woman, who he later marries. It emerges that the man he killed was Laios, and the woman he married, Jokasta, was his mother.

to materialise, Member States started withdrawing from regional arrangements. Tanzania withdrew from the East African Navy, believing it did not benefit from the navy as it was based in Mombasa. Uganda, for its part, withdrew from East African Tourist Travel Association, claiming that its contributions to the association were disproportionate to the benefits it received. The aforementioned decision to discontinue the East African shilling was the death knell of the East African Common Market.[31] Since Kenya had accepted the Kampala Agreement on condition that the common currency was maintained,[32] the separation of the shilling gave Kenya the excuse to withdraw from the Agreement.

In June 1965, Kenya gave formal notice under the Common Services Agreement calling for a review of the agreement and for discussions on all aspects of the cooperation. The heads of state, meeting in Mombasa in August 1965, established a commission on the common market and common services under the chairmanship of Professor Kjeld Philip.[33] This commission started work in January 1966, and in May of the same year, submitted a report which formed the basis of the Treaty for East African Cooperation.

II. THE SECOND ATTEMPT

The Treaty for East African Cooperation was signed in June 1967, adopting the recommendations of The Philip Report, and came into force on 1 December 1967. The Philip Commission was a vehicle for negotiation between the three governments, and consisted of three ministers from each country, with a chairman to act as an initiator of ideas and conciliator. The new treaty codified and confirmed existing arrangements and was a demonstration of the three countries' willingness to work together, if for nothing else than the fear of the consequences of splitting apart. This was done by basing the Treaty on three broad areas of cooperation: harmonisation of economic policy, common institutions and a common market.[34] These are discussed briefly below.

A. Harmonised Economic Policy

The international harmonisation of economic regulation is the process by which countries work to eliminate or narrow differences among their respective regulatory regimes.[35] It has also been defined as making the regulatory requirements

---

[31] Hazlewood, *Economic Integration* (n 3) 64.

[32] Paragraph (c) of App 3 to the Kampala Agreement: Statement by Kenya.

[33] The Commission on East African Cooperation. (Hazlewood, *Economic Integration* (n 3) 70).

[34] See also: M Nyirabu, *Deepening Regional Integration of the East African Community*, Workshop Report of 'Deepening Integration in the East African Community', Development Policy Management Forum, 8–9 September, Addis Ababa.

[35] J Nakagawa, *International Harmonisation of Economic Regulation* (Oxford, Oxford University Press, 2001) 1.

and governmental policies of different jurisdictions identical or at least more similar,[36] and refers to the idea that taxes and regulatory rules in countries belonging to economic blocs should be made to converge over time. These definitions have three immediate implications for countries belonging to economic blocs.

The first is that rules, especially relating to trade, the economy, taxation, etc, are the subject of harmonisation. The second implication is that there should be convergence, and this signifies a tendency for two or more economies to become increasingly similar.[37] It is arguable whether the rules must be the same across the borders, or whether it is sufficient to have them similar (but not identical). The third implication is that harmonisation takes place over time. While a treaty might create harmonisation as a goal, the process of harmonisation takes a while, and requires adjustments at the domestic level in tandem with what has been agreed at the regional level.

Policy coordination and harmonisation are a common trait in regional integration initiatives, and can take place either on a functional basis outside an RTA or within the framework of a regional integration arrangement.[38] In an economic union, members pursue some degree of harmonisation of national economic policies in order to remove discrimination due to disparities in these policies.[39] Against this background, this chapter turns to consider the harmonisation of economic policy under the Treaty for East African Cooperation (the 1967 Treaty).

Article 2 of the 1967 Treaty made it the aim of the Community to strengthen and regulate the industrial, commercial and other relations of the Partner States, to the end that there would be accelerated, harmonious and balanced development, and sustained expansion of economic activities. It was agreed that the benefits of these would be equitably shared. In pursuit of this, the community would ensure the harmonisation of the monetary policies of the Partner States in order to ensure the proper functioning of the Common Market.[40] This signified a desire to avoid a disintegration similar to the one suffered by the EAC just the previous year.

The 1967 treaty had a 'general undertaking as to implementation,' embodied in Article 4, and its tone points heavily to the harmonisation of policies:

> The Partner States shall make every effort to plan and direct their policies with a view to creating conditions favourable for the development of the Common Market and the achievement of the aims of the Community, and shall coordinate, through

---

[36] D Leebron, 'Lying Down with Procrustes: An Analysis of Harmonisation Claims' in J Bhagwati and R Hudec (eds), *Fair Trade and Harmonisation*, Vol 1: *Economic Analysis*, (Cambridge, Mass, The MIT Press, 1996) 41–117, 43.

[37] J Black, Nr Hashimzade and G Myles, *Oxford Dictionary of Economics*, 4th edn (Oxford, Oxford University Press, 2012).

[38] Kimbugwe et al, *Economic Development Through Regional Trade* (n 2) 14.

[39] ibid 15.

[40] Article 2(2)(f) of the Treaty for East African Cooperation.

the institutions of the Community, their economic policies to the extent necessary to achieve such aims and shall abstain from any measure likely to jeopardise the achievement thereof.

This Article, although worded more persuasively than compulsorily, is clearly an indication of a desire to move, if not at the same pace, in the same direction. It can be argued that this aspiration is further reflected in the intention to create a common market, or at least a customs union, and this is illustrated by the adoption of a common external tariff[41] and the prohibition of external trade arrangements that do not benefit the entire Community.[42] In Article 19 of the Treaty, the Partner States indicated a commitment to agree upon a common scheme of fiscal incentives towards industrial development which would apply within the Community. This was a further testament to the intention to coordinate on policies across the board. The 1967 Treaty was, indeed, riddled with provisions that enjoined such cooperation, including on monetary policies,[43] taxation, commercial laws, and surface transport.[44]

It can be argued that the harmonisation rhetoric was given even more emphasis than the Common Market itself. This can be inferred from the number of common institutions, services, and Community corporations[45] that were created by the Treaty. It is, however, difficult to say whether this harmonisation goal was achieved. The common services, institutions and corporations did not specifically deal with economic harmonisation, although they were targeted at harmonising the running of services in the Community. The literature is silent on the economic harmonisation in the community, either because the non-occurrence of economic harmonisation went by unnoticed, or because it was not considered worth noting at the time. However, there is still evidence in the 1967 Treaty of the effort made. For example, Article 2(2) provided for several forms of harmonisation. This included the harmonisation of monetary policies required for the proper functioning of the Common Market, the coordination of economic planning, and the approximation of the commercial laws of the Partner States. These aspirations were further reflected in the Annexes to the treaty.

Annex X lists matters with respect to which Acts of the Community may be enacted, and Annex XIV deals with decentralisation and related matters. This annex creates, for example, the East African Customs and Excise Department, with a Commissioner of Customs and Excise in each Partner State, and headed by a Commissioner General. Similar positions are created for other institutions and departments, such as Civil Aviation and the Community corporations.

---

[41] ibid, Art 5.
[42] ibid, Art 7.
[43] ibid, Art 27(2).
[44] ibid, Art 29.
[45] Section II.B.iii below discusses the corporations established jointly by the three states under the Treaty for East African Cooperation.

However, while common structures were created, there were no common policies put in place on which they could base their operations.

Unlike the EAC today (discussed below),[46] which has made specific provisions in the constituting Treaty, Protocols and Community Acts, the 1967 Community did not specifically provide for economic harmonisation. It remained more of an aspiration or principle of the Community, and did not become a binding commitment towards which the Partner States could work. Possible reasons for this are explored in subsequent sections,[47] but it is worth noting that as discussed later, economic harmonisation would be difficult to achieve in a milieu with divergent economic and political aspirations.

B. Common Institutions

Common institutions were a hallmark of the 1967 Treaty, and it can be argued that the prominence of these institutions had both good and adverse results. These can be categorised into three groups: the 'Inner Institutions,' 'outer organs,' and the corporations.[48] This section selects some of those institutions and discusses them based on their relevance to this study.

i. The 'Inner Institutions'

The inner institutions included those that were within the 'Principle Common Market Machinery', created under Part III, and the 'Functional Institutions', created under Part IV of the Treaty. The Principal Common Market Machinery were the Common Market Council and the Common Market Tribunal, while the Functional Institutions included, at the pinnacle, the East African Authority,[49] the East African Ministers,[50] the East African Legislative Assembly,[51] and five councils.[52] These were supported in their functioning by the Central Secretariat. Although the Treaty did not provide extensively for their functions, they are discussed briefly below.

The East African Authority was the Community's principle executive organ.[53] It was made up of the Presidents of the three countries, and would be assisted in its functions by the Councils and the East African Ministers. In carrying out its executive functions, the authority could give directions to the Councils and to the ministers as to the performance of any functions conferred upon them.

---

[46] Section III.
[47] Section II.D.
[48] See also: P Sebalu, 'The East African Community' (1972) 16(3) *The Journal of African Law* 345–363, 349.
[49] Treaty for East African Cooperation, Art 46.
[50] ibid, Art 49.
[51] ibid, Art 56.
[52] ibid, Art 53.
[53] ibid, Art 46.

The East African Ministers was a body of three cabinet ministers, nominated from each country, and their responsibilities were laid down in Article 51 of the Treaty for East African Cooperation. They were charged with assisting the Authority in the exercise of its executive functions, as directed by the Authority. In addition, they were expected to chair one or two Councils, and as permanent members of the Councils, the ministers acted as a continuity link between the previous and new councils.[54]

The East African Legislative Assembly (EALA) was composed of the three East African Ministers and their three Deputies, along with the EAC Secretary General, the Counsel to the Community, and 27 members, with each Partner State appointing nine representatives.[55] It was presided over by a Chairman, and was the principle legislative organ of the bloc.

The Common Market Tribunal was created to ensure the observance of law and of the terms of the Treaty in the interpretation and application of the treaty as far as the Common Market was concerned.[56] It was composed of a chairman and four other members, all of whom were appointed by the Authority. Under Article 35 of the Treaty, the Tribunal was competent to accept and adjudicate upon all matters which would be referred to it under the Treaty, and any other jurisdiction specifically conferred upon it by the treaty. This Tribunal was the only judicial body created specifically for Common Market affairs; all other matters involving the Community or based on the Treaty were referred first to the domestic courts, and then, through a system of appeals, to the East African Court of Appeal. From a reading of Article 36, only Partner States had standing before the Tribunal, and this would, arguably, go a long way in further streamlining the Tribunal's jurisdiction. Decisions of the Tribunal were not subject to appeal[57] and were made by majority verdict.[58]

There were five Councils: the Common Market Council, the Communications Council, the Economic Consultative and Planning Council, the Finance Council, and the Research and Social Council.[59] Each Council consisted of the three East African Ministers, together with a varying number of members (three on the Communications and Finance Councils, and nine on all the other Councils). Each of the other members of the Councils had to be Cabinet Ministers in their respective governments, and specifically, the members of the Finance Council were Finance Ministers, while the members of the Communications Council were ministers responsible for communications in their respective governments. As with all the other organs, each country appointed an equal number of members to represent it on the Councils.[60]

---

[54] Sebalu, 'The East African Community' (n 48) 349–350.
[55] Treaty for East African Cooperation, Art 56(2).
[56] ibid, Art 32(1).
[57] ibid, Art 37(1).
[58] ibid, Art 37(2).
[59] ibid, Art 53.
[60] ibid, Art 54(1).

It can be argued that the Councils were a forum for ensuring cohesion in the integration process. This is illustrated by the role of the Common Market Council, which, as the one of only two Institutions in the Principle Common Market Machinery, was arguably the most important Council. It was established to settle problems concerning the Common Market that arose from the implementation of the Treaty. This Council was also tasked with ensuring the function and development of the Common Market in accordance with the Treaty, and keeping its operation under review. It also played a dispute resolution role with relation to the Common Market, where any action or omission was alleged to be in contravention of the Treaty.[61] The other Councils had similar cohesion enhancing roles, centred around consultation, negotiation and joint decision making on the matters that fell under their respective dockets.[62]

The Central Secretariat was composed of the Secretary General's office, the three Secretariats of Finance/Administration, Common Market/Economic Affairs, Communications/Research/Social Services, and the Chambers of the Counsel to the Community.[63] The Secretariat was created to keep the functioning of the Common Market under continuous examination, and could act in relation to any particular matter which appeared to merit examination, either on its own initiative or upon the request of a Partner State made through the Common Market Council.[64] Sebalu notes that the powers previously exercised by the Secretary General, as the principal executive of EACSO, had been pared down and allocated to the three ministers. This left the Secretariat with the principal responsibility of continuously examining the functioning of the Common Market.[65]

ii. The 'Outer Organs'

The 'outer organs' included the East African Court of Appeal, the Common Market Tribunal, the East African Development Bank, and the East African Industrial Court. For purposes of this section, the first three are the most relevant.

The Court of Appeal for East Africa was established as a successor to the Court of Appeal for Eastern Africa, which was established by the EACSO[66] between 1961 and 1966.[67] The Court had jurisdiction to hear and determine appeals from the courts of each Partner State, and had powers in connection with such appeals. The Court was the final Court of Appeal in East Africa for both civil and criminal matters, with the exception of constitutional appeals

---

[61] ibid, Art 30.
[62] ibid, Art 61, and Sebalu, 'The East African Community' (n 48) 351.
[63] ibid, Sebalu 352.
[64] Treaty for East African Cooperation, Art 31(1).
[65] Sebalu, 'The East African Community' (n 48) 352.
[66] See section I, above.
[67] Treaty for East African Cooperation, Art 80.

from the High Court of Uganda and appeals from the High Court of Tanzania in treason cases.[68]

The East African Development Bank (EADB) was established under Article 21 of the Treaty, and is one of the only Community institutions that had a separate Charter agreed upon to provide for its running. It was established to provide financial and technical assistance in order to promote the industrial development of Partner States, giving priority to industrial development in the relatively less developed Partner States, and thereby endeavouring to reduce the industrial imbalances between them.[69] The bank was intended to finance projects designed to make the economies of the Partner States increasingly complementary in the industrial field,[70] and to supplement and cooperate with the national development agencies of the Partner States as well as other institutions concerned with industrial development.[71]

An indication of the intention to level the playing field can be deduced from the territorial distribution of funds to be invested. Only 22.5 per cent of the funds could be invested in Kenya, while Tanzania and Uganda could benefit from 38.75 per cent each.[72] This was one of the first codified implementations of flexible integration in the EAC. The Bank was, perhaps, the most independent organ of the Community. Article 27 of the EADB Charter vested all powers of the Bank in the Board of Directors, while, under Article 35 of the Charter, the Bank reported directly to the East African Authority and the Bank's shareholders. By comparison, the Corporations (discussed below) submitted their annual reports and statements of account to the Communications Council for presentation to the Assembly.[73]

iii. The Corporations

The Corporations established by the Treaty were, under Article 2, considered institutions of the Community. Although they are all defunct today, it is important to note them, even briefly, for comparative purposes. In understanding the evolution of the EAC and relations between the Partner States, it will be useful to understand why some institutions, especially the Corporations, no longer exist. As such, it will be useful to at least have a general knowledge of the Corporations and their nature.

Article 71 of the Treaty established four corporations: the East African Railways Corporation, the East African Harbours Corporation, the East African Posts and Telecommunications Corporation, and the East African

[68] Sebalu, 'The East African Community' (n 48) 352.
[69] Charter of the East African Development Bank, Art 1(1)(b).
[70] ibid, Art 1(1)(c).
[71] ibid, Art 1(1)(e).
[72] ibid, Art 13(c).
[73] Article 79 of the 1967 Treaty.

Airways Corporation. On the back of experience from the EACSO, the corporations were established as semi-autonomous, each with its own Act.[74] Article 72 of the Treaty was repeated in each Act, and sets out the principles that govern the operations of the corporations. Perhaps most relevant for this book is the emphasis on spreading investment. Under Article 72(4), the corporations were required to regulate the distribution of their non-physical investments, to ensure an equitable contribution to the foreign exchange resources of each of the Partner States. They were also expected to arrange their purchases within the Partner States so as to ensure an equitable distribution of the benefits thereof to each of the Partner States, taking into account the scale of their operations in each Partner State.[75]

The existence of these institutions was a step in the right direction for the Community, although they faced a great challenge in the lack of underlying policy to guide their operation. In stark contrast from the EAC today, the 1967 Community created institutions and expected them to be mostly independent, developing their own regulatory structure, with only minimal central control at the regional level. The EAC today, as will be seen below, focuses on creating rules, agreeing protocols, and harmonising policies that the institutions are expected to follow. To this end, they have made a commitment to give regional agreements and policies precedence over national laws and policies[76] – a position which would have, other factors being constant, gone a long way in ensuring the endurance of the 1967 Community.

C. The Common Market

The treaty created a common market between the three states.[77] It aimed to strengthen and regulate the industrial, commercial and other relations of the Partner States for accelerated, harmonious and balanced development and sustained expansion of economic activities, with benefits to be equitably shared.[78] This tongue twister of an objective reflects a desire to avoid or even resolve the conflicts that led to the downfall of the original customs union. Although it singled out 'industrial' and 'commercial' relations, it left room for 'other' relations that could be enjoyed by the Partner States.

The creation of a common market was a compromise agreed to when it became clear that the dream of a federation could not be achieved.[79] In addition, the emphasis on 'harmonious and balanced development' and 'equitable sharing of benefits' is indicative of a resolve to avoid the inequalities that led

---

[74] Sebalu, 'The East African Community' (n 48) 354.
[75] Article 72(5) of the 1967 Treaty.
[76] Article 8(4) of the EAC Treaty.
[77] Article 1(1) of the 1967 Treaty.
[78] ibid, Art 2(1).
[79] Sebalu, 'The East African Community' (n 48) 348.

to the grumbling of the early 1960s. 'Accelerated development' and 'sustained expansion of economic activities' show that the leaders of the 1967 EAC – or at least the drafters of the Treaty – were bent on improving the welfare of the Community. It was hoped that these objectives could be achieved by the establishment of the East African Common Market.

However, neither the Treaty nor the practice of the states created an actual common market. Instead, a customs union was established, since no provision was made for the free movement of factors of production. On the contrary, provision was made for their regulation and even restriction in some cases. As Hazlewood comments, the term 'common market' had been applied for so long to the East African arrangements that the niceties of the terminology escaped the draftsmen of the Treaty.[80] This section investigates this claim by briefly revisiting the nature of a common market,[81] and weighing this against what was established and indeed applied by the EAC in the 1967 Treaty.

As the EAC would later define it, a common market means the integration of the Partner States' markets with the free movement of capital, labour, goods and services.[82] This integration presupposes that the regional group has already established a customs union, which under Article XXIV(8) of GATT, requires:

i)   elimination of duties and other restrictive regulations of commerce on substantially all trade between the constituent territories of the union; and

ii)   application of the same duties and other regulations to trade with third countries not included in the union.

For the common market to be realised, there must be, in addition to the above, free movement of capital, labour, goods and services within the union.

The question then, is two-fold. The first is an assessment of whether the 1967 Treaty created a common market, and the second is whether, according to history, a common market was implemented.

Article 1(1) of the 1967 Treaty established the East African Community, and 'as an integral part of such Community, an East African Common Market'. There is a clear effort to distinguish between the Community and the Common Market,[83] an indication that possibly in practice the two were expected to run side by side, rather than as one unit. The Treaty established institutions to run the Community, but also established specific institutions to handle matters related to the Common Market. These (the Common Market Council and the Common Market Tribunal) have been discussed in the previous section. Of particular interest, however, is whether the Treaty provided for the above-mentioned features.

---

[80] Hazlewood, *Economic Integration* (n 3) 72.
[81] Defined in ch 2, section I of this book.
[82] Article 1(1) of the EAC Treaty.
[83] Article 2(2) of the 1967 Treaty.

The first feature is the subject of Article 11 of the Treaty. This Article provides that no Partner State shall impose a duty in the nature of a customs duty or import duty in respect of goods which originate in the Partner States. The Rules of Origin under the treaty are quite simple and laid out in Paragraph 3 of the same Article. Apart from goods wholly produced in the Partner States, goods could be considered East African if they had been produced in the Partner States, and the value of materials imported from a foreign or undetermined country, and used in the production of the goods, does not exceed 70 per cent of the ex-factory value of the goods. There was even a blanket removal, with exceptions,[84] of quantitative restrictions on East African Goods.[85]

It is also easy to find satisfaction of the second feature in Article 5(1):

> The Partner States, recognising that a common external customs tariff is a basic requirement of the Common Market and subject to paragraphs 2 and 3 of this Article, agree to establish and maintain a common customs tariff in respect of all goods imported into the Partner States from foreign countries.

This desire for interactions with third parties on common terms is manifested further in Article 7 of the 1967 Treaty, where the Partner States agree not to enter into any arrangements with any foreign country in which tariff concessions are available to that Partner State and not available to the other Partner States. Related principles were laid down in Article 9 of the Treaty to provide that no customs duties would be charged on goods from foreign countries if they had been charged upon entry into one Partner State and then transferred to another Partner State.

On the face of it, therefore, the Treaty made provision for the establishment of a customs union. However, nothing in the Treaty points to an intention to fulfil the third feature of a common market – free movement of the factors of production. Admittedly, Article 1 of the Treaty does create the East African Community with the East African Common Market as an integral part thereof, and even provides for 'freedom of capital account payments necessary to further the aims of the Community'.[86] Additionally, the Treaty creates institutions such as the Common Market Council and the Common Market Tribunal, but aside from these, no provision is made for the implementation of the said Common Market. And even then, the Common Market Council, which in a perfect world should have been tasked with pursuing free movement of factors of production, was tasked with dispute resolution and external (other states and international

---

[84] ie security laws; control of arms; the protection of human, animal or plant health or life, or the protection of public morality; transfers of gold, silver and precious and semi-precious stones; the control of nuclear materials and radioactive products; and the protection of revenue under Art 17(2). Partner States also reserved the right to impose quantitative restrictions on some agricultural products set out in Annex III to the Treaty (Art 13).

[85] Article 12(1) of the 1967 Treaty.

[86] ibid, Art 2(2)(e).

organisations) relations.[87] As Sebalu wrote on free movement of capital and labour:

> ... all the Partner States have imposed exchange controls. These have seriously inter-fered with the movement of capital and disrupted trade within the Community. *The Community provides for no free movement of labour except the employees of the Community* (emphasis added).[88]

Several implications can be deduced from this situation. The most obvious is, as Hazlewood has noted, that after decades of using the term 'Common Market', it was included in the Treaty without a proper appreciation of its import. Second, the question can be asked, 'could the Common Market have failed if it did not even exist?'. This one is, of course, purely academic, as for practical purposes, the Hazlewood approach – treating the bloc as the Customs Union that it was – would suffice. Another vital implication can be drawn from this: more than likely, this version of the EAC crumbled a few years after it began because there was a lack of clarity on which direction should be pursued. Finally, the EAC appears to be notorious for the functionalist approach to integration,[89] where the leaders create systems and let the market do the rest of the work in the integration process.

'Niceties of a common market' aside, the resurgence of the EAC did endure for a decade, and during this time, several gains and losses were registered. While Kenya gained because the continued existence of the bloc meant continued access to the Tanzanian and Ugandan markets, it lost because the Treaty, in remedying the imbalances of the past arrangements, curtailed Kenya's free-dom of trade.[90] Tanzania and Uganda benefited from the continuation of the common services (airways, harbours, rail, post and telecommunication, etc) and from the decision to decentralise and relocate the headquarters of the services.

Tanzania's and Uganda's best gains, however, were predicted to have been the Transfer Tax and the East African Development Bank (EADB).[91] Under Article 20 of the 1967 Treaty, industrially less-developed Partner States could impose a tariff on imports of manufactures from the relatively more developed ones in order to protect their own manufacturing industries. Transfer taxes could be imposed only by a country with an overall deficit in intra-regional trade in manufactures, and only on imports from a country with which it had a deficit. The prevailing pattern of intra-East African trade in manufactures at the time of the Treaty gave Tanzania a deficit with each of the other countries, and Uganda a deficit with Kenya. Under the Transfer Tax system, Tanzania was therefore able to impose transfer taxes on imports from both Kenya and Uganda, and Uganda was able to impose them on imports from Kenya. Kenya was not entitled to impose any Transfer Taxes.

---

[87] Article 30(e) of the 1967 Treaty.
[88] Sebalu, 'The East African Community' (n 48) 360.
[89] Functionalism and other methods of integration are discussed in ch 2, section II.C.
[90] Hazlewood, *Economic Integration* (n 3) 86.
[91] ibid 87.

D. The Second Collapse

The 1967 Treaty did not properly resolve the differences that existed between the three states, though it attempted to remedy the past imbalances. In addition to the 'equalisation' under the EADB Charter, it created a complex system of taxation that sought to protect Uganda and Tanzania from the inequitable development of Kenya at their expense, as had happened in the past. These provisions only serve to illustrate that there were attempts at resolving the mistakes of the past.

However, as history testifies, the 1967 Treaty did not survive for long, and in 1977, the Community was dissolved with even greater finality than the first collapse. The reasons for this failure included the complexity of the regime created by the Treaty, which Hazlewood described as a 'regulated customs union'. Free trade between the Partner States was to be limited by transfer taxes in an attempt to protect manufacturing in the less-developed states with the aim of promoting industrial balance.[92]

The Treaty had other shortcomings, arising in part out of a lack of clarity on the intentions of the provisions. It did not help matters that the Treaty appeared to restrict more than liberalise trade, especially from Kenya to the other Partner States. Mismatched political expectations also had a role to play. The Common Market survived before independence because it was being coordinated more or less by a central power – England – represented by the colonial governments. After independence, however, each state had its own interests to look out for, and the failure of the governments to realise the constraints arising out of this has been blamed for the troubles of the Community.[93]

The move towards independence in the 1950s and early 1960s coincided with a reduction in efforts to bring about greater economic integration on the African continent. The newly independent countries faced difficulty in surrendering their hard-earned sovereignty, as African independence leaders viewed cross-border institutions and initiatives as an erosion of their sovereign power and a mild form of re-colonisation.[94] In the EAC, this was exacerbated by the fact that citizens also lacked managerial skills, which led to the demise of many cross-border institutions.[95] Additionally, the EAC suffered a fate that plagues regional groupings in Africa, even today: African notions of economic integration were not tailored to the day-today practical realities of the continent's economic and political life.[96] None of this was helped by the fact that until recently, integration

[92] Article 20(1) of the 1967 Treaty.

[93] Hazlewood, *Economic Integration* (n 3) 142.

[94] A Adejeji, *History and Prospects for Regional Integration in Africa*, Paper presented at the Third Meeting of the African Development Forum, UNECA, Addis Ababa, 5 March 2002.

[95] F Kahnert et al, *Economic Integration Among Developing Countries*, 1969, OECD Development Centre, Paris.

[96] A Goldstein and C Quenan, 'Regionalism and Development in Latin America: What Implications for Sub-Saharan Africa?' in *Regional Integration in Africa* (Paris, African Development Bank and OECD, 2002) 47–76.

was not employed as an effective tool in coping with the competitive demands of a rapidly globalising world,[97] but rather as a means to achieving other goals through regional collaboration.

As with the East African Common Market which collapsed in 1961, the post-independence governments of the three Member States adopted different governmental and economic systems, especially in light of growing feelings of nationalism. Kenya pursued a market economy, Tanzania formed an Africanised version of socialism, while Uganda opted for a mixed economy.[98] This, coupled with personal and ideological differences between the leaders[99] (particularly Julius Nyerere of Tanzania, and Idi Amin of Uganda[100]), inevitably made it impossible to pursue regionally harmonised policies. Weak regional institutions – which could not act or function independent of the political backing of heads of states – did not help as they had limited control over national policy in each country, and the national assemblies lacked the commitment to implement the economic and development policies that the regional bodies promulgated.[101]

The differences between the three countries were, not however, only due to merely divergent approaches, but also due to opposing views and interests. As Agrippah T Mugomba narrated in 1978:

> The collapse of this once highly acclaimed experiment in regional cooperation is the result of actions taken by the Partner States themselves over a period of years. Since 1975, a three-dimensional verbal 'guerrilla' war has been waged by Kenya, Tanzania, and Uganda against one another; indeed, sometimes it has come close to physical combat.[102]

Mugomba gives several reasons for the frosty relations between the three states. The ball was set rolling by Tanzania's progressive 'drift' southwards as conflicts in Southern Africa intensified. Julius Nyerere, then president of Tanzania, sought to play a pivotal role in resolving this crisis, and this, combined with growing disillusionment with Tanzania's traditional partners (Kenya and Uganda), and the emergence of a group of regional actors with which Nyerere and his ruling party (TANU) shared ideological affinity, decisively shifted the country's political, economic, and ideological interests.[103] This 'move to the south' remained evident even when the EAC was revived in its current form. Tanzania remains a member of the Southern African Development Community (SADC),[104] and for years after the EAC was revived, South African brands remained dominant

---

[97] J Omutunde, 'Economic Integration in Africa: Enhancing Prospects for Success' (1991) 29(1) *Journal of Modern African Studies* 1–26.

[98] Kimbugwe et al, *Economic Development Through Regional Trade* (n 2) 67.

[99] P Anyang' Nyong'o, *Regional Integration in Africa: Unfinished Agenda* (Nairobi, African Academy of Sciences, 1990).

[100] Kimbugwe et al, *Economic Development Through Regional Trade* (n 2) 69.

[101] ibid.

[102] Mugomba, 'Regional Organisations and African Underdevelopment' (n 8) 263.

[103] ibid.

[104] Kenya, Uganda and Rwanda are concurrently members of COMESA.

in the Tanzanian market while East African brands struggled to make their way into the market. For example, in retail services, South African retail chain, Shoprite, was the dominant player in the Tanzanian Market, while Kenya-based Nakumatt only opened its first Tanzanian branch in July 2014.[105] By comparison, Nakumatt entered the Ugandan market in June 2009, five years before opening in Tanzania.

While Tanzania embraced SADC, Kenya – the most capitalist of the three countries – formed alliances with the US, in part to enhance its security and limit the effects of its political, economic and diplomatic isolation within the region. Unfortunately, this divergence between Kenya and Tanzania happened during Idi Amin's reign over Uganda, a period marked by so many ideological somersaults that Uganda could not play the potential role of a moderating force to balance the 'extreme' positions of Kenya and Tanzania.[106] These conditions provided a perfect environment for relations to sour along multiple planes:

> Long-harboured fears of domination by one or the other of the partners; resentment by Kenya over the need to 'carry' the poorer members; long-strained relations between Uganda and Tanzania over Nyerere's refusal to recognise Amin's military regime; markedly different foreign policy concerns and approaches; and the concentration of foreign capital in the industrial and commercial 'core' which long threatened to turn the two 'peripheral' states into economic satellites and the principal victims of Kenyan 'sub-imperialism'.[107]

These conflicts culminated in competing nationalisms, which combined with other 'purely psychological' and 'inexplicable' factors[108] to cause a decentralisation of Community organs. States either monopolised the running of common service institutions, or set up separate or parallel bodies, so that by the early 1970s, centralisation was no longer the general pattern in East Africa. The first step in this disintegrative direction was the 1966 end of the common monetary unit and the consequent establishment of separate currencies for each country. This was closely followed by the break-up of the University of East Africa, which had existed since 1963 and was replaced by national institutions in 1970. In 1973, the East African Income Tax Department ceased to operate, with each country setting up its own revenue authority. In February 1977, the Nairobi-based regional carrier, East African Airways collapsed, and out of its ashes rose Kenya Airways.

---

[105] The East African, *Nakumatt Eyes Tanzania's Emerging Retail Business*, 2 August 2014, available at www.theeastafrican.co.ke/business/Nakumatt-eyes-Tanzania-s-emerging-retail-business-/2560-2405950-4c7cl6z/index.html (last accessed 6 December 2016).

[106] Mugomba, 'Regional Organisations and African Underdevelopment' (n 8) 263.

[107] ibid.

[108] Mugomba does not explain the 'psychological' or 'inexplicable' reasons, but considering that this was written during/soon after the disintegration, this might be a reference to matters that were still sensitive at the time. It could also be a reference to political or diplomatic information, the publication of which might have been considered detrimental.

The final blow to the integration process came from external shocks. Kenya had a balance of payments crisis in 1971–72, and there were oil price shocks in 1973, to which the EAC countries reacted differently. Members also reacted differently again to the commodity boom in 1976–77, adopting radically different economic management tactics.[109] In 1977, the bloc finally collapsed, and a Mediation Agreement was signed to resolve the division of the EAC's assets and liabilities. Under the agreement, the parties agreed to explore areas of future cooperation and to establish concrete arrangements to facilitate such cooperation.[110] It was on the basis of this planned future cooperation that efforts to rekindle the EAC began in 1993, as discussed below.

III. THE EAC TODAY

The EAC today is the result of negotiations between Kenya, Tanzania and Uganda in 1993, resulting in the Agreement for the Establishment of a Permanent Tripartite Commission for East African Cooperation (PTCEAC).[111] The Commission was charged with the coordination of economic, social, cultural, security and political issues among the members. Chapter five offers a more detailed history of the events leading up to the establishment of the PTCEAC and the negotiation of the EAC Treaty.[112] For this chapter, it is sufficient to note that in April 1997, the heads of states of the three countries directed the Commission to commence negotiations for upgrading the 1993 Agreement into a Treaty.[113]

The resultant EAC Treaty was signed on 30 November 1999, and entered into force on 7 July 2000. The Republics of Burundi and Rwanda acceded to the EAC Treaty on 18 June 2007 and became full members of the Community on 1 July 2007.[114] The Republic of South Sudan acceded to the Treaty on 15 April 2016 and became a full member on 15 August 2016.[115]

The EAC became a customs union on 1 January 2005 following the 2 March 2004 signing of the Protocol for the Establishment of the EAC Customs Union (the EAC-CU Protocol). Given the EAC's multi-speed integration, Burundi and Rwanda only became bound by this Protocol from 1 July 2009. The Protocol provided for a common external tariff to be applied by the Partner States, among other provisions. It provided for a five-year transition period to allow the Partner States to make the necessary adjustments to their internal

---

[109] Kimbugwe, *Economic Development Through Regional Trade* (n 2) 66.
[110] ibid 70.
[111] Preamble to the EAC Treaty.
[112] Chapter 5, section I.
[113] Preamble to the EAC Treaty.
[114] EAC, *About the Treaty*, available at www.eac.int/treaty (last accessed 12 October 2016).
[115] EAC, *Overview of the EAC*, EAC website, www.eac.int.

customs and tariff regimes.[116] This meant the customs union only became fully fledged on 1 January 2010.[117]

On 20 November 2009, the Protocol for the Establishment of the EAC Common Market (the EAC-CM Protocol) was signed and it entered into force on 1 July 2010. This Protocol provided for the removal of barriers to trade that remained between the Partner States. The most notable of these were hindrances to the free movement of factors of production, especially persons. As this section will show, this Protocol has yielded varying results, with some Partner States being more open to trade and the movement of factors of production than others.

On 30 November 2013, the Partner States signed the Protocol for the Establishment of the EAC Monetary Union (EAC-MU Protocol). This Protocol will enter into force upon ratification and deposit by all the Partner States,[118] and the EAC has set a target of 2024 for the introduction of a single currency across the bloc.[119] Several activities have been laid out towards the achievement of this goal, including the establishment of institutions, coordination and harmonisation of fiscal, monetary and exchange rate policies, as well as the integration of financial systems amongst the Partner States. It is arguably premature, given the relative shallowness of the bloc's integration, to pursue a common currency. However, given the EAC's history in this chapter,[120] it is understandable why the EAC would be heavily invested in establishing a regional currency.

The following sections evaluate the bloc's progress along three planes: policy harmonisation, institutions, and trade under the Customs Union and Common Market.

A. Policy Harmonisation

As with its predecessor, the Treaty for East African Cooperation, the EAC Treaty and Protocols emphasise the centrality of policy harmonisation. While mostly avoiding the use of the word 'harmonisation', the emphasis is on 'cooperation'. The Treaty defines cooperation as:

> The undertaking by the Partner States in common, jointly or in concert, of activities undertaken in furtherance of the objectives of the Community as provided for under the Treaty or under any contract or agreement made thereunder, or in relation to the objectives of the Community.[121]

---

[116] Article 11 of the EAC-CU Protocol.

[117] EAC, *History of the EAC*, available at www.eac.int/eac-history (accessed 20 December 2018).

[118] Article 30, EAC-MU Protocol.

[119] EAC, *Monetary Union*, available at www.eac.int/monetary-union.

[120] Section I details how the collapse of the East African Shilling sped up the collapse of the bloc in 1966.

[121] Article 1(1) of the EAC Treaty.

Arguably, this definition is a more in-depth definition of harmonisation, as it defines not just the goal (furtherance/achievement of the objectives of the Community) but also the method of achieving the goal, ie an undertaking of activities jointly or in concert in furtherance of those objectives. This convergence goal is pursued further in Article 47 of the Common Market Protocol, where the Partner States undertake to approximate their national laws and to harmonise their policies and systems for purposes of implementing the Protocol.

Semantics aside, the current EAC appears to be making greater efforts at policy harmonisation than the 1967 bloc. To quote Kimbugwe:

> The three countries are pursuing similar market-oriented economic policies in restructuring their economies. Moreover, the private sector has been actively involved in the formulation of policy and in participating in regional organisations.[122]

Some of the bloc's achievements include the introduction of an East African passport, an important objective in achieving the free movement of people within the Community; full convertibility of the national currencies and agreement to liberalise capital accounts; pre- and post-budget consultations, as well as the synchronisation of budget speeches. Others include the development of a regional macroeconomic framework as a route to economic convergence; reduction in border delays, due to the harmonisation of customs documentation, and execution of a tripartite agreement on avoidance of double taxation. The bloc has also established an East African Stock Exchange and East African Investment Authority to promote cross border trade and investment, in order to create an environment conducive for trade and investment; and has developed an integrated transport and communications network.

All these milestones have been achieved on a regional basis, or at least, at national level concurrently. In April 2010, the Council of Ministers and the Heads of States Summit directed Partner States to enact enabling legislation to integrate the provisions of the Common Market Protocol into domestic law by 21 August 2010, and to review their domestic laws to ensure that they were consistent with the EAC Treaty. This was an ambitious goal, but the Partner States established national task forces or similar bodies which were charged with the duty to audit their national laws and to ascertain any conflicts with the Common Market Protocol.[123]

Gathii gives a specific example of this harmonisation effort. In 2010, the EAC Secretariat commissioned a project to identify and inventory commercial laws that relate to the implementation of the Common Market. This project was interrelated with the work of the Committee on the Approximation of Laws, which also launched a study on the harmonisation of commercial laws. By April 2010, 45 pieces of legislation on trading, business registrations, investment,

---

[122] Kimbugwe, *Economic Development Through Regional Trade* (n 2) 73.
[123] J Gathii, *African Regional Trade Agreements as Legal Regimes* (New York, Cambridge University Press, 2011) 200.

insurance and banking had been identified.[124] Although it was happening at different speeds, all of the EAC's members appeared to be taking some action to approximate, reform or revise their laws in conformity with the Common Market Protocol and the EAC Treaty.[125]

Going by the definitions of harmonised economic policy discussed earlier in this chapter,[126] it is safe to suggest that the EAC, in its current form, is making significant efforts at economic harmonisation. It is possible to weigh the treatment of policy in the region against the three implications cited earlier: that rules relating to trade, the economy, and taxation are the subject of harmonisation; that there should be convergence; and that harmonisation is gradual.

The first implication is relatively easy to satisfy. In addition to the adoption of a common external tariff, thereby establishing a single customs territory, the EAC has created a common market, and is in the process of working out the modalities to satisfy the four freedoms.[127] All five Partner States (as of 2013) started the implementation of various measures geared towards establishing the single customs territory. As part of this aim, regional legislation and policy have been passed geared at centralising aspects of trade, in order to operate a harmonised policy regime. For example, in 2004, the bloc passed the EAC Customs Management Act and adopted the Framework for the Attainment of the EAC single customs Territory in November 2013.[128] Additional efforts can be observed from 'minor' ones like coordinated fiscal planning, denoted, among others, by the Partner States having their annual budgets read on the same day of each year (usually the second Thursday of June).

The second implication of harmonised economic policy is that there should be convergence, or a tendency for two or more economies to become increasingly similar. While an in-depth analysis of this aspect would extend far beyond the scope of this chapter, it is possible to find some pointers from regional agreements and documents that indicate that this convergence is being pursued. The most significant is the general undertaking as to implementation in Article 8 of the EAC Treaty. Under this Article, Partner States are required to plan and direct their policies and resources in order to create favourable conditions for the development and achievement of the objectives of the Community. This Article also enjoins them to coordinate their economic and other policies and abstain from measures likely to jeopardise the achievement of Community objectives.[129] Critically, Community organs, institutions and laws take precedence over similar national ones, at least on matters pertaining to the implementation of

---

[124] ibid 201.

[125] ibid.

[126] Section II.A above.

[127] Free movement of goods, free movement of persons and labour, free movement of services, and free movement of capital.

[128] Annex XXI to the Report on the 28th Meeting of the EAC Council of Ministers.

[129] Article 8(1) of the EAC Treaty.

the Treaty.[130] This surrender of national sovereignty over policy points to an intention to achieve the convergence of policy through the centralisation of policy and concurrent subjugation of national objectives to Community objectives.

The third implication of harmonised economic policy is that harmonisation takes place over time. The current EAC has attempted to pursue a gradual process of integration and harmonisation of policy. This can be deduced from the numerous transitional periods that have been provided for at each stage of closer cooperation. For example, as mentioned above,[131] with both the EAC Customs Union and the EAC Common Market, transition periods of five years were used to enable the Partner States to make the necessary adjustments for the implementation of the new Protocols. In addition, the EAC admits that the goals of integration can only be achieved in the long term, and as such, did not wait for the 'full' achievement of a customs union before it started pursuing a common market. A similar trend is being followed with the establishment of the EAC monetary union. While the Monetary Union Protocol was signed in 2013, a common currency is not expected to be introduced until 2024, with domestic and regional policy adjustments being made during this transitional period.

On the three implications, therefore, it seems believable that the EAC is, at least in some ways, working towards the attainment of harmonised economic policy.

B. EAC Institutions

The governance of the EAC is set up across various organs and institutions. Departing from 'Inner Institutions' and 'Outer Organs' structure under the 1967 Treaty, the 1999 EAC Treaty created seven organs[132] and provided for an open ended number of Institutions that may be created by the Summit.[133] Unlike the 1967 Treaty, the 1999 Treaty did not create corporations, possibly due to the acrimony they caused in the previous Community and the neo-functionalist approach adopted by the present bloc.[134] Instead, it provides for close cooperation on areas that were previously common services or services provided by Community Corporations. For example, under Article 91, the Partner States shall establish and maintain coordinated railway services that will efficiently connect the Partner States within the Community, and where necessary, construct additional railway connections. This section briefly highlights some of the organs and institutions created by the 1999 Treaty.

---

[130] ibid, Art 8(4).
[131] Section III.
[132] Article 9(1) of the EAC Treaty.
[133] ibid, Art 9(2).
[134] See ch 2, section II.C for a detailed exploration of approaches to integration.

i. The Organs

Article 9 of the EAC Treaty creates the organs of the Community to perform the functions and act within the limits of the powers conferred upon them by or under the Treaty.[135] These organs are the Heads of States Summit, the Council of Ministers, the East African Court of Justice, the East African Legislative Assembly, and the Secretariat. The Article also creates a Coordination Committee and Sectoral Committees, and authorises the Summit to establish additional organs.

a. The Summit

The Heads of States Summit consists of the heads of state or government of the Partner States,[136] and gives general directions and impetus as to the development and achievement of the objectives of the Community.[137] As the de facto pinnacle of power in the EAC, the Summit reviews the state of peace, security and good governance within the Community and the progress achieved towards the establishment of a Political Federation of the Partner States.[138] The summit meets at least once a year[139] (traditionally in November – which is why a lot of the agreements and protocols are signed on or around 30 November), and makes its decisions by consensus.[140] While some of its powers can be delegated, four functions are exclusively reserved for the Summit: giving general direction and impetus; the appointment of judges to the EACJ; the admission of new members and granting of Observer Status to foreign countries; and assent to Bills.[141] The Summit is led by a Chairperson, who is a President of a Partner State appointed for one year on a rotational basis.

b. The Council

The Council of Ministers is composed of the minister responsible for East African Community Affairs of each Partner State, the Attorney General of each Partner State, and one other minister as each Partner State may determine.[142] Each Partner State therefore has three representatives on the Council, and these form the policy organ of the Community.[143] The Council is responsible for the promotion, monitoring, review and implementation of the programmes of the Community, and ensures the proper functioning and development of the Community.[144] To this end, it is the Council's responsibility to make policy

---

[135] Article 9(4) of the EAC Treaty.
[136] ibid, Art 10(1).
[137] ibid, Art 11(1).
[138] ibid, Art 11(3).
[139] ibid, Art 12(1).
[140] ibid, Art 12(3).
[141] ibid, Art 11(9).
[142] ibid, Art 13.
[143] ibid, Art 14(1).
[144] ibid, Art 14(2).

decisions for the efficient and harmonious functioning and development of the EAC.[145]

Apart from making policy decisions, the Council is responsible for the initiation of Bills, which it then submits to the Assembly,[146] and also makes regulations, issues directives and takes decisions on matters concerning the Community.[147] It is the ministers' collective duty to give direction to the Partner States and all organs and institutions of the Community other than the Summit, the Court and the Assembly.[148] The Council also considers the Community's budget,[149] and consider measures that should be taken by Partner States in order to promote the attainment of the objectives of the Community.

The Council is accountable to the Summit, and in this respect, submits annual progress reports to the Summit.[150] Similarly, the Council implements the decisions and directives of the Heads of States Summit.[151] In order to streamline its performance, the Council constitutes itself into Sectoral Councils to deal with matters that arise under the Treaty. The decisions of these Sectoral Councils are deemed to be decisions of the Council.[152]

Unlike the Summit, the Council meets at least twice a year, with one of the meetings being held immediately before a meeting of the Summit.[153] Like the Summit, decisions are by consensus,[154] although the leader of a Partner State's delegation can effectively veto a decision by recording an objection to a proposal. When this happens, the decision on that proposal is submitted to the Summit for consideration, unless the objection is withdrawn.[155] All decisions, regulations and directives of the Council are binding on the Partner States, and on all Organs and Institutions other than the Summit, the Court and the Assembly within their jurisdictions.[156] This ensures the separation of powers, so that, for example, the Council cannot enjoin the EALA to decide in a specific way in the conduct of the Assembly's affairs.

c. The Court

The East African Court of Justice (EACJ/the Court) is the Community's judicial body, and it ensures adherence to law in the interpretation and

---

[145] ibid, Art 14(3)(a).
[146] ibid, Art 14(3)(b).
[147] ibid, Art 14(3)(d).
[148] ibid, Art 14(3)(c).
[149] ibid, Art 14(3)(e).
[150] ibid, Art 14(3)(h).
[151] ibid, Art 14(3)(k).
[152] ibid, Art 14(3)(i).
[153] ibid, Art 15(1).
[154] ibid, Art 15(4). However, under the Protocol on Decision-Making by the Council, some decisions may be by simple majority.
[155] Article 15(3) of the EAC Treaty.
[156] ibid, Art 16, ibid.

application of – and compliance with – the Treaty.[157] Sitting in Arusha (Tanzania), the Court has both a First Instance Division and an Appellate Division.[158] The First Instance Division is composed of a maximum of ten judges,[159] with each Member State appointing no more than two judges.[160] The Appellate Division is composed of five judges,[161] with one appointed from each of the Member States.[162] The composition of both courts is likely to change as the membership of the bloc increases with the accession of the Republic of South Sudan to the EAC Treaty.

The Court is headed by a President and Vice President, who are both judges of the Appellate Division,[163] and a Principle and Deputy Principle judge, who are judges of the First Instance Division.[164] None of these positions may be held by more than one national of the same Partner State at the same time.[165] Judges in both Divisions hold office for a maximum of seven years, and retire at the age of 70 years.

The First Instance Division has jurisdiction to hear and determine, subject to a right of appeal, any matter before the Court,[166] which, under Article 27(1), covers the interpretation and application of the Treaty. This jurisdiction is applied in several ways, and can be employed by different parties under the Treaty. A Partner State can bring a reference to the Court on two possible grounds under Article 28. The first is where a Partner State considers that another Partner State or an Organ or Institution of the Community has failed to fulfil an obligation under the Treaty, or has infringed a provision of the Treaty. The second is where a Partner State would like to challenge the legality of any Act, regulation, directive, decision or action, on the ground that it is ultra vires, or unlawful, or an infringement of the Provisions of the Treaty or any rule of law relating to the Treaty's application, or where it amounts to a misuse or abuse of power.[167]

The Secretary General of the Community also has standing before the Court, albeit after exhausting other channels prescribed for resolving the matter. Under Article 29, where the Secretary General considers that a Partner State has failed to fulfil an obligation under the Treaty, or has infringed a provision of the Treaty, he or she shall submit his or her findings to the Partner State concerned for that Partner State to submit its observations on the findings. Where the Partner State does not submit its observations to the Secretary General within four months, or if the observations submitted are unsatisfactory, the Secretary General shall

---

[157] ibid, Art 23(1).
[158] ibid, Art 23(2).
[159] ibid, Art 24(2).
[160] ibid, Art 24(1)(1)(a).
[161] ibid, Art 24(2).
[162] ibid, Art 24(1)(b).
[163] ibid, Art 24(4).
[164] ibid, Art 24(5).
[165] ibid, Art 24(6).
[166] ibid, Art 23(3).
[167] ibid, Art 28(2).

refer the matter to the Council, which then decides whether the matter should be referred to the Court, or that it should be resolved by the Council. If the matter remains unresolved, the Council then directs the Secretary General to refer the matter to the Court.

Both natural and legal persons resident in a Partner State may refer, for determination by the Court, the legality of an Act, regulation, directive, decision or action of a Partner State, or an Institution of the Community on the grounds that such Act, regulation, directive, decision or action is unlawful or is an infringement of the provisions of the Treaty.[168] Curiously, this is the only category of persons with standing before the Court that is required to institute proceedings within two months of the enactment, publication, directive, decision or action complained of.[169] A special category of natural persons with jurisdiction before the Court is provided for under Article 31 of the Treaty. It gives the Court jurisdiction to hear and determine disputes between the Community and its employees that arise out of the terms and conditions of employment of the employees, or the application and interpretation of the staff rules and regulations and terms and conditions of service of the Community.[170]

The Court has a special jurisdiction to deal with arbitration. There are three possible categories of matters that can be brought before the Court for arbitration: matters arising from an arbitration clause contained in a contract or agreement which confers such jurisdiction to which the Community or any of its institutions is a party; matters arising from a dispute between the Partner States regarding the Treaty, if the dispute is submitted to it under a special agreement between the Partner States concerned; and matters arising from an arbitration clause contained in a commercial contract or agreement in which the parties have conferred jurisdiction on the Court.[171]

While the Treaty does not oust the jurisdiction of national courts on disputes involving the Community, it gives two provisos. The first is that national jurisdiction would not supersede the Court's jurisdiction if the Treaty confers specific jurisdiction on the Court, and the second is that decisions of the Court on the interpretation and application of the Treaty shall have precedence over decisions of national courts on similar matters.[172] Another way in which the relationship between national courts and the Court can be used, is by requests made to the Court for preliminary rulings on the interpretation of the Treaty.[173] Such requests are lodged in the Appellate Division by way of a case stated.[174]

The Appellate Division has an appellate and a limited original jurisdiction. It hears and determines appeals from judgments of the First Instance Division,

---

[168] ibid, Art 30(1).
[169] ibid, Art 30(2).
[170] ibid, Art 31.
[171] ibid, Art 32.
[172] ibid, Art 33.
[173] ibid, Art 34.
[174] Rule 76(1) of the EAC Rules of Procedure.

and even this appellate jurisdiction is limited under Rule 77 of the EACJ Rules of Procedure. Appeals may only lie on points of law; on grounds of lack of jurisdiction; or procedural irregularity, and the Court's decisions are not subject to further appeal. The Appellate Division sits as a court of original jurisdiction to entertain requests from national courts of the Partner States for the EACJ to assist those (national) courts to authoritatively interpret the Treaty in cases brought before them.[175] The Division also has original (and therefore final) jurisdiction to provide advisory opinions under Article 36 of the Treaty.[176] One of the most prominent decisions delivered by the Court arose out of one such request for an advisory opinion, and is also one of the motivations for this study. In *The Matter of a Request by the Council of Ministers of the EAC for an Advisory Opinion on Variable Geometry*,[177] the Court determined, among others, whether the principle of variable geometry can apply to guide the integration process, the requirement on consensus in decision-making notwithstanding.

d. The Assembly

The East African Legislative Assembly (EALA) is comprised of nine members elected by each Partner State, and ex-officio members (the Minister and Deputy Minister responsible for East African Community Affairs from each Partner State, the Secretary General and the Counsel to the Community).[178] As the name suggests, the Assembly is the legislative organ of the Community, and is also responsible for the approval of the Community's budget, among other responsibilities.[179] Members of the Assembly are elected from the National Assemblies of each Partner State, and are expected to represent, as much as it is feasible, the various political parties, shades of opinion, gender and other special interest groups in that Partner State.[180] The procedure for this selection is determined by each Partner State, though the qualifications for members are laid down in the Treaty.[181] Each member of the Assembly can hold office for a maximum of two five-year terms.[182] The Assembly is presided over by a Speaker, who is elected from among the members of the Assembly,[183] and all decisions are determined by a majority of the votes of the members present and voting (ex-officio members of the Assembly are not entitled to vote).[184]

In line with the Community's policy of popular participation in the achievement of its objectives, and to enable the Council to take account of public

---

[175] Article 35 of the EAC Treaty and Rule 76 of the EACJ Rules of Procedure.
[176] Rule 75(1) of the EACJ Rules of Procedure.
[177] EACJ Application No. 1 of 2008. This case and its implications are in ch 6, section II.A.
[178] Article 48 of the EAC Treaty.
[179] ibid, Art 49.
[180] ibid, Art 50(1).
[181] ibid, Art 50(2).
[182] ibid, Art 51(1).
[183] ibid, Arts 53 and 56.
[184] ibid, Art 58.

opinion,[185] the Assembly is required to keep close relations with the National Assemblies of the Partner States. To achieve this, the Clerk of the Assembly sends records of all debates and Bills before the Assembly to the National Assemblies, and these are laid before the National Assemblies by the respective Ministers for East African Community Affairs.[186] Similarly, the Clerks to the National Assemblies must transmit to the Clerk of the Assembly records of the relevant debates,[187] and the Clerk sends these on to the Secretary General for the information of the Council.[188]

e. The Secretariat

The EAC Secretariat, based at the headquarters in Arusha, Tanzania, is the executive organ of the Community.[189] It is headed by the Secretary General, Deputy Secretaries General, Counsel to the Community, and such other offices as may be deemed necessary by the Council.[190] The Secretary General is appointed by the Summit for a five-year rotational term,[191] and is the principle executive officer of the Community. As principal executive officer, the Secretary General is the head of the Secretariat; the Accounting Officer of the Community; and the Secretary of the Heads of States Summit.[192] The Secretary General can only serve one five-year term.[193] The Counsel to the Community is a contractually appointed member of the Secretariat and is the principle legal adviser to the Community.[194]

The Secretariat is responsible for the day-to-day running of the Community, in addition to administrative responsibilities, and the initiation, coordination and harmonisation of policies and strategies relating to the development of the Community. It is the custodian of all Community property, and serves as a coordination point between the different organs and offices in the Community. It is also responsible for finances, both in a budgetary role, and in a resource mobilisation capacity in order to fund the implementation of projects of the Community. The Secretariat proposes agendas for the meetings organs of the Community, excluding the Court, and reports on the activities of the Community to the Council.[195] In the performance of the Secretariat's roles, its staff members are regarded as international civil servants and are responsible only to the Community. As such, they do not seek or receive instructions from any Partner State or any other authority external to the Community.[196]

[185] ibid, Art 65.
[186] ibid, Art 65(a) and (b).
[187] ibid, Art 65(c).
[188] ibid, Art 65(d).
[189] ibid, Art 66.
[190] ibid.
[191] ibid, Art 67(1).
[192] ibid, Art 67(3).
[193] ibid, Art 67(4).
[194] ibid, Art 69.
[195] ibid, Art 71.
[196] ibid, Art 72.

f. The Coordination Committee

The Coordination Committee consists of the Permanent Secretaries responsible for East African Community Affairs in each Partner State and such other Permanent Secretaries of the Partner States as each may determine.[197] The Committee submits reports and recommendations on the implementation of the Treaty to the Council, and implements its decisions as the Council may direct. In addition, the Committee oversees and coordinates the activities of the Sectoral Committees, which it can also request to investigate any particular matter.[198] The Committee meets at least twice a year, before the meetings of the Council, and may hold extraordinary meetings at the request of the Chairperson of the Committee.

g. Sectoral Committees

The Sectoral Committees are established by the Council on an ad hoc basis.[199] In accordance with the directions of the Council, Sectoral Committees are responsible for the preparation of a comprehensive implementation programme and the setting out of priorities with respect to their sectors.[200] They also monitor and constantly review the implementation of the programmes of the Community in their respective sectors.[201] The Committees are responsible to the Coordination Committee,[202] and meet as often as necessary for the proper discharge of their functions.[203]

ii. The Institutions

The Community has created several semi-autonomous institutions in order to implement its mandate.[204] These appear to be a blend of the 'outer organs' and the corporations created by the 1967 Treaty. While not all are relevant here, these institutions are listed below:

- the Civil Aviation Safety and Security Oversight Agency (CASSOA);
- the East African Development Bank (EADB);
- the East African Health Research Commission (EAHRC);
- the East African Kiswahili Commission (EAKC);

---

[197] ibid, Art 17.
[198] ibid, Art 18.
[199] ibid, Arts 14(3)(j) and 20.
[200] ibid, Art 21(a).
[201] ibid, Art 21(b).
[202] ibid, Art 21(c).
[203] ibid, Art 22d.
[204] EAC Website, *EAC Institutions*, www.eac.int/about/institutions (accessed 19 December 2016).

- the East African Science and Technology Commission (EASTECO);
- the Inter-University Council for East Africa (IUCEA);
- the Lake Victoria Basin Commission (LVBC); and
- the Lake Victoria Fisheries Organization (LVFO).[205]

For purposes of this chapter, the most relevant of these institutions is the EADB for its historical significance. The Bank was subsumed as a Community Institution by Article 9(3) of the EAC Treaty, as a 'surviving institution of the former East African Community'. While the Treaty does not define 'surviving institutions', it lists four institutions falling in this category: the East African Civil Aviation Academy; the EADB; the East African School of Librarianship; and the IUCEA. The literature is silent as to why these institutions remained operational after the 1977 collapse of the East African Community, though the EADB suggests its survival was due to the commitments made by the Member States which were signatories to the EADB Treaty. This survival prompted the shareholders to reorganise and strengthen the Bank's mandate. In 1980, the Bank was re-established under its own Charter,[206] with a broader, more robust mandate in which Member States sought to liberalise and loosen state control.[207]

When it reopened, the Bank pursued a decentralised structure, opening country offices in each of the Partner States, although the headquarters remained in Kampala, Uganda.[208] This enabled the Bank to broaden its reach across the region, spurring investment and recovery as it could finance a broader range of enterprises in agriculture, energy and telecommunications.[209] The 1980 EADB Charter reads like a company's Memorandum and Articles of Association, providing for the Bank's membership and objectives, among others. Under Article 1, these objectives include the provision of financial assistance to promote the development of the Member States, and to generally promote the development of the region. The Bank was set up to give attention, in accordance with its operating principles, to economic development in the Partner States, in such fields as industry, tourism, agriculture, infrastructure and similar or related fields.[210] This is done by supplementing the activities of national development agencies of the Partner States, by joint financing operations and technical assistance, and by the use of such agencies as channels for financing specific projects.[211]

---

[205] ibid.

[206] The Treaty Amending and Re-enacting the Charter of the East African Development Bank, entered into at the same time as the Charter of the East African Development Bank on 27 July 1980.

[207] EADB Website, *History*, www.eadb.org/about-us/history (accessed 20 December 2016).

[208] Article 32, EADB Charter.

[209] EADB Website, www.eadb.org/about-us/history.

[210] Article 1(c) of the EADB Charter.

[211] ibid, Art 1(e).

One remarkable difference between the 1967 EADB and the revived Bank is the absence of variable geometry in the allocation of resources. Under Article 13(c) of the 1967 EADB Charter, the bank was required to ensure that for every five-year period, Tanzania and Uganda would each receive 38.75 per cent of the total sum of loans, guarantees or investments made during that period, while Kenya was only entitled to receive 22.5 per cent. The 1980 Charter does not have this provision. It is possible that there was no need to 'level the ground' in favour of Tanzania and Uganda, or that in fact, the percentages made the Bank's operations difficult. This is particularly likely, given the political and economic challenges Uganda was going through in the 1970s, and the socialist approach Tanzania adopted during the same period. This would effectively mean that the Bank could only use up to 22.5 per cent of its potential loan portfolio, and that would not bode well for its profitability.

These organs and institutions are essential components of the EAC today, and should, hopefully enable the current Community to outlive its predecessors. While similar organs, or organs with similar responsibilities, were created by the 1967 Treaty for East African Cooperation, they had several challenges. As discussed earlier, the divergent political and economic aspirations held by the three integrating states would make it difficult to pursue a common goal. In addition, the absence of skilled personnel to fill the positions created by the 1967 Treaty meant that it could not be adequately implemented, even if it had been clearer and aspirations had been convergent.

Hopefully, the inclusion of asymmetry and variable geometry in the current revival of the bloc should facilitate an integration process less impeded by the differences of the past. This process would require organs and institutions whose roles and powers are clearly specified, avoiding the vagueness of the 1967 Treaty – whose organs and institutions the 1999 Treaty has made efforts to create.

C. The EAC Customs Union and Common Market

The EAC Treaty establishes a Customs Union between the Partner States,[212] and this is operationalised by the Protocol on the Establishment of the East African Customs Union (the Customs Union Protocol). By weighing this Customs Union against the definition of a Customs Union adopted earlier in this chapter,[213] it is possible to estimate whether indeed a customs union has been established.

---

[212] Article 75 of the EAC Treaty. It can be argued that this Article only indicates an agreement to establish the Customs Union, but a reading of Art 76 on the intended establishment of a Common Market shows, from the different wording used, that Art 75 does the actual establishment. A similar argument in favour of Art 75 only indicating an intention can be found in the fact that in Art 2(1) of the Customs Union Protocol, the Partner States 'hereby establish a customs union ...'. The present author adopts the interpretation that while the Treaty established the Customs Union, it was only operationalised by the Customs Union Protocol, entered into five years after the Treaty was signed.

[213] Section II.C, and Art XXIV(8) of GATT.

Article 75(1) of the Treaty provides for the details to be contained in the Customs Union Protocol, which adopts Article 75(1) *in toto*, and with some additions.[214] Among others, these Articles provide for the elimination of internal tariffs and other charges of equivalent effect; the elimination of non-tariff barriers; the establishment of a common external tariff; rules of origin; subsidies and countervailing duties; competition; customs cooperation; re-exportation of goods; and the simplification and harmonisation of trade documentation and procedures.

The Community has passed Acts and established institutions to facilitate the implementation of the Customs Union. For example, the East African Community Customs Management Act creates the Directorate of Customs, which is responsible for the initiation of policies on Customs and related trade matters in the Community and the coordination of such policies in the Partner States.[215] This Directorate is responsible for, among others, the administration of the Common External Tariff; enforcement of the Customs law of the Community; administration of the Rules of Origin and other aspects of the Customs Union.[216] Further implementation of the Customs Union between Partner States can be found in the set-up of facilities such as one-stop border posts, to enable the faster clearance of goods through borders, depending on whether they are goods produced in the region or imported. For example, under the EAC One Stop Border Posts Act, no border controls are carried out in the Partner State of exit, unless there is an express agreement with the adjoining Partner State.[217]

There are several examples in support of the implementation of the Customs Union, and similarly, for the Common Market. Article 76 of the EAC Treaty signals the intention to establish a Common Market among the Partner States. This was done in July 2010, when the Protocol on the Establishment of the EAC Common Market (the Common Market Protocol) came into force. This Protocol created what is now known as the four freedoms and two rights: free movement of goods; free movement of persons; free movement of services; free movement of capital; the right of establishment; and the right of residence.[218] Again, the actual existence of a Common Market can be assessed by checking the progress of the bloc against the definition of a common market adopted by this study.

As a starting point, this study concedes that at least, there is a customs union comprised of the EAC Partner States. What remains to be ascertained is whether, in addition to the Customs Union, there is free movement of factors

---

[214] Article 2(5).
[215] East African Community Customs Management Act, s 3.
[216] ibid, s 4(1).
[217] East African Community One Stop Border Posts Act, s 6.
[218] Article 2(4) of the Common Market Protocol, and Arts 76(1) and 104(1) and (2) of the EAC Treaty.

of production, and the two rights created by the Treaty. While an in-depth examination of these phenomena would be beyond the scope of this chapter, it is possible to identify activities in the Community that are in line with the Common Market's aspirations. The aforementioned One-Stop Border Posts Act is one example of how free movement of goods is being pursued by the Partner States. More specifically, the Common Market Protocol is an agreement to eliminate tariff, non-tariff and technical barriers to trade; harmonise and mutually recognise standards and implement a common trade policy for the Community.[219] It also seeks to ease cross-border movement of persons,[220] an aspiration which has led to the launch of the East African Passport.[221]

The Common Market Protocol also provides for the free movement of workers within the EAC. Thus, Article 10 requires non-discrimination of the workers of the other Partner States, based on their nationalities, in relation to employment, remuneration and other conditions of work and employment. The free movement of workers entitles a worker, among other things to: apply for and accept offers for employment; move freely within the territories of the Partner States for the purposes of employment; and enjoy the rights of workers in a Partner State, including social security and collective bargaining rights.[222]

To this end, the Partner States undertook to mutually recognise the academic and professional qualifications granted, experience obtained, requirements met, licences and certifications granted in the other Partner States.[223] While, admittedly, this would not happen in an instant, efforts have been made to achieve this goal. For example, it is now possible for lawyers to practice their trade across borders if they have qualified in some of the Partner States (Kenya and Uganda, mainly), and have gathered the requisite experience. This is, in part, due to successful lobbying by professional bodies, such as the East African Law Society.

Today, negotiations continue for the implementation of the Common Market Protocol. These negotiations are not on the terms of the Common Market, as these are enshrined in the Treaty and the Protocol. The negotiations are on the details of what needs to be done in order to ensure the freedoms and rights created by the Community in pursuit of a common market. One example has already been mentioned with cross-border legal practice. Taking professional services as an example, similar negotiations are going on for other professions to conclude Mutual Recognition of Qualification Agreements, with the fine print as to how to harmonise qualifications. As provided for under Article 11(1)(b) of the Common Market Protocol, this will involve the gradual harmonisation

---

[219] Article 5(2)(a) of the Common Market Protocol.

[220] ibid, Art 5(2)(b).

[221] Joint Communiqué from the 17th Ordinary Summit of the EAC Heads of State Summit, March 2016, available at www.eac.int/communique/374-446-526-joint-communique-17th-ordinary-summit-of-the-east-african-community-heads-of-state (accessed 20 July 2021).

[222] Article 10(3) of the Common Market Protocol.

[223] ibid, Art 11(1)(a).

of curricula, examinations, standards, certification and accreditation of educational and training institutions.

For a Common Market which has only existed since 2010, the EAC has made some considerable progress. Full existence of the freedoms and rights will take a while to realise, as there are many remaining constraints. These mainly stem from the differences in institutional and regulatory structure that the Partner States have developed over a long period of time. There is, however, hope. The Common Market and Customs Union both enjoy a fair amount of political goodwill, even though such goodwill is limited in some Partner States. It is on the back of such diversity of opinion that the Coalition of the Willing emerged.

IV. LOOKING FORWARD

By early 2019, the EAC was going through some upheavals in its relations. Some of the reasons for these upheavals are discussed in chapter six,[224] and appear to be a direct consequence of the use of flexible integration in the bloc. On 30 November 2018, for example, the 20th Ordinary Meeting of the EAC Summit ended in disarray after Burundi boycotted it, angry at how its concerns had been handled by the EAC Chairman, Uganda's President Yoweri Museveni.[225] A new date (27 December 2018) was agreed, but this did not materialise, with a postponement to early 2019. This time, it was claimed consultations were on-going as to an appropriate date.[226]

While this meeting was eventually held on 1 February 2019, this is the first time, under the current treaty, that a Heads of State Summit has been postponed on the basis of differences between political leaders or conflicting national interests. Given the history of the EAC described in this chapter, this does not bode well for the continued existence of the bloc. While these conflicts are mostly recent and still developing, it would be unwise not to mention them, however briefly.

Tensions simmered between the Partner States and their leaders along different planes between 2015 and 2018. As noted in chapter six, there is growing friction between Kenya and Tanzania, between Kenya and Uganda, and on and off between Tanzania and Uganda. There are also frosty relations between Burundi and Rwanda, Rwanda and Uganda, and more recently, between Uganda and Burundi. While the first three are considered in chapter six, it is important

---

[224] Chapter 6, section III.B.

[225] The East African, *Nkurunziza, Now Isolated, Creates Crisis All by Himself*, www.theeastafrican. co.ke/news/ea/Pierre-nkurunziza-now-isolated-creates-crisis-all-by-himself-/4552908-4886924-view-asAMP-m2hqqi/index.html?__twitter_impression=true (accessed 27 December 2018).

[226] The East African, *EAC Integration in Doubt as Summit Aborts Second Time*, www. theeastafrican.co.ke/news/ea/EAC-integration-in-doubt-as-summit-aborts-second-time/4552908-4906704-gwcew6/index.html (accessed 27 December 2018).

to have a brief look at the latter three conflicts, even if only to provide an indication to future writers on why the EAC faltered nearly twenty years after its reestablishment.

The East African cited differences between Presidents Paul Kagame of Rwanda and Pierre Nkurunziza of Burundi, and between Nkurunziza and President Yoweri Museveni of Uganda.[227] These differences are not independent of each other, but are interlinked, much like a Mexican standoff. According to Harold Achemah, a retired Ugandan diplomat, the Burundi-Uganda tensions stem mainly from the region's responses to the political challenges in Burundi. In May 2015, while President Nkurunziza was attending an EAC Summit meeting in Tanzania, there was an attempt to oust him as Burundi's president in a coup that failed upon his hurried return before the end of the meeting.[228]

In the aftermath of the coup attempt, President Museveni was appointed to mediate between Nkurunziza and other factions in Burundi, which were opposed to his third term bid. It was generally felt that Museveni did not perform adequately in this role, since he was heading into his most challenging election year at the time, and needed to concentrate on consolidating his position at home. Former Tanzanian President, Benjamin Mkapa, was the direct facilitator of the talks on behalf of Museveni.[229]

Mr Mkapa submitted a report which ignored Burundi's indictment of Rwanda for its involvement in the coup. This prompted Nkurunziza to decree that no outsider would interfere in the country's internal matters. In response to this, Museveni accused Nkurunziza of manipulating the EAC – using it when it suits him and discarding it when it does not.[230] Things came to a head when, in a letter dated 4 December 2018, Nkurunziza wrote to Museveni:

> In addition to the fact that Rwanda prepared and supervised the coup d'état of 2015, the coup perpetrators and other criminals have taken up residence in Rwanda where they receive support to attack Burundi … It is, therefore, urgent for the EAC to focus on the real problem that is jeopardising peace and security throughout Burundi. It is Rwanda, a state party to the EAC Treaty, which is not at its first attempt to destabilise its neighbour, Burundi, in violation of the fundamental principles of the Community … Rwanda is the only country in the region that is one of the main destabilisers of my country, and therefore, I no longer consider it a partner country, but simply as an enemy country.[231]

---

[227] The East African, *Nkurunziza* (n 225).

[228] BBC News, *Burundi President Nkurunziza Faces Attempted Coup*, www.bbc.co.uk/news/world-africa-32724083 (accessed 27 December 2018).

[229] A Bagala, *Museveni, Nkurunziza in Strong Exchange*, The Daily Monitor, www.monitor.co.ug/News/National/Museveni--Nkurunziza-strong-exchange/688334-4894670-rl9ijuz/index.html (accessed 27 December 2018).

[230] ibid.

[231] The East African, *Nkurunziza meets His Match as Museveni Answers Letter*, www.theeastafrican.co.ke/news/ea/4552908-4897182-12sjxww/index.html (accessed 27 December 2018).

This, of course, was not the only source of conflict between the two states. In December 2018, Rwanda blamed Burundi for the death of two Rwandans, after unknown assailants attacked a village in the south of Rwanda.[232] In the same week, Burundi accused the Rwandan marine forces of kidnapping four of its fishermen on Lake Rweru.[233] Just two days after this accusation, Rwanda's president Kagame warned enemies of Rwanda that they would be dealt with decisively if it became necessary.[234] These are just three reports in the space of six days, and are indicative of a rather tense neighbourhood.

There were also reports that citizens of the two countries do not go to each other's capitals.[235] It is not clear whether this is a result of state policy on either side, or whether it is the citizens themselves feeling unsafe on the other side of the border. Whichever it is, however, is not a sign of healthy relations between the two states, and, as seen from the postponement of Summit meetings, there is a regional spill-over of the acrimony.

At the same time as the spat between Burundi and Rwanda, which has inevitably dragged in Uganda as above, Rwanda and Uganda were not particularly hosting a party. While for the most part these have stayed below the surface, they have regularly become public spectacles with Uganda deporting Rwandans it accused of espionage and illegal entry, and Rwanda accusing Uganda of supporting dissidents. A meeting on 25 March 2018 between Presidents Kagame and Museveni to ease the tensions seem to have yielded little fruit, with the situation appearing to worsen. Rwanda accuses Uganda of arbitrarily arresting Rwandans in Uganda and seeking to destabilise Rwanda, with local media accusing the Ugandan president of speaking to and supporting David Himbara, one of Rwanda's most vocal critics. For its part, Uganda alleges segregation of Ugandan workers in Rwanda, with reports that some have lost their jobs without tangible explanations, disregarding the EAC Common Market Protocol.[236]

These tensions have, of course had implications for both countries' regional and continental relations. Early in 2018, Rwanda's president missed a summit of the EAC Heads of States in Uganda's capital, Kampala, and only weeks later, Uganda's President skipped the signing of the AfCFTA[237] Treaty in Kigali,

---

[232] The East African, *Kagame Blames Neighbours as Two are Killed in Attack*, www.theeastafrican.co.ke/news/ea/Kagame-blames-neighbours-for-deadly-attack/4552908-4897942-43wvpsz/index.html (accessed 27 December 2018).

[233] The East African, *Burundi Accuses Rwanda of Abducting Four Fishermen*, www.theeastafrican.co.ke/news/ea/Burundi-accuses-Rwanda-of-abducting-fishermen/4552908-4889312-11r6p78/index.html (accessed 27 December 2018).

[234] The East African, *Jitters in Region as Kagame Fires Military Action Warning*, www.theeastafrican.co.ke/news/ea/Jitters-in-region-as-Kagame-fires-military-action-warning/4552908-4892284-e4wry7z/index.html (accessed 27 December 2018).

[235] The East African, *Nkurunziza* (n 225).

[236] The East African, *Uganda, Rwanda Yet to Restore Cordial Relations*, www.theeastafrican.co.ke/news/ea/Uganda-and-Rwanda-yet-to-restore-cordial-relations/4552908-4697068-ubitdrz/index.html (accessed 28 December 2018).

[237] The Africa Continental Free Trade Area. This new bloc and its implications for the EAC are the subject of ch 7 in this book.

despite the absence of pressing engagements back home. It later emerged that Mr Museveni's handlers advised him to miss the AU meeting, mainly because efforts by his advance security and protocol teams to establish his accommodation and travel arrangements were frustrated by Rwandan security.[238] It is, perhaps, telling that Uganda is still one of the initial signatories to the AfCFTA Treaty, which indicates that it was not the Treaty that Museveni was opposed to, but more the venue of its signing, or rather, the hosts.

Tensions between Uganda and Rwanda culminated in Rwanda's closure of the main border post at Gatuna (Katuna on the Ugandan side) in February 2019.[239] Goods and passenger traffic was diverted to Mirama Hills-Kagitumba border post, nearly 114 kms away. At the time of the closure, it was under the guise of construction works going onto complete the One Stop Border Post,[240] the consistent diplomatic efforts to resolve the impasse suggest otherwise.[241] These have not yielded much fruit as, by July 2021, the border post remains closed, more than two years later, and the back-up border posts have been closed too.[242]

This three-way standoff has, as this section has shown, brought the EAC back to an all too familiar and concerning precipice. With leaders snubbing Summit meetings and trading accusations of the nature being reported on a nearly daily basis, it is a wonder how the bloc is still held together. Some in the corridors of power point at Burundi being the main problem, especially since it seems to be adamant that the EAC has not done enough to allay, or is the source of, its internal problems.[243] In fact, some commentators propose that Burundi should be expelled from the EAC, and only be readmitted when it is ready to play by the rules.[244]

With a new President at the helm in Bujumbura, there are indications that the direction of travel might change. In February 2021, he attended the 21st Summit of the EAC Heads of State, the first one to be held since he took office, and the first attended by a Burundian President since 2015. It can be argued that this was easier to do since this Summit was held via video conference[245] as a result of the

---

[238] The East African, *Focus on Kagame, Museveni in Simmering Diplomatic Cold War*, www.theeastafrican.co.ke/news/ea/Focus-on-Kagame-Museveni-in-simmering-diplomatic-cold-war-/4552908-4355428-e9qiehz/index.html (accessed 28 December 2018).

[239] All Africa, *Tension Builds Up Between Uganda, Rwanda Over Border Closure*, https://allafrica.com/view/group/main/main/id/00066601.html.

[240] Daily Monitor, *Traders Count Losses as Uganda-Rwanda Border Impass Persists*, www.monitor.co.ug/uganda/news/national/traders-count-losses-as-uganda-rwanda-border-impasse-persists-1810472.

[241] Daily Monitor, *We're Using Diplomatic Means to Resolve Rwanda Row – Minister*, www.monitor.co.ug/uganda/news/national/temporal-opening-of-uganda-rwanda-border-ends--1833388.

[242] All Africa, *Rwanda, Uganda Border Remains Shut Two Years Since Talks Began*, https://allafrica.com/view/group/main/main/id/00077425.html.

[243] The East African, *Nkurunziza* (n 225).

[244] For example, C Onyango-Obbo, *EAC, Just Let Burundi go, We Can Always Remarry*, The East African, www.theeastafrican.co.ke/oped/comment/EAC-just-let-Burundi-go-we-can-always-remarry/434750-4889314-8dwp20z/index.html (accessed 28 December 2018).

[245] The East African Community, *Communique of the 21st Ordinary Summit of the East African Community Heads of State*, 27 February 2021.

Covid-19 pandemic. It therefore remains to be seen whether this return to closer cooperation will continue in the future.

Another threat to the continued existence of the EAC is, of course, the lack of funding. Each Partner State is expected to contribute US$8.3 million to the EAC budget for 2018–2019, as decided by the EALA in June 2018. However, with Burundi and South Sudan in arrears from previous years, and none of the other Partner States up to date with their payments, the EAC was facing, by December 2018, a budgetary shortfall of US$1.4 billion.[246] As has been argued in chapter three, equal contributions to a bloc's budget can be unfair or impractical, and should be approached with some flexibility.[247] It is short of sensible to expect Burundi – a country that is a fraction the size of Kenya in area, population and economy – should make the same contribution as Kenya.

V. SUMMARY

This chapter has followed the evolution of the EAC from its establishment as a matter of convenience for the colonial governments of British East Africa, through the post-independence tumult, to the hopeful rebirth of the bloc at the dawn of the new millennium. It has, hopefully, laid the ground for an in-depth study of the issues discussed. The most important of these issues is, of course, the use of flexible integration in the EAC and other parts of Africa and the world. The history given in this chapter is revisited in chapters five and six of this volume, and more reference is made to the bloc's history in chapter seven, which studies integration in Africa on a continental level.

---

[246] The East African, *$1.4 Billion Budget Deficit Could Ground EAC Operations*, www.theeastafrican.co.ke/news/ea/billion-budget-deficit-could-ground-EAC-operations/4552908-4880340-fu91e0/index.html (accessed 28 December 2018).

[247] Chapter 3, section IV.

5

Flexible Regional Economic Integration in the East African Community

THIS CHAPTER STUDIES the historical, political, legal and economic context that led to the adoption of the East African Community's version of flexible regional economic integration – variable geometry. To this end, the first section gives a brief history of Article 7(1)(e) of the EAC Treaty,[1] looking at the negotiation process and documents leading up to the Treaty. It also relates the provision to Africa-wide integration efforts in the context of the African Economic Community. On the back of this, the second section considers the reasons for the inclusion of Article 7(1)(e) in the Treaty.

I. A BRIEF HISTORY OF ARTICLE 7(1)(E) OF THE EAC TREATY

In order to establish at which point variable geometry was introduced, the draft versions of the Treaty were studied in reverse chronological order. Article 7(1)(e) was found, in its current form, in every draft that was produced between 1997 when the first outline of the treaty was produced by the Permanent Tripartite Commission for East African Cooperation (PTCEAC), and 1999, when the resultant Treaty was signed. This necessitated looking further back to documents before the 1997 decision to revive the EAC Community.[2] The proposed outline for the Treaty is contained in the Report of the eighth Meeting of the PTCEAC (28 August 1997) and lists the principle of variable geometry as one of the proposed operational principles.[3] While this outline was the first step in the drafting of the EAC Treaty, it was not the earliest official document to contain the principle. The First EAC Cooperation Development Strategy (1997–2000),[4] launched in April 1997, contains the following paragraph:

> In order to facilitate the success of the East African Cooperation initiative, regional integration is also being viewed within the framework of the larger regional

---

[1] The Treaty for Establishment of the East African Community.
[2] Chapter 4 discusses the history of the EAC in detail.
[3] Paragraph 2.0, *Outline of Issues for Possible Inclusion in the Proposed Treaty*, contained in Annex IX to the Report of the 8th Meeting of the PTCEAC (EAC/C8/1/97).
[4] The East African Cooperation Development Strategy 1997–2000 EAC/DS/4/97.

integration schemes such as the Common Market for East and Southern Africa (COMESA). Recent experiences in regional integration have indicated that the approach to larger regional integration should allow for flexibility and incorporate the "principle of variable geometry". *This principle allows for progression in cooperation among a sub-group of members in larger integration schemes in a variety of areas and at different speeds.* To be successful, integration in the East, Central and Southern Africa region will therefore need to proceed on a multi-speed basis with a variety of focal points. The East African Cooperation is therefore bound by this principle and forms one of the multi-speed focal points (emphasis added).[5]

Two main things arise out of this paragraph. First, it suggests that the EAC (and not the EAC Partner States) is the intended 'subgroup' within the context of a continent-wide integration. Second, the definition of variable geometry in the 1997 Development Strategy is, verbatim, the same as it is in the Treaty today. These two issues warrant some further discussion.

A. The Double-Edged Context

The first issue is the possibility that for purposes of variable geometry, the EAC was meant as a sub-group of Africa-wide integration efforts. This idea is considered again in chapter seven in the context of continent-wide integration,[6] so this section limits itself to the concept and how it relates to the EAC.

Paragraph 32 of the EAC Development Strategy is silent on the origin of variable geometry, but it is a clear reference to the idea that the EAC would be only a smaller part of a larger integration effort across the African continent.[7] This is a reference to the 1980 Lagos Plan of Action, the Final Act of Lagos, and the 1991 Treaty Establishing the African Economic Community (AEC), signed in Abuja, Nigeria.[8] While this latter treaty does not expressly provide for variable geometry, it lays the foundation for a multi-centric approach to economic integration in Africa. For example, in Article 4(1)(d), one of the main objectives of the AEC is to coordinate and harmonise policies among existing and future economic communities in order to foster the gradual establishment of the Community. In Article 4(2)(a) and (b), the AEC aims to gradually strengthen the existing regional economic communities and establish others where they do not exist, as well as conclude agreements aimed at harmonising and coordinating policies among sub-regional and regional economic communities. In addition, the Abuja Treaty specifically provided for a gradual approach to integration (Article 6(1)), which is the approach adopted by the EAC.

---

[5] ibid, para 32.
[6] Chapter 7, sections I.B and III.
[7] This pan-African context is discussed further, ibid.
[8] To avoid mixing it up with the EAC Treaty, this Treaty is referred to as the Abuja Treaty.

Gradualism[9] and its attendant flexibility, as used by the AEC and eventually, the EAC, are based on the 1980 Lagos Plan of Action (LPA) and the Final Act of Lagos (FAL),[10] agreed to by the then members of the Organisation of African Unity (OAU) – now the African Union (AU). Under Paragraph II.B.1 of the FAL, the plan was to strengthen existing regional economic communities and establish other economic groupings in other regions of Africa, so as to cover the continent as a whole (Central, Eastern, Southern and Northern Africa). This was to be done during the decade of the 1980s but, as can be deduced from the establishment of the EAC in 1999, this aspiration was not achieved. This failure notwithstanding, it is clear that variable geometry (even before it was so-called) was intended to be used in the context of continental economic integration, with regional economic groups assuming the role of 'smaller economic groupings'.

This is important for several reasons. In the first instance, it suggests that at least within the context of the EAC, and consequently in this book, variable geometry has been misconstrued, since it has been used to refer to a collection of states within the EAC rather than the EAC as a subset of the AEC. It can, however, be argued that this interpretation has been drawn from the practice of the EAC. Second, it shows the vital link between the EAC's variable geometry and the Africa-wide integration efforts. This is useful in understanding the origin of the principle, since the EAC documents and interviews do not directly reveal it. Described in linear form, the history of variable geometry in the EAC looks like this:

Image 5.1 Timeline of Variable Geometry in the EAC

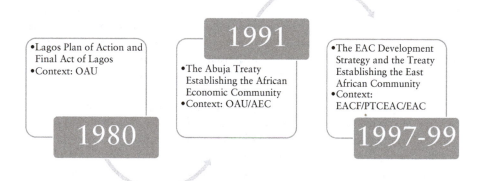

From this timeline, variable geometry – or at least some form of flexible regional economic integration – was conceived by the OAU in 1980, and included in the

---

[9] Gradualism is defined and discussed in section I.B below, as a synthesis of variable geometry, asymmetry and consolidation, all of which are forms of flexible integration.

[10] Annex 1 to the Lagos Plan of Action.

Lagos Plan of Action and the Final Act of Lagos. In 1991, the AEC adopted the gradualist approach for its establishment, relying on the existing and future regional blocs as building blocks for the establishment of a continent-wide trading community. The EAC took this approach a step further, defining it as variable geometry in the 1999 EAC Treaty, and applying it to even smaller units – states.

B. The Unchanging Clause

The premise that variable geometry was imported into the EAC context at some point between 1991 and 1997 leads to the second issue arising out of Paragraph 32 of the EAC Development Strategy. While much of the EAC Treaty evolved during the negotiation process, Article 7(1)(e) is one of the few provisions that remained unchanged. Some articles were expanded to cover a wider scope, or streamlined, and a few were abandoned altogether. For example, the 1997 strategy provides for the following objectives of the East African Cooperation in Paragraph 13 which were to:

- strengthen and consolidate cooperation in agreed fields with a view to bringing about equitable development among the Member States and thereby uplift the living standards and quality of life of the people;
- promote sustainable utilisation of the region's natural resources and put in place measures for effective protection of the environment;
- enhance the role of women in development; and
- promote peace, security and good neighbourliness in the region.

By the time of the final text, the objectives of the Treaty had been merged into one paragraph, and the above four were modified and included as strategies for achieving the main objective. As stated in Article 5(1) of the EAC Treaty:

> The objectives of the Community shall be to develop policies and programmes aimed at widening and deepening cooperation among the Partner States in political, economic, social and cultural fields, research and technology, defence, security and legal and judicial affairs, for their mutual benefit.[11]

The four original objectives, which became strategies for achieving the objective, are now included in Article 5(3) of the EAC Treaty, which reads, in relevant part:

> For Purposes set out in paragraph 1 of this Article and as subsequently provided in particular provisions of this Treaty, the Community shall ensure:
>
> a) the strengthening and consolidation of cooperation in agreed fields that would lead to equitable economic development within the Partner States and which would in turn, raise the standard of living and improve the quality of life of their populations;

---

[11] Article 5(1) of the EAC Treaty.

b)   the promotion of sustainable utilisation of the natural resources of the Partner States and the taking of measures that would effectively protect the natural environment of the Partner States;

c)   the mainstreaming of gender in all its endeavours and the enhancement of the role of women in cultural, social, political, economic and technological development;

d)   the promotion of peace, security, and stability within, and good neighbourliness among, the Partner States.[12]

This Article alone shows that considerable work was done to transform the ideas of the PTCEAC into actionable and binding treaty provisions, which can probably be expected of any treaty making process. It therefore seems curious that Article 7(1)(e) would be a guiding principle in the Cooperation and Development Strategy, survive through multiple drafts, and end up in the final Treaty unchanged.

It is important to point out that there are two articles defining variable geometry in the EAC Treaty, and that the two differ slightly. The first is the interpretation section of the Treaty (Article 1), and the second is Article 7 itself, the latter of which provides for the operational principles of the Community. Even then, the first article only differs from the original version by the conversion of 'larger integration schemes' to the singular form:

> the 'principle of variable geometry' means the principle of flexibility which allows for progress in cooperation among a sub-group of members in *a larger integration scheme* in a variety of areas and at different speeds.[13] (emphasis added)

The second provision, Article 7(1)(e), dispenses with the express statement that variable geometry is a principle of flexibility:

> The principles that shall govern the practical achievement of the objectives of the Community shall include the principle of variable geometry, which allows for progression in cooperation among groups within the Community for wider integration schemes in various fields and at different speeds.

By juxtaposing the three versions, it is easy to see that although there might be a slight difference in the wording, the meaning is essentially the same. In table 5.1, **bold type** represents the part of the definition that relates to the desire to keep the integration process in motion. Text in *italics* relates to the part of the provision that allows some members to implement treaty provisions amongst themselves, while ***italicised bold type*** refers to the possibility of subject-specific flexibility. <u>Underlined</u> text, which appears in exactly the same words in all three versions, refers to the time-scope flexibility of variable geometry.[14]

---

[12] ibid, Art 5(3).
[13] ibid, Art 1(1).
[14] Chapter 3, section I explores these elements at length.

Table 5.1 Juxtaposition of Varying Definitions of Variable Geometry

Development Strategy[15]	Interpretation Section Version[16]	Operational Principles Version[17]
This principle allows for **progression in cooperation** *among a sub-group of members in larger integration schemes in a variety of areas* and at different speeds.	The 'principle of variable geometry' means the principle of flexibility which allows for **progress in cooperation** *among a sub-group of members in a larger integration scheme in a variety of areas* and at different speeds.	The principle of variable geometry, which allows for **progression in cooperation** *among groups within the Community for wider integration schemes in various fields* and at different speeds.

The consistency or unchanging nature of the principle of variable geometry and its definition is an indication of two things. First, variable geometry was not as contentious as the other principles and articles might have been, and all parties agreed with its inclusion right from the start of the negotiation process. Nothing in the PTCEAC reports during the negotiation period shows that it ever caused contention, and it does not seem to have led to much discussion in civil society circles during this time.[18] Second, the principle clearly predates the EAC's earliest documents, and can only have been introduced before the negotiation process commenced.

Understanding the origin of variable geometry requires a look back beyond the bloc's earliest documents and history. An interview with Professor Sam Tulya-Muhika, former chairperson of the East African Cooperation Forum (EACF)[19] revealed that variable geometry was introduced into the EAC Treaty in two ways: first as a working method for the EACF, and second, as a proposed principle for the integration process. In order to achieve the goal of reviving the EAC, the EACF adopted a 'willing party' approach:

> … we initiated a process of variable geometry, not by country but by groups. We teamed up with the private sector, and said, 'If the presidents will not do it, the people are going to do it.' The primary driver in Tanzania was not the government; it was the CTI (Confederation of Tanzanian Industries). KAM (Kenyan Association

---

[15] Paragraph 32 of the East African Development Strategy.

[16] Article 1(1) of the EAC Treaty.

[17] ibid, Art 7(1)(e).

[18] Reports of workshops and conferences held by, among others, the East African Law Society.

[19] The EACF was a cross-sectoral forum, bringing together academics and the private sector in Kenya, Uganda and Tanzania. Started in 1989, the Forum had one goal: the revival of the EAC. It was a private sector initiative started in 1989 by academicians, industrialists, businessmen, professionals, consultants and some politicians (in their private capacity) from the three East African states, who believed there was a case for re-integration of the East African countries. (See *Report of the Third Meeting of the East African Cooperation Forum*, Nairobi, Kenya, July 1992, p 1).

of Manufacturers) and UMA (Uganda Manufacturers Association), joined in. We decided the private sector is now going to push the politicians, and we did. It (the EACF) was academia, people who worked with the East African Community before, and the private sector. This is also a variable geometry in the route to integrate: those who are ready do it. You are ready, you want to expand, let's start. Let's go and tell government, 'I want to trade across the border. I have these problems, and you can't solve them by quarrelling with the next country all the time, because you are hurting me.'[20]

This approach proved effective in getting more bodies and eventually, governments on board. Coupled with the realisation that flexibility was necessary for integration, it led to its inclusion in the proposals made to the governments and eventually the PTCEAC. Tulya-Muhika is quick to acknowledge that the current theory of regional integration has been largely informed by the process of European integration. He notes that the principle of variable geometry has always been on the books for Europe:

> There was a time between completion of the European Customs Union in 1958 and the Single European Act of 1986 when there was sharp disagreement partly because of differences in linguistics or punctuation. In the CAD (Common Administration Document), there was a dispute between the French and the Germans. I was told this story by a German, so there must be a German slant in it (laughter). The disagreement was about the meaning or use of a coma and a semi-colon. The difference was so sharp, it held this up for a long time, and so it was decided as an interim arrangement that for goods destined to Germany, the French use their interpretation of the Convention until the difference was sorted out. There was this accommodative undercurrent, that where we disagree, let us for the time being act as disagreed or as agreed to disagree, until we sort it out, rather than endanger the bigger purpose.[21]

In the view of the EACF, variable geometry (by whatever name, at the time) had been useful even beyond the EU. According to Tulya-Muhika, it was an old principle that was derived from the process of the formation of the US, which is the most complete (though not entirely complete) common market:

> ... there are still some cities, like Evanston, Illinois, where no hard drinks are sold.[22] There are parts of the United States where you cannot import alcohol into that city and so on. When I first flew to the US, there were even some dry states! There are always these kinds of accommodations, so that rather than leave you out, we'll keep you in, but you can keep your idiosyncrasies.

---

[20] Interview with Prof Sam Tulya-Muhika.

[21] ibid.

[22] Cross-checking this showed that Evanston has allowed the sale of liquor since 1972. However, many counties in the US are still 'dry communities', and three states (Kansas, Mississippi and Tennessee) outlaw the sale of alcohol by default, though they permit counties/cities to authorise such sales.

The economic benefit of flexibility in Malaysia was also cited in the adoption of variable geometry in the EAC:

> The states of Sabah and Sarawak in Malaysia on the island of Borneo practice Sharia Law, and Malaysians from the mainland need a visa[23] to go to these two states. Malaysia is a federation, and even though the two states want to keep their pure Islamic principles, they agreed to keep the union. It is a bit idiosyncratic to think like that, 'as long as economically you are with us, that's fine. You can determine your principles of Islam, we'll have our own.'

> It is mixed. You go to a supermarket and drinks are there, *toa*![24] They also have Christians and a Chinese society, who are the captains of industry and capital. They'll have the halal section and the non-halal, where there's pork (and alcohol). They have a big section of drinks in the supermarket, not for sale to Muslims. I don't know how they tell who's a Muslim and who's not (laughter), but they've tried to accommodate everybody, so that they can achieve a common objective.

These experiences were the thinking behind the flexibility in the EAC Treaty. The EACF felt that no country should be left behind, whether because it lacks capacity, or is reluctant to integrate, or for any other reason. There was a clear desire to take everybody along, accommodate social and socio-political differences, and focus on economic integration. As the EACF admitted, the processes of integration are quite complex, especially if the states are already formed.[25] Existing states have existing structures, and integration would mean coordinating these from multiple centres of power. As Tulya-Muhika says,

> [The old EAC] was a beautiful arrangement, because it had been organised and arranged by the British, who managed it from Whitehall. It had one policy centre.[26] The problem of integrating or trying to manage a common market with different governments as actors is that management of the economy is one of the three principal functions of government (law and order, regulation of the market, and service delivery). If you regionalise any of those three, you need a [regional] government. It does not matter if it is a weak one, a federation, or a commission like the EU. You need somebody who can call everybody to order and regulate the market.

As states would not be willing to cede sovereignty to a regional body, variable geometry became an inevitable alternative, in order to allow them the flexibility to implement the treaty provisions on their terms. Until the EAC integrates politically, variable geometry will remain essential.

---

[23] This is a reference to the formation of the Malaysian federation in 1963. In the period immediately after, some parts of the federation, notably Sabah and Sarawak had differentiated immigration requirements for the citizens of other states, requiring citizens to present a passport or identity card at the border before admission.

[24] Kiswahili for remove/take.

[25] This sentiment is reminiscent of Tanzanian founding father, Julius Nyerere's desire to postpone Tanzanian independence in favour of creating a unified EAC in the 1960s (ch 4, section I on the history of the EAC).

[26] This perspective is briefly explored in ch 4, section I of this study.

Variable geometry in East Africa would have been unnecessary if there was some kind of due political process of integration. There would have been a political decision-maker at the regional level, listening to Uganda, to Tanzania, and saying, 'why don't we accommodate you this way or that way, so that we move together?'[27]

It is safe to say that the EACF achieved its goals,[28] since its work was taken over by the PTCEAC in 1993. The PTCEAC drafted the aforementioned East African Cooperation Development Strategy of 1997, which contained variable geometry as a guiding principle.[29] Variable geometry was introduced as one of three aspects of the 'Gradualism Principle',[30] the other two aspects being the principle of subsidiarity and the consolidation approach. The principle of subsidiarity emphasises multi-level participation and the involvement of a wide range of stakeholders in the process of integration.[31] According to the PTCEAC, 'subsidiarity' relates to the appropriate division of responsibilities between the regional layers of governance on one hand, and national governments on the other.[32] It is worth noting that subsidiarity in the EAC context differs slightly from the EU context, in which the Union only acts if the objectives of a proposed action cannot be sufficiently achieved by Member States. The EU resorts to subsidiarity where the scale or effects of a proposed action would be better achieved at Union level.[33]

The consolidation approach did not expressly make it into the Treaty as an operational principle, but arguably, it was not entirely discarded. The PTCEAC defined 'consolidation' as a method of integration which starts with low-cost or free projects with high success being an expectation. The early successes are then consolidated through strong regional institutions to avoid any reversals, and are built up into refined and consolidated, larger projects and programmes.[34] This is, possibly, the thinking behind the gradual approach to integration adopted by the EAC, which aims to evolve from a Customs Union into a Political Federation.[35]

Gradualism, then, is a synthesis of the principles of variable geometry, subsidiarity and consolidation, and is similar to Ernst Haas' disjointed incrementalism.[36] This is a way of making decisions under conditions of uncertainty, in a setting of bargaining among sets of participants with partly convergent and partly opposing interests. It is a 'rational' second-best strategy

[27] Interview with Prof Sam Tulya-Muhika.
[28] *cf* History of the EAC, in ch 4.
[29] PTCEAC Secretariat, *Synopsis on East African Cooperation,* April 1999, Arusha, Tanzania p 15.
[30] ibid, p 18.
[31] Article 7(1)(d) of the EAC Treaty
[32] PTCEAC Secretariat (n 29) p 18.
[33] Article 5(3) of the Treaty on European Union.
[34] ibid.
[35] Article 5(2) of the EAC Treaty.
[36] Discussed as a theory of integration in ch 2, Section II.C.

under these constraints, which is valued as a process by certain analysts and actors because it is participatory and consensual, and is accepted by decision makers as a reality, good or bad.[37]

In addition to these three principles, one other was introduced into the Treaty during the drafting process. The 'principle of asymmetry' seeks to address variances in the implementation of measures in an economic integration process for the purposes of achieving a common objective.[38] While this is clearly a principle of flexibility, it appears in neither the Development Strategy nor the initial Treaty Outline. According to Tulya-Muhika, asymmetry differs from variable geometry in that while variable geometry excludes slow or unwilling partners, asymmetry seeks to include them by encouraging them to implement treaty provisions, albeit at a slower pace.[39] Effectively, variable geometry is an exclusionary approach to flexibility, while asymmetry is an inclusive approach.

While 'asymmetry' has not been used much in practice, it can be argued that the current state of the Economic Partnership Agreement (EPA) with the European Union is a reflection of this brand of flexibility. The EPA is not in force until all EAC Partner States have signed it. However, Kenya and Rwanda signed the Agreement in 2016, while the other four EAC Partner States have not signed for various reasons. In line with the principle of asymmetry, Kenya and Rwanda have shown their readiness to cooperate with the European Union by signing the EPA, but this cooperation will not start until the other four members have signed. This differs from variable geometry because in variable geometry, Kenya and Rwanda would have had the option to start the cooperation with the EU, and the rest would join whenever they were willing or ready.

This 'gradualism' and flexibility adopted by the PTCEAC, coupled with the inclusive asymmetry approach of the EACF, were regarded as remedies to the past failures of integration in the EAC. For its part, the EACF wanted a process which would avoid the decline of the 1970s, and therefore pushed the governments of the three countries to integrate in a manner that would avoid a repeat of the 1976–77 crisis.[40] Flexibility was considered the best way to do this. When the PTCEAC took over the process and it became a formal negotiation process, its mandate was to produce a treaty that was not rigid enough to buckle under possible political pressure or conflict. It is increasingly clear that this is how variable geometry and its 'flexibility cousins', such as asymmetry and gradualism, were adopted by the EAC.

---

[37] EB Haas, 'Turbulent Fields and the Theory of Regional Integration' (1976) (30) *International Organisation* 173–212, 183.
[38] Articles 1(1) and 7(1)(h) of the EAC Treaty.
[39] Interview with Prof Sam Tulya-Muhika.
[40] Discussed in ch 4, section II.D.

C. The Connection between the Unchanging Clause and the Africa-wide Link

The preceding sections have shown two main things: first, that the EAC imported the principle from the AEC, and second, that the EAC version of the principle of variable geometry remained unchanged from the first time it appeared. What has not been discussed is the transformation it underwent as the EAC imported it into its own documents. This study found no document older than the 1997 EAC Development Strategy that uses similar wording to define variable geometry, or even call it by this name. Although it is possible to infer, from the wording of the Development Strategy, that the principle is based on the AEC ideals, the AEC wording is not as clear as the EAC definition. This could mean one of two things. First, the current definition of variable geometry, as used by the EAC, might in fact be an EAC creation – a consolidation of the AEC aspects of flexibility into what is now called variable geometry. Alternatively, the EAC Development Strategy quotes an uncited source for the definition of variable geometry, and this uncredited source is lost to memory as no records appear to exist between the AEC (1991) and the EAC (1997).

Regardless of what the case may be, this rather circuitous journey has been an attempt to understand the history of variable geometry in the EAC. The connection between the unchanging clause and the Africa-wide link is the necessity of the principle itself. Whether it was imported from the AEC to enable the EAC to be a cog in the continental process of integration, and then misconstrued, or borrowed and modified to fit the EAC context – hence the unique interpretation and application – the fact that it remained unchanged shows how vital it was to the reestablishment of the EAC. The only other logical explanation for the principle's unchanged nature would be that its impact was so minor that it went through three years of negotiations unnoticed and therefore unchanged.

This connection is revisited in chapter seven, where the use of the gradualist approach to regional economic integration is demonstrated by the incremental establishment of the Africa Continental Free Trade Area (AfCFTA). That chapter shows how flexible regional economic integration continues to play an invaluable role in continent-wide integration, more than forty years since its inception in the Lagos Plan of Action and the Final Act of Lagos.

II. WHY FLEXIBLE REGIONAL ECONOMIC INTEGRATION IN THE EAC?

This section considers two aspects of the EAC's history that may have led to the negotiation and inclusion of variable geometry in the EAC Treaty – the political and economic factors. While these reasons have already been considered in some detail,[41] the following pages synthesise the African experience of economic

---

[41] Chapter 4, on the History of the EAC, ch 2, section III, on an 'Africanisation' of Integration Theory, and ch 3, section IV on the reasons for flexible regional economic integration.

integration with the theory of flexible integration and the history of the EAC to explain the region's variable geometry.

A. Political Factors

At the reinstitution of the EAC, one of the primary goals was to avoid a repeat of the factors that led to the bloc's collapse in 1977. The preamble to the EAC Treaty attributes this collapse, in part, to the lack of strong political will from the Partner States. This realisation led to the determination to 'strengthen their economic, social, cultural, political, technological and other ties for their fast, balanced, and sustainable development by the establishment of an East African Community'.[42]

The most glaring political factor responsible for the existence of variable geometry in the EAC Treaty is the differing, often divergent political aspirations present in the Partner States. As reported in chapter four,[43] Kenya adopted a mixed system in order to attract foreign investment and foster a growing private sector. Tanzania preferred a socialist approach, while Uganda sought to nationalise the private sector, as demonstrated by President Idi Amin's expulsion of Asian traders in 1972. Remnants of divergences remained while the current EAC Treaty was being negotiated in the late 1990s, although in different forms. For example, while Tanzania was still holding on to a form of socialism, Uganda had taken on ambitious structural reform spurred on by the World Bank, and the birth of the WTO. Variable geometry would therefore be an appropriate safety valve in case political ambitions led the Partner States down different individual paths. This way, they could cooperate where possible, without necessitating a collapse of the bloc as was experienced in the 1970s.

Related to this is the fact that variable geometry is a safe way to deal with opposing sovereignties. With each state attempting to push for its interests and the interests of its citizens, it is often necessary for one to yield its sovereignty in favour of another or the others. In an interview with Lilian Awinja,[44] it was revealed that sovereignty adds to the complexity of integration. Governments prefer to make their own decisions rather than be handed policies that have been agreed at the regional level – especially at the highest political level – and are not necessarily good for national governments and their countries. Many times, implementation of treaty provisions and regional decisions stalls because of such issues. When this happens, resort is often had to variable geometry, in the hope to both continue the process of integration and to preserve the sovereignty of the states involved.

---

[42] The Preamble to the EAC Treaty.
[43] Chapter 4, section II.D.
[44] Lilian Awinja, Executive Director, East African Business Council.

As the preamble to the EAC Treaty admits, the EAC enjoys a rich history of colonial and pre-colonial cooperation. This history has had some impact on the nature of the relations between the EAC states.[45] For example, the colonial distribution of the Community's organs and institutions in the 1940s and 1950s led, inevitably, to a varied and imbalanced distribution of resources between the Partner States, which also led to imbalanced development. In the current bloc, this has been ameliorated by keeping the headquarters of EAC Institutions in one place – Arusha in Tanzania – while ensuring that each state enjoys the benefits of the institutions equitably. Variable geometry allows the bloc to keep one centre of power (unlike the 1967–1977 bloc that had multiple centres of power) even though the Partner States may be at different stages of integration for different aspects of the integration process.

Another reason variable geometry exists in the EAC Treaty is to create a safety valve in case relations between the Partner States get frosty as they did in the 1970s.[46] With variable geometry, a collapse can be avoided when interests become divergent or even opposite. Arguably, this is exactly what has happened in the EAC. When Tanzania preferred a slower, more cautious approach to integration, Kenya, Uganda and Rwanda instead chose an accelerated schedule, resulting in the creation of the NCIP.

Variable geometry in the EAC Treaty helps accommodate the multi-faceted approach to integration used by the bloc. The ultimate goal of the EAC is to create a political federation comprising the Partner States.[47] The Community's main objective is:

> to develop policies and programmes aimed at widening and deepening cooperation among the Partner States in political, economic, social and cultural fields, research and technology, defence, security, and legal and judicial affairs, for their mutual benefit.[48]

Clearly, this covers a wide scope of activities and areas of collaboration. Moving at the same pace on all of them for six Partner States would be a herculean task, and so the pragmatic approach would be to allow an à la carte model, in which Partner States can focus on select areas for cooperation. In the EAC, the most cooperation has been on trade matters, and even then, the depth of integration varies from country to country, as the NCIP demonstrates. This is, of course, understandable, since boosting intra-regional trade would go a long way in achieving the bloc's goals of economic growth and development. The focus has been on the reduction of tariff and non-tariff barriers to trade, as discussed in chapter four.[49]

---

[45] See ch 4, sections I, and II.D.
[46] Chapter 4, section II.D, and AT Mugomba, 'Regional Organisations and African Underdevelopment: The Collapse of the East African Community' (1978) 16(1) *Journal of Modern African Studies* 261–272, 263.
[47] Preamble to the EAC Treaty.
[48] Article 5(1) of the EAC Treaty.
[49] Chapter 4, section III.A.

One reason for the existence of flexible integration cited in chapter three is the varied objective capacity and subjective political will to integrate.[50] Flexible integration as envisioned in the EAC Treaty enables states to pursue integration at different speeds and degrees, and in spite of their differences. This provision therefore exists due to lessons from the past, and as an attempt not to 'test the depth of the water with both feet.'

B. Economic Factors

Economic reasons for the existence of Article 7(1)(e) would come down to the practicalities surrounding the integration process, such as the distribution of responsibilities, resources and benefits. This section outlines these.

A recurrent theme in this study has been and continues to be the unequal benefits that accrue from integration. Predictably, this is a natural consequence when countries with differing economic capacities and levels of political commitment attempt to meet in the middle as a bloc. Determining this 'middle' can be a great challenge, especially when the integrating economies are varied in size and type. Distributional equity is not only a question of the asymmetrical economic benefits of trade integration, but also a function of unequal 'networks of power, information and knowledge' between African economies.[51]

The EAC Treaty identifies disproportionate sharing of benefits of the Community as a contributing factor to the 1977 collapse of the bloc.[52] This disproportion was due to differences in levels of development, and the attendant lack of policies to address this situation. The details of these inequalities have been discussed in chapter four,[53] and while mechanisms to redistribute the gains of integration were put in place from time to time,[54] none seems to have sufficiently settled the inequality. It is, arguably, in response to this issue, that variable geometry was introduced in order to allow states to participate as and when their economies would allow them, so that no injustice – perceived or actual – is caused.

Closely related to the distribution of benefits is the distribution of responsibilities and costs of integration. Prior to the 1967 Treaty for East African Cooperation, Kenya was dissatisfied with bearing an unequal burden within the Community.[55] Although the 1967 Treaty did away with some of this discontent,

---

[50] Chapter 3, section IV.A, and N Koenig, *A differentiated View of Differentiated Integration,* Policy Paper 140, Jacques BelorInstitut, Berlin, 23 July 2015, p 7.

[51] J Gathii, *African Regional Trade Agreements as Legal Regimes* (Cambridge, Cambridge University Press, 2011) 37.

[52] Preamble to the EAC Treaty.

[53] Chapter 4, section II.D.

[54] ibid and A Hazlewood, *Economic Integration: The East African Experience* (London, Heinemann, 1975) 39–45.

[55] See ch 4, section I.

the inequality was not properly assuaged, leading to the bloc's dissolution in 1977. This introduced the need for a two-pronged approach to equalisation – with costs on the one hand and benefits on the other. The EAC found variable geometry, which permits both voluntary participation and voluntary restraint from participation in some integration projects, as an appropriate approach to dealing with both inequalities.

Another economic factor that would lay the ground for the adoption of variable geometry in the EAC Treaty is the nature and volumes of trade between the Partner States. As previously discussed,[56] the EAC Partner States trade in small volumes of different goods and services. The result of this situation is that apart from unequal national gains, integration based on a classical free trade/comparative advantage model does not necessarily create new opportunities that induce a greater number of people to enjoy the benefits of growth in poor economies that share the same characteristics.[57] The adoption of such a model without adapting it to the African context of huge disparities in export and economic power is one of the reasons for the failure and ultimate disbandment of the original EAC in 1977.[58] It would therefore be difficult to aggregate trade in order to benefit from external markets, while there would also be complexities deciding which sectors to favour across the region. Therefore, the most logical solution would be to adopt policies that allow domestic economies to thrive while allowing for closer regional cooperation for external trade. Variable geometry has enabled this.

Chapter four shows that the final blow to the earlier integration process in East Africa came from external shocks, principally in the form of Kenya's balance of payment crisis in 1971–72, the global oil price shocks of 1973, and the commodity boom of 1976–77, to which each Partner State reacted differently.[59] Given that at the time, all three Partner States had to make joint or at least similar economic decisions, these events led to a rapid disintegration. With the current treaty, however, it is possible, in theory at least, for the bloc to survive such shocks. For example, in the event that Uganda's trade in coffee (worth US$402.6 million in 2015[60]) would collapse, it would experience a significant shortfall to its economy. Rather than risk an end to the bloc's existence due to Uganda's reduced participation, variable geometry would permit it to participate within its reduced sphere of capability, thereby enabling the continued existence of the Community.

---

[56] Chapter 4, section III.
[57] CV Vaitsos, 'Crisis in Regional Economic Cooperation (Integration) Among Developing Countries: A Survey' 1(978) 6 *World Development* 719–769, 739.
[58] Gathii, *African Regional Trade Agreements* (n 51) 40.
[59] Chapter 4, section II.D.
[60] Wits – COMTRADE Data at www.wits.worldbank.org (accessed 6 February 2017).

III. SUMMARY

This chapter has attempted to create a meeting point between the theory on flexible integration and the history of the EAC, explaining why and how the EAC included the principle of variable geometry in its constituent treaty. It has also shown the origins of Article 7(1)(e) of the EAC Treaty, and its basis on continent-wide integration. Chapter six evaluates the most significant application of Article 7(1)(e) of the EAC Treaty so far: the establishment of the Northern Corridor Integration Projects (NCIP). It considers the reasons for the establishment of the NCIP as they flow from relations between the EAC Partner States, and attempts to evaluate the impact the initiative has had on the integration process.

6

The Northern Corridor
Integration Projects

T HE NORTHERN CORRIDOR Integration Projects (NCIP) was the formal name of what had previously been referred to as the Coalition of the Willing (CoW). Although the project appears to have been abandoned,[1] both terms are still used interchangeably. The first section of this chapter is an overview of the NCIP participating states, and briefly looks at the structure, objectives and other aspects of the initiative. The second section considers the events that led to the establishment of the NCIP, and the reasons for it. This section also summarises opposition to the NCIP from Tanzania and other criticisms of the initiative. The final section attempts to evaluate the effects NCIP has had on the integration process so far. This is assessed on three fronts: trade patterns, relations between the EAC states, and relations between the EAC and third-party states.

I. AN INTRODUCTION TO THE NCIP

The NCIP is a collaboration between the Republics of Kenya, Rwanda, Uganda, and South Sudan. It was established in June 2013 as the Tripartite Initiative for Fast Tracking the East African Integration (TIFTEAI) by a Memorandum of Understanding (MoU) between Kenya, Rwanda and Uganda. Whether by design or accident, this Memorandum and other documents about the initiative have not been made public,[2] with the result that in the public domain, its name has evolved from TIFTEAI, to CoW, and finally, to the NCIP.

The NCIP takes its name from an existing structure for the improvement of transport links across Eastern Africa. The structure creates 'corridors' intended to link different parts of the region's hinterland to the Indian Ocean. The Southern Corridor connects Zambia to Dar es Salaam, while the Central Corridor connects Rwanda and Burundi to Dar es Salaam (Tanzanian coast) via Central Tanzania. The Northern Corridor links Burundi to Mombasa (Kenyan coast), and runs through Rwanda, Uganda, and Southern Kenya. Farther to

---

[1] Section III considers the outlook of the NCIP and its current status.
[2] This criticism is discussed further in section II.D below.

the north, the proposed Lamu Corridor connects Juba in South Sudan to the Kenyan port of Lamu. This has recently been combined with the proposed Addis Ababa-Nairobi connection and the proposed Addis Ababa-Juba connection to form the Lamu Port, South Sudan, Ethiopia Transport corridor (LAPSETT).[3]

The NCIP was based on a desire to create a conducive environment and greater opportunities for the participating states and their citizens by building on the advantages of the EAC integration process.[4] It was driven by the 'ultimate necessity to urgently implement high impact/quick win projects in order to meet immediate and long term development needs'.[5] This signified the need to counter what had been perceived as a lull in the process of integration brought on by external and internal challenges[6] – a reference to Tanzania dragging its feet and Burundi's struggles with meeting EAC obligations. The leaders of the three TIFTEAI states showed a commitment to fostering integration in the customs union, the common market, infrastructure, common foreign policy, trade, defence and security in order to enable sustainable development and long-term stability of the region.[7] From the MOU between the parties, it is clear that there was a need to speed up the integration process, in both economic and political terms. The three countries intended to foster and promote greater integration driven by economic development and political federation[8] – a goal reminiscent of the destructive zeal that plagued the EAC in 1966.[9]

Under Article 3 of the MOU, the parties agreed to fully implement the EAC Common Market and establish a single customs territory (SCT), in addition to establishing a common foreign policy. They also pledged to enter a Common Defence and Security Pact in order to coordinate regional security, and collaborate on infrastructure projects. All this would be done in an 'appropriate political structure' for the parties in order to fast track the region's integration.[10] From Article 12 of the MOU, the 'appropriate political structure' seems to be a political federation between the States Parties. With the stroke of a pen, the MOU sought to immediately and fully implement the EAC Common Market Protocol, including the immediate free movement of people and labour, and 'further deepening of the free movement of capital, services and goods'.[11] As part of this goal, the parties intended to establish an e-identification system and

---

[3] Discussed in section III.B below.

[4] Preamble to the Memorandum of Understanding between the Republic of Kenya, the Republic of Rwanda and the Republic of Uganda on the Tripartite Initiative for Fast Tracking the East African Integration.

[5] ibid.

[6] ibid.

[7] ibid.

[8] ibid.

[9] Chapter 4, section I explains that the desire to create a federation between Kenya, Tanzania and Uganda inadvertently led to the collapse of the common market.

[10] Article 3, TIFTEAI Memorandum of Understanding.

[11] ibid, Art 4.

other means of easy identification to ease movement of their nationals across borders with effect from the beginning of 2014.[12] This venture yielded mixed and delayed results, as discussed in section III.A below.

From the outset, NCIP was an ambitious project. The MOU was signed in June of 2013, but had a short timeline for its implementation. For example, Under Article 4, it set a June 2014 (12 months) deadline for full implementation of the EAC Common Market Protocol by all the parties. While, admittedly, this was an arrangement between three countries that sought to build on the existing success of the EAC, twelve months would not be enough time to put in place everything required for the establishment of a common market. Considering that the customs union between the five EAC states was only just finding its feet, and the Common Market Protocol had only existed for three years by the time the MOU was signed,[13] trying to eliminate all the barriers to free movement in such a short period was bound to be a gargantuan task. Section III.A.ii below examines the NCIP's success in establishing the SCT and implementing the Common Market Protocol, as well as its success in other areas covered by the MOU.

At its second summit on 28 August 2013, the initiative was expanded to include the newly formed Republic of South Sudan, which had not formally acceded to the EAC Treaty. From the third summit, other countries attended NCIP meetings, and requested or were invited to participate in NCIP projects. These countries include Burundi, which is an EAC Partner State, in addition to Ethiopia and the Democratic Republic of Congo (DRC), which are not EAC Partner States. This chapter focuses on the activities of the members of the NCIP that were also members of the EAC, ie Kenya, Rwanda, Uganda and South Sudan. Burundi's role in the NCIP was limited to the status of an observer, and therefore limited reference is made to it. What follows is an introduction to the NCIP, considering the relationships between the NCIP states, and the factors and events that led up to the commencement of the collaboration.

A. The Projects

The Participating States identified 16 areas of cooperation, distributing their coordination between themselves as the following paragraphs describe. This chapter only focuses on a few of the projects because not all of them took off or bore any fruit, thereby having no bearing on the history or the process of EAC integration. Due to their non-occurrence, they remained irrelevant, and so writing about them would not be an efficient use of resources.

---

[12] ibid, Art 6.

[13] Chapter 4, section III.C gives a more detailed evaluation of the EAC Customs Union and Common Market.

Uganda was responsible for five projects. These were the standard gauge railway, ICT infrastructure, oil refinery development, fast tracking political federation, and financing. The most successful of these, relatively speaking, was the standard gauge railway. In August 2013, Kenya, Rwanda and Uganda signed the Tripartite Agreement for the Development and Operation of a Standard Gauge Railway (SGR) between Mombasa, Kampala and Kigali. South Sudan acceded to this agreement in 2014 in order to facilitate an extension of the line to Juba. Kenya reported that regional economic interests worked in favour of the project, which attracted funding from the Chinese Government.[14] As reported in section III.B.i below, the SGR was only partially successful. Kenya constructed most of the railway it had pledged to construct, upgrading an existing line from Mombasa to Kisumu. Uganda and Rwanda, on the other hand, did not commence construction, despite agreements to secure funding and the completion of preliminary studies.[15]

Kenya was responsible for the coordination of six projects: power generation, transmission and interconnectivity, crude oil pipeline development, refined petroleum products pipeline development, commodities exchange, human resource capacity building and land. Of these, the most important were the oil-related ones: crude oil pipeline development and refined petroleum products pipeline development. These two were important because as reported in section III.B.i below, the failure of these two – due to Uganda shifting goal posts at the last minute – led to the abrupt collapse of the NCIP. Since infrastructure was the mainstay of the initiative, faltering on both the SGR and the oil pipeline project rendered the coalition more or less worthless.

Like Uganda, Rwanda was expected to coordinate five projects: immigration, tourism, trade, labour and services (ITTLS), single customs territory, defence cooperation, peace and security cooperation and air space management. The most significant of these were tourism and the establishment of the single customs territory. As with the projects coordinated by Kenya and Uganda, the results on this front were measly. The biggest success out of the five, and perhaps the NCIP's greatest achievement, was the establishment of the 'East African' Tourist visa. While it is named after the region, it only allows tourists to access Kenya, Rwanda and Uganda on a single visa which is valid for 90 days. The other EAC states still issue separate visas to tourists visiting their countries. Contrary to the aspirations of the TIFTEAI MOU, the three states did not establish a single customs territory between themselves, since this had been established at the EAC level by the time the MOU was signed. This is discussed in section III.A.ii below.

---

[14] D Kaunda, *Against All Odds: Mega-Railway Project Becomes a Reality*, in Uchukuzi (Magazine by Kenya's Ministry of Transport and Infrastructure), Issue 1, June 2014, 6–8.

[15] Memorandum of Understanding Between Kenya, Rwanda and Uganda and the African Development Bank/Africa 50 on the Financing of the Standard Gauge Railway Project from Mombasa-Kampala-Kigali (19 February 2014).

B. Participating States and a Brief Review of Relations between them

A detailed history of the EAC has already been considered,[16] which touched on the relations between Kenya and Uganda. Rwanda and South Sudan are relatively new in the arena of EAC politics. To avoid a lengthy history of relations between the states, this section concerns itself with the political and economic relations between the four states immediately before and during the initiation of the NCIP.

C. The Politics of the East African Community

East African political relations, though scarcely written about, are relatively complex. There is a mixture of influences shaping the region's relations. These include shared cultural backgrounds, economic interests, centres of power and military involvement. Kenya is usually hailed as the region's big brother, owing to its status as a lower middle-income economy,[17] and the region's biggest exporter. It is also the most 'aggressive' in the region, in terms of investment and expansion, with involvement in all the economies of the EAC in at least one industry or services sector.

While Kenya enjoys a stronger economic position, Uganda has considerable political and military influence in the region, having intervened in many conflicts in the region in recent years. These have included military interventions in Rwanda (1990, 1994), Democratic Republic of Congo (1996–2003, 2013), Somalia (2007 to date), South Sudan (2013), and other political interventions in the region and beyond. It is because of these interventions, most of which have been successful, that the current president of Uganda makes an unconventional bedfellow for the West. In spite of his questionable democratic record spanning more than 35 years in power, he is credited, especially by the US, with maintaining peace in the Great Lakes Region.[18]

Rwanda's role in the region is relatively new, but cannot be downplayed. It is the second fastest growing economy in the EAC with an annual GDP growth rate of 6.1 per cent (Tanzania leads at 7.1 per cent).[19] It is also quite progressive especially in the fields of technology and investment, and has an inclusive

---

[16] Chapter 4, section III.

[17] The World Bank, *World Bank Country and Lending Groups*, available at https://datahelpdesk.worldbank.org/knowledgebase/articles/906519-world-bank-country-and-lending-groups (accessed 10 February 2017).

[18] The Great Lakes Region is the area of east and central Africa surrounding a number of freshwater lakes, and is made up of Rwanda, Burundi, the Democratic Republic of the Congo (DRC), Uganda, Tanzania, Zambia, Republic of Congo, Central African Republic (CAR), South Sudan, Kenya and Sudan.

[19] World Bank Data https://data.worldbank.org/indicator/NY.GDP.MKTP.KD.ZG?locations=TZ-RW-BI-KE-SS-UG&name_desc=false (accessed 22 January 2019).

government that appears more accountable than its East African counterparts.[20] In the EAC, Rwanda has the highest ranking in the 2017 *Doing Business Rankings*, with an overall position of 56.[21]

Uganda is the apparent 'convener' of the NCIP, as seen below.[22] The way the Coalition of the Willing began shows that Uganda is a considerable influence in the region. It is possible to explain why Uganda has such influence over Kenya, Rwanda and South Sudan. Kenya's case is easier to understand, given that the two countries have relied on each other for trade and other purposes since as early as 1917 in 'the original Common Market'. They have adopted similar economic models and political systems, and have, generally, enjoyed a peaceful relationship over the years.[23]

South Sudan's role is also fairly direct, with Uganda having a lot to do with the resolution of conflicts between Juba (South Sudan) and Khartoum (Sudan); and South Sudan's eventual independence from Sudan. The two countries have enjoyed close ties on trade, with South Sudan being Uganda's biggest export market. Before South Sudan became independent, Uganda and the Sudan People's Liberation Movement collaborated on flushing the Lord's Resistance Army (LRA) rebels out of Uganda and into the Central African Republic.

Rwanda has had a similar relationship with Uganda. Predating independence, Uganda has been home to refugees from Rwanda from as far back as the Rwandan Revolution of 1959. Closer to present times, however, Uganda's Government was instrumental in the creation of the Rwanda Patriotic Front (RPF), which took power in July 1994 after a four-year long civil war, which culminated in the infamous genocide in Rwanda.

All these events point to the fact that Uganda is at the centre of the NCIP, politically at least. The participating states have enjoyed close relations with Uganda, and in some cases, owe Uganda a debt of sorts. With the two centres of power – Kenya, being the economic, and Uganda, the political one – the Coalition appeared to be made up of some strong fibre.

II. MILESTONES TO NCIP'S ESTABLISHMENT

A. EACJ Advisory Opinion No. 1 of 2008

The earliest hints on the implementation of Article 7(1)(e) in the EAC were in Minute 8 of the 16th Ordinary meeting of the Council of Ministers, held on 13 December 2008 in Arusha, Tanzania. At this meeting, the Council directed

---

[20] A comparison of EAC states' governance is done below.

[21] The World Bank, *Doing Business 2017: The EAC*, Washington, 7.

[22] Sections II.B and III.C.

[23] In November 2017, tensions between the two started brewing, so this might change. See ch 4, section IV.

the Secretariat to seek an advisory opinion of the East African Court of Justice (EACJ) on the application of the principle of variable geometry.[24] The request for this opinion arose during negotiations on details of the common market. There was lack of agreement on some aspects of the draft Protocol Establishing the EAC Common Market, and since Community decisions are made by consensus,[25] there were two options available to the Council of Ministers. The first was to delay the negotiations until consensus was reached, and the second was to agree to proceed in a manner that accommodated the differences.[26] According to the Council, interpreting variable geometry as permitting progression of the different activities, projects and programmes at different speeds was contestable based on the fundamental requirement for consensus under the Treaty and its annexes.[27]

This advisory opinion was promptly filed before the Court, with three main questions:

1. Whether the principle of variable geometry is in harmony with the requirement for consensus in decision making.
2. Whether the principle of variable geometry can apply to guide the integration process, the requirement on consensus in decision-making notwithstanding.
3. Whether the requirement on consensus in decision-making implies unanimity of the Partner States.

The Court opted to treat the first two questions jointly, concluding that variable geometry was in harmony with the requirement for consensus if applied appropriately. It stated as follows:

> Consensus is purely and simply a decision-making mechanism in Summit, Council and other executive organs of the Community, while variable geometry as used therein is a strategy for implementation ... Decisions in any of the executive organs of the Community are made with two aspects in mind. The first aspect is that a decision is made on the basis of it being consistent with the objectives of the Treaty and desirable at the time. At this level, the basis of making the decision is consensus. The second aspect is the implementation of what has been decided as, in our view, a decision that will not be implemented is not worth the paper on which it is written. With this aspect of implementation comes the practical realities such as the vital national interests, the negotiations, the give and take and consultations that each Partner State will inevitably have to take care of for the good of the Partner State and ultimately, that of the Community. Consensus ... will then be tailored to the elements

---

[24] Decisions of the EAC Ministerial Council Meeting of 13 September 2008, *East African Community Gazette*, 30 December 2008, Arusha.

[25] Articles 12(3) and 15(4) of the EAC Treaty.

[26] J Gathii, *African Regional Trade Agreements as Legal Regimes* (Cambridge, Cambridge University Press, 2011) 51.

[27] The EAC Council of Ministers, *Proposal for Requesting Advisory Opinion of the East African Court of Justice*, 13 September 2008.

just above highlighted and a suitable operational principle, which may well be variable geometry, will be agreed upon to govern the practical implementation of that particular decision. Partner States may agree on implementation at different speeds due to different readiness levels or different priorities, some may choose to opt out of implementation altogether due to national realities, yet others may decide to 'opt out' and at a future time they will 'opt in'. All these will be agreed by the Partner States, by consensus.[28]

This decision was an important turning point for the EAC. It provided an interpretation of the Treaty that allowed Partner States to implement Community decisions at different paces, rather than uniformly. It is a significant decision because it provides an existing route within the Treaty framework for states like Tanzania, which are deeply suspicious that they will be economically disadvantaged by relatively more economically powerful states like Kenya. For those states willing to continue in the common market stage of the integration process, the decision also provides a legal basis for their deeper cooperation. Objecting states will not be regarded as wielding a veto under the rule of consensus decision-making, but rather as exercising their right to opt out of commitments under the principle of variable geometry.[29]

Curiously, there is a break in activity and literature from the time the decision is given, until the Entebbe meeting in 2013. Other than Gathii's comments in 2011,[30] there appears to be no mention of variable geometry, especially its implementation, in the EAC. An examination of communiqués from the Heads of States Summits and Reports from Council of Ministers Meetings between 2009 (when the EACJ decision was delivered) and June 2013 show no explicit mention of the implementation or invocation of Article 7(1)(e). This could mean that some of the discussions, understandably, were held behind closed doors, and that consequently, the records of such discussions are not made available to the public. Alternatively, and more likely, it could point to the fact that during this period, implementation of Community decisions was, generally speaking, harmonious. What then, caused the turn of events witnessed in 2013?

B. The Entebbe Meeting of 25 June 2013 and Subsequent NCIP Summits

The NCIP was conceived on 25 June 2013, when the three presidents of Kenya, Rwanda and Uganda met in Entebbe, Uganda to discuss how to cooperate and speed up development in the region.[31] This meeting started as a bilateral one between President Uhuru Kenyatta of Kenya, and his host, Yoweri Kaguta

---

[28] EACJ, *In the Matter of a Request by the Council of Ministers of the East African Community for an Advisory Opinion*, Application No 1 of 2008, 29–30.

[29] Gathii, *African Regional Trade Agreements* (n 26) 61.

[30] ibid.

[31] About Us – Northern Corridor Integration Projects, www.nciprojects.org/about/about-us (last accessed 17 October 2016).

Museveni of Uganda. They noted that non-tariff barriers, including movement of labour, continue to hinder intra-EAC trade and full implementation of the Common Market. They also noted delays in the clearing of goods at Mombasa port and the Malaba border, and agreed to take immediate measures to improve management of the port and expedite clearance by the Uganda Revenue Authority (URA) at Malaba.[32] The two presidents agreed to:

- implement a programme for Uganda to collect customs duties before goods are released from Mombasa port. For goods destined for warehousing in Uganda, importers would continue to execute the general bond security;

- jointly develop the Kapchorwa-Swam-Kitale road (linking Eastern Uganda to Western Kenya);

- explore the possibility of Kenya investing in Quality Chemicals, a company which manufactures HIV/AIDS and malaria drugs in Uganda;

- coordinate joint disarmament of cattle rustlers on both sides of the border and encourage other countries in the region to complement these efforts;

- establish a mechanism for mutual recognition of standards within the EAC framework and other internationally recognised standards in which Kenya and Uganda are members; and

- establish a joint permanent commission for regular consultations.

President Paul Kagame of Rwanda joined the meeting, and further agreement was reached on the following:

- revamp the existing railway network and also construct a new standard gauge railway line and extend it to Rwanda, by joint mobilisation of resources;

- develop an oil pipeline for finished products from Eldoret to Kampala and extend to Rwanda, with a link to South Sudan;

- explore the possibility of EAC Partner States investing in the oil refinery to be constructed in Uganda;

- enhance electricity generation and distribution by exploring and utilising the resources within each Partner State, including the exploration of alternative sources like renewable energy, nuclear, and geothermal energy;

- strengthen the SCT and implement all the provisions therein where taxes will be collected at the entry points, including Mombasa, Mpondwe and Oluhura;

- fast track political federation by setting up a committee that will draft an EAC Political Federation Framework, which will be considered and discussed by all relevant parties;

---

[32] Communiqué by H.E. Uhuru Kenyatta, President of the Republic of Kenya, after a working visit to his counterpart, H.E. Yoweri Kaguta Museveni, President of the Republic of Uganda, on 24–25 June 2013, at State House, Entebbe, Uganda.

- introduce EAC e identity cards (already in use in Kenya and Rwanda) to ease the movement of persons and services; and
- fast track the establishment of the EAC single tourist visa to facilitate the tourism industry in the region.[33]

The meeting further allocated responsibilities between the three Partner States: the Republic of Rwanda would take the lead on customs, the single tourist visa and the EAC e-identity card; Kenya would focus on energy issues (electricity generation/distribution and oil pipeline development) while Uganda would be responsible for railway development and political federation.[34] It is possible to argue that each country bore the responsibilities that were of greatest interest to it.

Rwanda has, over the last several years, touted itself as a tourist destination, an industry previously dominated by Kenya, Tanzania and Uganda. Uganda's interest in improved transport links would arise principally out of the costs of trade associated with being a landlocked country. A railway line would help expedite the import and export process, especially if the customs collection mechanism were streamlined. In particular, if customs duties were collected at the port of Mombasa there would be no need for the goods to stop again at the Kenya-Uganda border. It has also long been suggested that the Ugandan President is the most interested in the political federation of the EAC,[35] one of the dreams he hopes to achieve before he retires from the presidency.[36] For Kenya's part, energy is necessary to sustain its growing industrial economy; it still imports electricity from Uganda.[37] In addition, the recent interest in oil and gas in the region would require investment in infrastructure in the sector. In the EAC, Kenya has the most experience with oil and gas, having had refineries in Mombasa for decades.

This meeting was followed by further meetings to review the decisions made, and to make even more decisions relating to the NCIP. By agreement between the three presidents,[38] meetings were to be held every two months to review progress of implementation of the decisions. Subsequent meetings were hosted by a different country (Kenya and Rwanda) on a rotational basis and were

---

[33] ibid.

[34] ibid. See also section I.A above for a detailed discussion of the projects.

[35] In a Statement to the Symposium of the Special Sitting of the East African Legislative Assembly, 30 June–2 July 2011, President Museveni made an impassioned case for fast tracking the political federation of the EAC, suggesting that rather than being an ultimate goal, it should be brought before economic integration, which is currently hindered by divergent political/sovereign aspirations.

[36] BBC News, *Yoweri Museveni – Uganda's President Profiled*, www.bbc.co.uk/news/world-africa-12421747 (last accessed 4 November 2016).

[37] Kenya imported 40.7 million units (kilowatt-hours) from Uganda, accounting for 96% of Kenya's electricity imports for the year ending June 2016. See N Otuki, *Kenya's Power Imports from Uganda now Rise 32 Percent*, Business Daily, www.businessdailyafrica.com/Corporate-News/Kenya-power-imports-from-Uganda-now-rise-32-per-cent-/539550-3371092-1xrsap/ (last accessed 18 October 2016).

[38] 1st NCIP Presidential Communiqué, supra.

gradually opened up to other countries. Thirteen meetings were held between the presidents of the three countries (including the Entebbe meeting), but only the first four and the last one are relevant here. The fifth to twelfth meetings were mainly reviews of what was agreed in the first four, and the thirteenth meeting, as described below, was the last NCIP meeting.

The second meeting, held in Mombasa, Kenya in August 2013, was attended by representatives from the Republics of Burundi and South Sudan. It also had a wider attendance, drawing in cabinet ministers and senior government officials from the five states.[39] This suggested an intention to give effect to the declarations of the first summit, with the inclusion of government officials and policy makers. While Tanzania's President neither attended this summit, nor sent a representative, this second summit was convened, in part, to integrate the Republics of Burundi and South Sudan into the NCIP. It could be argued that this accelerated the process of accession for the Republic of South Sudan into the EAC, since it could participate in the NCIP better as a member of the EAC.

The third summit was held in Kigali, Rwanda, in October 2013. It was attended by the Presidents of Rwanda (hosting), Kenya, Uganda, South Sudan, and senior officials from the four states.[40] The meeting considered the Ministerial Report and the recommendations therein, taking account of various Memoranda of Understanding and the One Stop Border Post Agreement signed during the Ministerial Meeting. This summit made several directions on the various projects, including agreements to be reached and projects to be undertaken. For example, with regard to power generation and transmission, it was agreed that each Partner State would provide comprehensive information on existing power generation capacities and investments programmes before each summit.

The states further agreed to finalise a Memorandum of Understanding on Geothermal Energy, to be run by the Geothermal Centre of Excellence in Kenya. This MOU was to be signed by the next summit. It was also agreed that further consultations would be carried out between the Republic of Uganda, the Republic of Kenya and the Republic of South Sudan on the joint development of the crude oil pipeline project. As this chapter will discuss, crude oil and its transport would later prove to be a contentious matter for both NCIP and the EAC.[41]

By the fourth summit in February 2014, decisions made in the third meeting had been mostly implemented, and further discussions had been held at the ministerial level. It was clear that the NCIP was gaining both ground and speed, but the most notable thing about the fourth summit is not even how much had been achieved or agreed under the NCIP. It was the first NCIP summit that was

---

[39] Joint Communiqué of the 2nd Infrastructure Summit between the Republics of Kenya, Burundi, Rwanda, South Sudan and Uganda, at the White Sands Beach Resort and Spa, Mombasa, Kenya, 28 August 2013.

[40] Joint Communiqué of the Integration Projects Summit between the Republics of Rwanda, Kenya, South Sudan and Uganda, at Urugwiro Village, Kigali, Rwanda, 28 October 2013.

[41] Section III.B below.

attended by all members of the EAC, in addition to South Sudan, which was not a member of the bloc at that time. Hosted by Uganda, Tanzania was represented by then Vice President, Mohamed Gharib Bilal. Burundi was in attendance too, represented by its 2nd Vice President, Gervais Rufyikiri. As with earlier summits, the states reviewed the progress of implementation of earlier decisions and made direction on further implementation of the projects.

While no mention is made of Tanzania's contribution to the fourth NCIP summit, a few points must be noted about how the first four (and subsequent) summits shaped the political landscape of the EAC over the next few months. Two core projects undertaken by the NCIP were the construction of a Standard Gauge Railway (SGR) linking the three landlocked countries (South Sudan, Uganda and Rwanda) to the Kenyan ports of Mombasa and Lamu, and the construction of oil pipelines from South Sudan and Uganda through Kenya to Lamu. In April 2016, however, only a few days before the 13th NCIP Summit Kampala, a deal was reached for the oil pipeline to be constructed through Tanzania, leading, instead, to the Tanzanian port of Tanga.[42] Kenya announced it would proceed with the construction of the pipeline, focusing instead on the branch to South Sudan.[43] In what was regarded as a subtle retaliation for this last minute moving of the goal posts by Uganda, Kenya stalled its construction of the SGR on the leg that connects Kisumu in Kenya to the border with Uganda.[44]

These two events are particularly important because they left the NCIP on quite shaky ground. The SGR and the oil pipeline projects were central items on the NCIP's agenda right from its inception. A reduction in cooperation on these two items, especially between the two centres of power – Kenya and Uganda – was a substantial impediment to the progression of the NCIP. A testament to this is the fact that there have been no further summits since the 13th NCIP summit, at which the two decisions were communicated.

The unfolding of these events is critical, not just for the research that led to this book, but to the progress of the EAC. The NCIP was the first time, under the new EAC Treaty, that variable geometry was implemented in the bloc. Although, as discussed below, it has been argued that the NCIP was outside the EAC framework, it was formed to fast-track the EAC's integration – and seemingly, to do so as flexibly as possible.[45] If indeed the initiative has stalled, it will provide a useful case study for the appropriateness of flexible integration, especially for lessons on what should or should not be done when flexibility is pursued in integration.

---

[42] F Musisi and MK Muhumuza, *Uganda: How Oil Pipeline Deal Slipped Out of Kenya's Hands*, All Africa, http://allafrica.com/stories/201604250062.html (accessed 20 February 2017).

[43] Joint Communiqué of the 13th Summit of the Northern Corridor Integration Projects, at the Munyonyo Commonwealth Resort, Kampala, Uganda, 23 April 2016.

[44] Discussed in section III.B below.

[45] R Ndege, *East Africa Integration: State of Play*, in Africa in Depth, www.africapractice.com/wp-content/uploads/2014/08/Africa-InDepth-East-African-integration-State-of-play-August-2014.pdf (accessed 20 February 2017).

C. Precipitating Factors

In order to avoid repetition of the reasons for variable geometry in the EAC Treaty,[46] this section specifically studies the events that led up to the creation of the NCIP. Inevitably, there are some similarities with previous sections and chapters, but the specific events reported here are useful to buttress the theories contained in previous sections and chapters.

i. Political Factors

One of the reasons the implementation of Article 7(1)(e) was considered in the EAC was the difficulty in reaching consensus. As discussed above, the interpretation of this Article was brought before the EACJ because there was lack of agreement on some aspects of the Common Market Protocol. This lack of consensus, however, arose from the hesitation to make certain decisions, rather than a rejection of such decisions.[47] According to the EACJ, the cause for this hesitation appears to be the requirement, inherent in the decisions made, for simultaneous implementation by *all* Partner States.[48] These differences created an environment in which Partner States could make joint integration decisions that carry varied implementation obligations. As the Court noted, simultaneous implementation is impracticable in some circumstances, and Partner States cannot be expected to operate within such a straitjacket or one-size-fits-all situations.[49]

The Coalition of the Willing, which established the NCIP, was a response to a lull in the integration process due, in large part, to hesitations from Tanzania. Several reasons have been advanced for these hesitations. Gordon Onyango Omenya suggests that given Tanzania's overlapping membership with SADC, many Tanzanians were concerned that the EAC's success, especially the political federation, would affect their close relationship with several SADC countries. This informed their aloof nature as far as their commitment towards a speedy EAC integration was concerned.[50] This aloofness came to the fore when Tanzania missed two EAC meetings in Entebbe and Mombasa in 2013. It thus raised serious questions about Tanzania's commitment towards fast-tracking the integration process.[51]

One of the final straws to break the proverbial camel's back came in the form of a conflict outside the EAC itself. Between 2012 and 2013, there was a

---

[46] Chapter 3, section IV, and ch 5, section II.

[47] EACJ (n 28) 35.

[48] ibid.

[49] ibid.

[50] GO Omenya, *Coalition of the Willing as a Pathway to African Future Integration: Some Reflections on East Africa Regional Integration*, Paper Presented at the 14th CODESRIA General Assembly, 8–15 June 2015, Dakar, Senegal.

[51] ibid.

rebel uprising in the Democratic Republic of Congo. The M23 rebels, as they were known, operated mainly in the Eastern Congo, along the western borders of Uganda, Rwanda, Burundi and Tanzania. Uganda and Rwanda had been accused of supporting the rebels, while Tanzania committed a large number of peacekeeping troops to the UN mission in the region, which was tasked with removing them.[52] This had several effects, but two are most relevant here.

The first and perhaps most obvious was the apparent uncoordinated movement in the region, with one state backing a foreign government, while two states backed the rebels trying to unseat that government. The second was a result of the inevitable clashes between Tanzanian troops on the UN/Congo side, and the Ugandan and Rwandan troops on the M23 side. This led to awkward relations between the three states, though perhaps the coldest shoulders were between Rwanda and Tanzania. In 2013, Tanzania expelled citizens of a few countries who did not have proper documents, including many from Rwanda. Authorities in Kigali took the issue seriously, although their government did not retaliate.[53] When talks between Kenya and Uganda started, proposing a fast tracking of the integration process, these issues were on hand to shape an alliance that would exclude Tanzania's participation.

Another reason for the existence of the NCIP is the realisation that the EAC Partner States had different national priorities with regard to integration. For example, Uganda and Rwanda – both landlocked countries – were keen on the development of infrastructure, especially in order to lower the costs of importing and exporting goods through Kenya,[54] while Tanzania believed more in the consolidation of regulation and institutions in order to lay a solid foundation for the process of implementation. Indeed, according to the Tanzanian Government, the projects under deliberation by the coalition should have been endorsed first by all the EAC Partner States.[55] The Tanzanian position is informed by Article 12(3) of the EAC Treaty, which requires the heads of states to make their decisions by consensus. However, where such consensus cannot be reached on matters of implementation, the next best option must be sought, and since the treaty provides for variable geometry, Tanzania was easily outnumbered in Rwanda and Uganda's preference for the emphasis on infrastructure.

ii. Economic Factors

There are several economic explanations for the gravitation of Kenya, Rwanda and Uganda towards each other. As the name of the NCIP suggests, the

---

[52] ibid 8–9.

[53] ibid 7–8.

[54] Communiqué by H.E. Uhuru Kenyatta, President of the Republic of Kenya, after a working visit to his counterpart, H.E. Yoweri Kaguta Museveni, President of the Republic of Uganda, on 24–25 June 2013, at State House, Entebbe, Uganda.

[55] GOmenya, *Coalition of the Willing* (n 50) 9, but also discussed in section II.D below.

three countries are linked by the Northern Transport Corridor, which runs from the port of Mombasa, through Nairobi, across Uganda and into Rwanda and beyond.[56] In addition, the discovery of oil in Uganda, Kenya and South Sudan provided inspiration for the three countries to have a common infrastructure for the processing and transportation of petroleum products. This, boosted by Uganda and Kenya's historical reliance on each other for trade, made the alliance only natural. As one of the main aims of the bloc was the development of infrastructure,[57] this partnership was the logical alternative to region-wide infrastructure development, especially with Tanzania dragging its feet.

The rise of the NCIP was, even if only subconsciously, linked with the afore-mentioned transport corridors in the region. Naturally, one would ask why, for example, the central or southern corridor did not rise as natural candidates for deepened integration. The first answer to that is the relatively closed nature of the Tanzanian economy, which has been variously discussed in this book. Second, the central and southern corridors would mainly serve Tanzania and central African states, but given the current state of play, there is only a limited amount of goods going in and out of Rwanda, Burundi and the Democratic Republic of Congo, especially via the southern and central routes.[58] Among transport routes in the EAC, the largest share of goods pass through the northern corridor, with some goods destined beyond the EAC and going into the Democratic Republic of Congo.[59] With significantly higher traffic (more than twice the amount of goods via the central corridor[60]) and relatively lower transport costs, the northern route provided a stronger pull factor for deeper integration in line with Ernst Haas' communications approach to integration discussed in chapter two of this study.[61]

While some reasons have already been advanced for Tanzania's reluctance with integration projects, one significant reason has been around the issue of land and mineral deposits. In Kenya[62] and Uganda,[63] citizens can own land,

---

[56] Omenya, *Coalition of the Willing* (n 50) 7.

[57] Chapter 15 of the EAC Treaty relates to cooperation in infrastructure and services, and provides for the development of infrastructure, especially for transport and communication.

[58] Stratfor, *East African Infrastructure Development, Part 1: The Central Corridor*, Worldview, https://worldview.stratfor.com/article/east-african-infrastructure-development-part-1-central-corridor (accessed 25 January 2019).

[59] Stratfor, *East African Infrastructure Development, Part 2: The Northern Corridor*, Worldview, https://worldview.stratfor.com/article/east-african-infrastructure-development-part-2-northern-corridor (accessed 25 January 2019).

[60] ibid.

[61] 'An intensive pattern of communication (transactions) between national units will result in a closer community among the units if loads and capabilities remain in balance.' Chapter 2, section II.C.

[62] Article 61 of the 2010 Constitution of the Republic of Kenya creates three classes of land: public, community and private.

[63] Article 237 of the 1995 Constitution of the Republic of Uganda vests all land in the citizens of Uganda, and creates four land tenure systems: customary, freehold, leasehold and *mailo* land, which is a hybrid of customary, freehold and leasehold.

while in Tanzania, land belongs to the state, and citizens use it communally.[64] This disparity remains a challenge to integration, at least as far as Tanzania is concerned. As discussed in a previous chapter, Tanzania has historically adopted socialist approaches, and these form the basis of their land tenure systems. This perception of land as a public/communal property is deep rooted and embraced by most levels of society. At a grass-roots level, there is a real fear that integration would put this communal land ownership at risk.[65] From Tanzania's perspective, there is a big problem surrounding land ownership in Uganda and Kenya, where 'the rich own the biggest chunks of land'.[66] From the perspective of Kenya and Uganda, ownership of land is important for investment purposes, and restrictions on land rights run contrary to the free movement of persons, capital and other factors of production envisaged by the EAC Common Market Protocol.

Another area of contention in which Tanzania and Burundi have been considerably embroiled is the free movement of persons. Even after the EAC Common Market Protocol came into force, they continued to impose stringent requirements for foreign workers. For example, EAC citizens still have to pay 3 per cent of their gross salary for a work permit in Burundi[67] and up to US$3,000 (professionals and consultants) for a work permit in Tanzania.[68] Meanwhile Kenya, Rwanda and Uganda have mutually waived work permit requirements for their citizens.[69] Negotiations have been ongoing for the removal of work permits for citizens across the region but they remain inconclusive. Omenya reports that because of the high costs of work permits in Tanzania, many people from neighbouring countries do not bother to get permits and so work illegally in the country. In October 2013, the Tanzanian Government deported over 4,000 Ugandan and Rwandan migrants, leading to even more tensions between Tanzania and the two countries.

South Sudan, the EAC's latest member, had a significant role in the development of the coalition between Kenya, Rwanda and Uganda. The 'South Sudan factors' are a mixture of political and economic factors but can be adequately considered in this section. Before South Sudan applied to join the EAC, it was Uganda's biggest trade partner after Kenya. South Sudan accounted for 11.69 per cent of Uganda's exports.[70] In addition, South Sudan had recently gained independence from Sudan, and therefore considered joining the EAC as an avenue to

---

[64] Section 4 of Tanzania's Land Act 1999 vests all land in the presidency, who holds it in trust and on behalf of all citizens of Tanzania.

[65] Based on the author's conversations with Tanzanians between 2010 and 2013, on their attitudes towards integration.

[66] Omenya, *Coalition of the Willing* (n 50) 7.

[67] ibid 10.

[68] Immigration Services Department of Tanzania, www.immigration.go.tz/module1.php?id=45 (accessed 10 February 2017).

[69] D Asiimwe, 'Uganda Joins Kenya, Rwanda in Abolishing Work Permits for Professionals', *The East African*, www.theeastafrican.co.ke/news/Uganda-joins-Kenya--Rwanda-in-abolishing-work-permits/2558-2750958-om9sh7/index.html (accessed 10 February 2017).

[70] WITS – COMTRADE Data at www.wits.worldbank.org (accessed 9 February 2017).

reduce its dependence on Sudan.[71] This was so not only for trade purposes but also for infrastructure development. For example, South Sudan plans to build domestic refineries to export petroleum products to regional markets such as Kenya, Uganda and Ethiopia. In conjunction with LAPSSET, NCIP projects were expected to benefit from the construction of an oil refinery and seaport in Lamu (Kenya) and a 1,400 km oil pipeline that would link Juba to Lamu. The NCIP also envisioned the construction of a new Mombasa-Kampala standard gauge railway line, with a link to Juba, the South Sudan capital, while investment is being made in a 1,130 km road to link Nairobi and Juba.[72]

All these factors contributed to the inclusion of South Sudan in the NCIP, even before South Sudan became a member of the EAC. Kenya and Uganda were particularly expected to benefit from the thousands of jobs created by these projects.[73] The inclusion of South Sudan in the NCIP (and eventually, the EAC) would also significantly increase the border of the bloc, with contiguous access to the markets of Ethiopia, Sudan and the Central African Republic.

D. Protestations from Tanzania and Other Criticisms

The NCIP did not proceed unchallenged, in spite of having the indirect blessing of the regional court. The most vocal opposition to the initiative was from Tanzania, which insisted that the NCIP was inconsistent with the EAC Treaty. In Tanzania's opinion, the NCIP was making (as opposed to implementing) decisions, and this was inconsistent with the Treaty's consensus requirements, since not all members were involved in the decision-making. For example, one of the areas of cooperation under the NCIP is on defence and security. In 2015, Kenya, Rwanda and Uganda signed the Mutual Peace and Security Cooperation Pact and the Mutual Defence Cooperation Pact.[74] Tanzania, which was not a party to these pacts, argued that there was already an EAC Defence and Security Protocol, and as such, whatever the other members were doing was outside the integration process.[75]

Further resistance to the NCIP resulted from some of the causes of its existence that have already been discussed in this chapter. For example, Tanzania was consistently against fast-tracked or deeper integration on the basis that the bloc would only be as strong as its institutions were. In addition, due to the divergent

---

[71] Omenya, *Coalition of the Willing* (n 50).

[72] ibid.

[73] TK Rusuhuzwa, *The Potential Implications of the Entry of the New Republic of South Sudan into the EAC,* 2014, African Research and Resources Foundation.

[74] 11th NCIP Presidential Communiqué.

[75] Tanzania's Deputy Minister for East African Cooperation, Abdallah Juma Saadalla, quoted in *Coalition of the Willing Emerges Again in EAC,* The Citizen, www.thecitizen.co.tz/News/Coalition-of-the-willing-emerges-again-in-EAC/1840360-2144030-100yaaz/index.html (accessed 15 February 2017).

political and economic aspirations of the EAC Partner States, Tanzania was of the view that fundamental principles needed to be agreed before further implementation of the integration decisions. For example, the Common Market Protocol, if fully implemented, would enable free movement of persons between the states. As discussed above, Tanzania has a more socialist approach to land ownership, while Kenya and Uganda permit individual land ownership. The coalition therefore appeared to pit, once again, the capitalist states against the socialist one. An interview with Duncan Karari[76] in May 2017 revealed that land is still a matter of contention for much of Tanzania, even though most of this apprehension is based on a lack of understanding of the law. According to him, the Tanzanian Constitution prevents the amassing of land, and this would protect land from being grabbed by foreign investors, as feared.

The NCIP was also criticised for being an ambitious undertaking. This ambition is two pronged. The first is the sheer quantity of projects (the 16 mentioned above) and what responsibilities, especially financial, they placed on the national governments and their agencies responsible for undertaking them. The second, of course, is the timelines the NCIP gave to achieve these projects. Some of them, such as the construction of the Mombasa-Kampala-Kigali railway, which was supposed to be completed by March 2018,[77] have proved to be bigger logistical nightmares than could be anticipated. According to Lilian Awinja,[78] the NCIP's ambition was part of its undoing:

> The other issue with NCIP is that it was too expensive. Holding Heads of States Meetings every two months was too expensive, even for the Partner States, and it affected the EAC because a lot of money was being diverted to NCIP. As a result, Partner States could not meet their obligations under the EAC, such as paying their contributions to make the EAC work. People criticised NCIP, saying they should have brought this energy to the EAC and brought change to the EAC instead of coming up with a parallel structure.

In his criticism of NCIP as an alternative to a slump in the EAC integration process, Karari also alluded to the 'parallel structure culture' that is common in African integration:

> There is no need to keep starting new initiatives. Starting a new bureaucratic institution is difficult and expensive. Making this one work should be the priority as opposed to making other organisations work .... Instead of creating one body that works, we create a new one every time an existing one does not work.

---

[76] Duncan Karari, Communications and Brand Manager (East Africa), Deutsche Gesellschaft für Internationale Zusammenarbeit (GIZ) GmbH. Mr Karari is based at the GIZ office at the EAC Headquarters in Arusha, Tanzania, where GIZ provides support to the EAC on the integration process.

[77] 2nd NCIP Presidential Communiqué.

[78] Lilian Awinja, Executive Director, East African Business Council (EABC). The Council is the EAC's apex body representing the private sector and its interests in the integration process.

In the case of the NCIP, it was started largely out of frustration with the slowness of the EAC but as was discovered sooner, rather than later, the slow integration is only part of the process, and no amount of ambition can rush it along.

A glaring oversight on the part of the NCIP was the lack of structure with which it operated. It was more or less informal, had no constituting document, no proper centre of power beyond the presidents of the three countries, and no real order for the way it was to operate. To quote Awinja:

> They did not come up with a legal structure. It was mainly a gentleman's agreement. What was agreed was written down but it was loose because it did not have a foundation in the way the EAC has a treaty that governs them. With this one, there is nothing that can be referred to. I do not even know if there was a Memorandum of Understanding. Countries would meet, and too frequently, with the topmost political leadership (the presidents and ministers) taking the lead, and the presidents would meet every two months. On the one hand, this looked like a good arrangement, because what people agreed in the presence of the presidents was implemented. It was good in a way that it made things move faster, but there was no trust established. This lack of trust is what broke it, because what was agreed in the meetings was not necessarily adhered to. People often met informally without even documenting what had been agreed, so you would find many bilateral meetings that would not involve the rest of the partners. Kenya would meet with Uganda, and then tomorrow, Kenya is meeting with another party. There was no forum for accountability. It became like a game.

This ad hoc nature of operations was inevitably the downfall of the NCIP, as there was no proper accountability process, forum, or even point of reference. This chapter mentioned that the NCIP agreements were not available to the public, whether by design or accident, and this quote is a demonstration of the effect of that secrecy.

An understanding of this point would benefit from a description of the East African Business Council (EABC). It is the regional apex body of private sector associations and corporations in the EAC, and brings together the private sector, EAC institutions, academia, and the business community.[79] The EABC is, essentially, the non-state part of the EAC, uniting civil society in advocacy for the private sector/business community's interests. If anyone should be involved in any integration agenda in order for that agenda to succeed, it should be the EABC.

The NCIP did the exact opposite, locking out the EABC and not making the initiative's affairs known to them, even at the EABC's request. The fact that the EABC's executive director was not sure about the constitutive structure of the NCIP speaks volumes about the secrecy in which it was shrouded, and the 'make it up as we go' approach that the NCIP adopted.

---

[79] EABC, *About EABC*, http://eabc-online.com/ (accessed 2 February 2019).

Closely related to this, the NCIP was unclear about its mandate and basis. It was unclear whether it was an EAC initiative – an intention that could be inferred from its initial name[80] – or just a collaboration between Kenya, Rwanda and Uganda. To quote Awinja again,

> What NCIP did was pick some EAC projects, particularly infrastructure, and say, 'we are fast tracking these ones.' At the beginning, they seemed to say they were operating under EAC, but slightly on the side. One thing they did was not involve the EAC. The EAC was invited to NCIP much later, when they were at the eighth or ninth Summit. Before that, the input of the EAC was not sought. They seemed to be saying, 'we want to show you how things are supposed to be done.' They had separate secretariats, with each country having its own.

From this statement, it appears that the NCIP only recognised the importance of the EAC structures when it began to look shaky. The first time the EAC Secretary General attended an NCIP summit was in December 2014, when he attended the eighth NCIP summit. This was only a few months before the NCIP's apparent demise, as it only held five further Summit meetings after this one.

In spite of these criticisms, the NCIP did proceed, and has had some impact both within the region and on relations with third parties. The next section reviews these effects and criticisms in some detail.

III. EFFECTS OF THE NCIP

The general perception at the time of writing this chapter appears to be that the impact of the NCIP was akin to that of a firework. It started loud and with pomp, rose incredibly fast, lit up the dark sky with its spectacular presence, and fizzled out, soon to be forgotten by its keen observers. Respondents in interviews consistently referred to the NCIP in the past tense, an indication that they did not deem it a current factor in the integration process. As if to remove any doubt of its demise, the NCIP website referred to throughout this book was not functional by July 2021 – a sign that no further need to update the public on its activities exists.

Even then, during its short existence, the NCIP claimed to have made some achievements. As discussed below, many of these are EAC projects, and while it can be argued that the NCIP fast-tracked them under Article 7(1)(e), it would be difficult to maintain that these achievements are purely due to the NCIP.

A. Trade Patterns

International trade, even at a regional level, is usually slow to respond to stimuli. Except in the case of significant internal or external shocks, it would usually

---

[80] Tripartite Initiative for Fast-Tracking East African Integration.

take at least a year for the market to change based on changes in policy and other changes affecting the market. The details of these relationships are discussed in chapter two[81] but it is worth pointing out that given the length of time during which the NCIP existed, its existence could not reasonably be said to have significantly affected trade patterns at the regional level. The following sub-section briefly considers trade between the EAC Partner States between over a five-year period between 2012 and 2016, reporting on available data and briefly discussing whether the observed patterns were significantly affected by the NCIP.

i. The Trade Data

The statistics on intraregional trade between EAC Partner States reveal no significant change between 2012 and 2016. Export, import, re-export and re-import figures for each of the six Partner States (where available) were taken from the World Bank's WITS-COMTRADE, and show that no notable changes were registered. A few things are worth noting about the data.

First, for the period under study (2012–2016) the data was scanty or incomplete, at best. There was no data available for any trade between South Sudan and the other EAC Partner States, and there was no re-import data available for Burundi, Rwanda and Tanzania, which also lacks re-export data. In addition, it is impossible to draw credible conclusions from this data, as there are some countries with data for only some of the years. Kenya, for example, only has data for 2013, and even this is incomplete, as it does not reflect re-import data.

Second, where the data was available, it is difficult to impute any changes – where they exist – on NCIP decisions. This is so for two main reasons. The first reason is that there are barely any changes in trade patterns between the EAC states in the period 2012–2016. Rwanda and Uganda have the most complete data,[82] and even the changes in the data from these two countries are not significant enough. Rwanda's exports to the other EAC states generally declined in 2015, with the exception of exports to Kenya, which grew in both 2015 and 2016. The most significant fall was in exports to Tanzania, which fell from US$217 million in 2013 to just US$2.7 million in 2016. While it would be tempting to argue that this fall is a result of the changing landscape in the EAC, due to the closer relationship between Rwanda and Kenya (to the exclusion of Tanzania), restraint is required by the second reason that these changes cannot be ascribed to NCIP decisions: correlation does not connote causation.

It can be argued that in the EAC case, changes in trade flows are not necessarily the result of attempts at closer integration between Kenya, Rwanda and

---

[81] Chapter 2, section II on Regional Integration Theory discusses, among others, why nations trade and how regional integration alters trade patterns at regional level.

[82] Data for at least four out of five years, representing at least three of the four categories (export, import, re-export and re-import).

Uganda. For trade flows to have been affected by the NCIP, the three countries would need to have made policy decisions that had real effect, something they could not do given the existence of the EAC's common trade policy under the EAC Customs Union and Common Market Protocols. In addition, most NCIP decisions focused on collaborations on infrastructure between the participating states, rather than on trade policy. As integration theorists would argue, this is not what drives intraregional trade, but rather, policy changes that lead to the liberalisation of trade between integrating states. While a detailed exploration of this issue is undertaken in chapter two, this quote from Mia Mikić is relevant for this argument:

> A regional integration will only be successful in achieving its goal of improved economic performance and increased real income if there is a simultaneous integration at both the policy and production levels. Regional integration typically involves the removal ... of barriers to cross-border flows of goods and services. As such, this type of integration remains relatively shallow. In contrast, the regional integration of production extends to the liberalisation of barriers to cross-border flows of factors of production and technology. The policies needed for such a deep form of liberalisation must necessarily go further than those policies merely designed to support the intra-regional free trade of goods and services. We can thus differentiate between policy-led integration and FDI-led integration.[83] Policy-led integration is that in which the initiatives towards integration flow from national economic policies. Policy measures typically focus on reducing trade barriers between members in order to create a free trade area or customs union ... The essential feature of such a process is that the institutional framework for integration precedes actual integration at the production level.[84]

The NCIP was little more than a collaboration on infrastructure projects between Kenya, Rwanda, Uganda and later, South Sudan. These states did not introduce any policies geared towards trade liberalisation although they did, to their credit, attempt to make trade easier by the reduction of non-tariff barriers to trade (NTBs). Even then, it would be difficult to sustain the argument that the reduction of NTBs between the four states is responsible for the fall in trade with non-NCIP states, as shown by the falling exports from Rwanda to Tanzania.

ii. Other Aspects of Trade

Although the NCIP did not have a significant effect on the EAC's trade flows, it still had some impact on other aspects related to trade. This was so especially with regard to non-tariff barriers (NTBs) and to a lesser extent, the free movement of persons between NCIP states. This section briefly reviews these effects.

---

[83] Or in the NCIP's case, infrastructure-led integration.
[84] M Mikić, *International Trade,* (New York, St. Martin's Press, 1998) 513.

One of the NCIP's biggest boasts is in the reduction of NTBs between the participating states.[85] NTBs are measures, other than tariffs, that restrict the importation of goods into an economy, generate additional costs, and can be quite diverse.[86] NTBs in the EAC can be placed in four broad categories: tax-like measures, quality and safety standards, import bans and customs and trade facilitation measures.[87] The trouble, again, with this claim from the NCIP, is that it appears to take credit for EAC achievements, something for which the initiative has been variously criticised.[88] In 2009 (four years before NCIP), the EAC established a Non-Tariff Barriers Monitoring Mechanism, to identify NTBs in the region and to pave the way for their removal. The EAC Secretariat was tasked with maintaining a regularly updated inventory of resolved and unresolved NTBs affecting regional trade.

As of June 2016, 104 NTBs had been removed out of 129 identified by the Monitoring Mechanism.[89] While it is true that Tanzania still maintains more NTBs than Kenya, Rwanda and Uganda, this is not based on the efforts of the NCIP but rather, on the fact that Tanzania has been the country imposing the largest number of tax-like and quality/safety measures and is the slowest at resolving reported NTBs.[90]

The NCIP claims to have established a Single Customs Territory (SCT).[91] As shown in chapter four, this is untrue.[92] Article 2(1) of the EAC Customs Union Protocol establishes a customs union between the EAC Partner States as an integral part of the Community. This protocol goes on to specify the nature of the relationships between the EAC states required to make the customs union operational. For example, it provides for the elimination of customs duties and other charges between the Partner States, the removal of NTBs, and the creation of a common external tariff in respect of all goods imported into the bloc.[93]

The NCIP did not, therefore, create an SCT between the participating states, and although it might have tried to take the implementation of the EAC Customs Union Protocol a step or two further, it did not do anything that was not already being implemented by the bloc. The NCIP did not make any agreements towards the establishment of an SCT between the participating states. While the NCIP

---

[85] NCIP Website – About us, at http://nciprojects.org/about/about-us and NCIP Website – Single Customs Territory at http://nciprojects.org/project/single-customs-territory (both accessed 23 November 2017).

[86] Mikić, *International Trade* (n 84) 323.

[87] L Calabrese and A Eberhard-Ruiz, *What Types of Non-Tariff Barriers Affect the East African Community?*, 2016, ODI Briefing, p 2, (www.odi.org/sites/odi.org.uk/files/resource-documents/11110.pdf (accessed 23 November 2017)).

[88] Interviews with Lilian Awinja and Duncan Karari, April–May 2017.

[89] Calabrese and Eberhard-Ruiz, *What Types of Non-Tariff Barriers* (n 87).

[90] ibid.

[91] NCIP Website – Single Customs Territory at http://nciprojects.org/project/single-customs-territory (accessed 23 November 2017).

[92] Chapter 4, section III.C.

[93] Article 2(4) of the EAC Customs Union Protocol.

website was replete with information about achievements towards this goal,[94] there is no evidence that it was achieved, or even of any documents or steps taken towards the establishment of the customs territory, outside what was envisioned at regional level.

The NCIP made an effort to ease the movement of persons between the participating states. While this was based on EAC aspirations in the EAC Common Market Protocol, the NCIP took steps to facilitate the free movement of persons, at least in Kenya, Rwanda and Uganda. For example, the three countries announced the reciprocal removal of work permit requirements for citizens of their states,[95] following the signature of an agreement on free movement.[96] It can be argued that this was nothing exceptional, since the EAC Partner States had agreed to liberalise the free movement of persons by the end of 2015.[97] However, considering that Tanzania and Burundi still maintain work permit requirements and fees for EAC citizens, it can be argued that in this regard, the NCIP may have taken a further step towards deeper integration than the rest of the EAC, although it did not involve all NCIP states. The three states also attempted to make it possible for their citizens to travel across each other's borders with only a national identity card.[98] However, this too is a claim the NCIP cannot make without attracting some criticism. According to Awinja, this project was not done well:

> The identity cards did not meet international requirements, as they needed to be electronic. Rwanda came up with electronic ones, which were rejected by IATA (the International Air Transport Association). They (Rwanda) had a chip which does not work, instead of a readable strip and barcode. IATA rejected it, and it could not be accepted as a travel document until they revised it. They refused to take that input, saying, 'this is local. It is our own arrangement, and it should work.' In addition, Kenya and Rwanda had never finalised the process in accordance with the required standard.[99]

While NCIP claims credit for the use of national identity cards across borders, it has not been as successful as it would have the world believe. Further, while the

---

[94] Clearance of goods under Home Consumption and Warehousing regime at the first port of entry (Mombasa); interfacing of Revenue Authorities Systems of the three Partner states (Rwanda, Uganda and Kenya); integration of Regional Customs Bond with Revenue Authorities Systems; deployment of partner states (Rwanda and Uganda) Revenue Authority officers at the port of Mombasa; waiver of port charges and demurrage fees on over stayed cargo at Mombasa port; training and accreditation of clearing agents form partner states; reduction of multiple customs bonds to a single bond; reduction of clearance and movement of cargo in the Northern Corridor; and reduction of multiple cargo declarations to a single declaration (NCIP Website (n 91)).

[95] 'Uganda Joins Kenya, Rwanda, in Abolishing Work Permits for Professionals', *The East African*, www.theeastafrican.co.ke/news/Uganda-joins-Kenya--Rwanda-in-abolishing-work-permits/2558-2750958-om9sh7/index.html (accessed 24 November 2017).

[96] The Northern Corridor Integration Projects Agreement on Free Movement of Labour (June 2015).

[97] ibid.

[98] NCIP Website – About Us (n 91).

[99] Interview with Awinja (n 88).

three states could claim this as a success of the NCIP under variable geometry, the idea is based on the EAC's decision to allow the use of machine-readable and electronic national identity cards as travel documents.[100] Additional scepticism for this claim can be found in the fact that all three states had had projects to issue new national IDs to their citizens long before the NCIP existed.[101] As it has been with other alleged achievements of the NCIP, this might have just been a series of convenient coincidences that could be claimed as a result of their efforts.

Closely related to the free movement of persons was the creation of the East African Tourist Visa, which enabled visitors to Kenya, Rwanda and Uganda to access the three countries using a single visa. The 90-day multiple entry visa could be obtained on arrival or in advance from any of the three countries, and cost US$100 regardless of which state was the first point of entry.[102] Although this visa did encounter some implementation problems at the start,[103] it appears to have taken root, as the immigration departments of all three NCIP countries are issuing it.[104]

As the perceptive reader may understand, the successes of the NCIP cannot entirely be credited to the NCIP. As Awinja puts it:

> I do not think there is anything specifically successful about the infrastructure projects because most of the roads and railways have been funded by the World Bank for the whole EAC, so there are some that join Kenya and Tanzania, Kenya and Uganda, etc. Many of them were funded by the African Development Bank. The SGR (standard gauge railway) is still under construction and all of them are constructing anyway, even Tanzania. There is no particular success you can say was theirs (NCIP), at least for the specific infrastructure projects.

B. Relations between the EAC Partner States

The NCIP had a bigger impact on the political scene than it did on the trade and economic affairs of the EAC. As seen in section II above, the NCIP was born

---

[100] Article 9(2) of the EAC Common Market Protocol.

[101] See, eg, T Butagira, 'Government Suspends National ID Project Again', *The Daily Monitor*, www.monitor.co.ug/News/National/Government-suspends-national-ID-project-again/688334-1966 618-ko3qd7z/index.html (accessed 25 November 2017).

[102] 'Single Tourist Visa: Things to Note', *The East African* www.theeastafrican.co.ke/news/ Single-tourist-visa--Things-to-note/-/2558/2217586/-/d2xlytz/-/index.html (accessed on 24 November 2017).

[103] 'Country Laws Hampering East African Single Tourist Visa', *The East African*, www. theeastafrican.co.ke/business/Country-laws-hampering-East-African-single-tourist-visa--/2560- 3231966-dkumeh/index.html (accessed 24 November 2017).

[104] Kenya's Directorate of Immigration and Registration of Persons, www.immigration.go.ke/ Information.html, Rwanda Directorate General of Immigration and Emigration, www.migration. gov.rw/index.php?id=233 and Uganda's Directorate of Citizenship and Immigration Control, http:// mia.go.ug/content/visas-and-passes (all accessed 25 November 2017).

out of strained relationships between EAC Partner States. At the start of this book/chapter, two possible effects on inter-EAC relations were expected from the establishment of the NCIP. The first expectation was that there would be a closer relationship between the NCIP states, and second, that there would be some distance between the NCIP states and the non-NCIP states, since there was a reluctance to work together at the start of the initiative anyway. This section studies these two premises by looking at how the relationships between the states in the two categories (NCIP vs. non-NCIP) have evolved.

i. Inter-NCIP Relations (and the End of the NCIP)

Relationships between NCIP states have evolved faster than expected at the start of this book. In the four years since the Entebbe Meeting that kick-started the process, a lot has happened, from the expected close relationship to strained relations between some of the NCIP states. The coalition held 13 summits between June 2013 and April 2016, meeting on average every two months.[105] A review of what transpired in these summits has already been covered in section II.B above, but it is still necessary to discuss briefly the relationships between Kenya, Uganda and Rwanda during NCIP, and shortly after its apparent demise.

Perhaps the single most significant matter that shaped the destiny of the NCIP was the construction of a pipeline to transport crude oil from Western Uganda to the East African coast on the Indian Ocean. Uganda, being a land-locked country, had two main options, and both involved the construction of a pipeline through either Kenya or Tanzania, to a port in either state. The Kenyan President, Mr Uhuru Kenyatta, had hoped for his country to snap up the deal, following the northern route to its port at Lamu. With an election looming, this project would win him favour with voters, as it would mean investments, jobs and other associated benefits.[106] Following several feasibility studies, Ugandan technocrats knew that the Kenyan route was not a good idea, in spite of the fact that Kenya was a long-standing bilateral partner, and their leader, a close ally of the Ugandan President. Consequently, both the Kenyan and Tanzanian routes were subjected to several re-inspections, re-assessments and feasibility studies, which were accompanied with several back and forth meetings between Uganda and either party.[107]

The Ugandan technocrats were not the only ones with second thoughts on the Kenyan route. The private sector, while split between the two routes, preferred the southern route for several reasons. To start with, the Kenyan route raised security concerns because of Lamu's closeness to Somalia, where

---

[105] The first meeting between the heads of state of Kenya, Rwanda, and their host, Uganda, agreed to meet every two months to review the progress of implementation of their decisions. Thirteen of these meetings were held, with the last one being on 23 April 2016.

[106] F Musisi and MK Muhumuza, 'Uganda: How Oil Pipeline Deal Slipped Out of Kenya's Hands', *All Africa*, http://allafrica.com/stories/201604250062.html (accessed 25 November 2017).

[107] ibid.

al-Shabab militia continue to operate. Second, the terrain along the proposed route was unfavourable, with slopes above 25 degrees, which would not be ideal for transporting oil. This worked against the Kenyan route, given that the route to the Tanzanian port of Tanga was, according to multiple studies, more viable and less challenging. In addition, Lamu was not an operational port yet, but it is scheduled to be constructed under the LAPSSET corridor,[108] a project that is already two years behind schedule. The Tanga port, on the hand, is already operational, and would have enabled Uganda to export oil as early as 2020, two years earlier than the Lamu port would be ready.

There were also challenges with basic infrastructure, especially the road network on the Kenyan side of the northern route. While the route to Lamu would be only 1,038 km as opposed to 1,239 km to Tanga, the northern route only had 183 km of tarmac roads, and 250 km of usable murram (dirt/unpaved) roads. The southern route, on the other hand, had 1,101 km of tarmac roads and 582 km of usable murram roads, in addition to a railway along the project route. All this was not helped by environmental concerns such as the ecologically sensitive nature of the northern route and Lamu itself, which is a UNESCO world heritage site.[109]

All these factors meant that the only logical choice was for Uganda to pursue the export of its oil through the southern route, going through northern Tanzania to Tanga. In March 2016, the Ugandan and Tanzanian Presidents met on the sidelines of the 17th Ordinary EAC Heads of States summit and agreed to use the southern route. This was less than a month before what would be the last NCIP summit. This pipeline decision appears to be what finally killed the NCIP. The manner in which the decision to use the southern route was reached, at a time when Kenya was in negotiations with Uganda over the same issue, led to an almost immediate loss of trust.[110] It is little wonder, then, that there has been no NCIP Summit or activity since April 2016.

The pipeline, though a major factor, was not the only cause of altered relationships between NCIP states. An even more significant factor was to be found in the nature of the NCIP and its structure – or more correctly, the lack of structure. In keeping with the way it started – from a state visit turned trilateral – NCIP was administered in an ad hoc manner that centred around the personalities of the three leading presidents. As Awinja puts it,

> NCIP has been led by the presidents themselves, and it seemed to be effective at some point, but it did not have roots, a foundation, a legal structure, or a framework that would make it have a strong foundation. That is where they went wrong. If that was to be brought to the EAC, I think it would move faster. The way the structure of the

---

[108] The Lamu Port, South Sudan, Ethiopia Transport Corridor, which consists of seven key infrastructure projects, with a port to be constructed at Lamu, and interregional highways linking major cities in the three countries (Welcome to LAPSSET –www.lapsset.go.ke/ accessed 25 November 2017).
[109] ibid.
[110] Interview with Awinja (n 88).

EAC is, the presidents meet just to endorse what has been agreed by the ministers. The ministers are the ones who are actually responsible for making decisions. They make the final decisions, brief the Heads of States, and then the Heads of States can make their own pronouncement on the same.

This quotation reveals two challenges with the modus operandi of the NCIP. The first is the lack of a constitutional structure, and this inevitably leads to the lack of direction, since there is no basis for the cooperation and no rules that exist to govern relations between the parties. The second is the lack of trust, which is an inevitable result of the unpredictability of an unstructured set up, as well as the series of backdoor and bilateral dealings that Awinja, other respondents,[111] and the pipeline story above disclose.

What this meant for relations between the NCIP states, then, was that although the NCIP was founded on optimism and an eagerness to make quicker progress of the integration process, there was insufficient openness between the participating states. This lack of transparency led to strained relationships, with each party seeking to satisfy its interest, and not willing to make any sacrifices that may be adverse to itself in case the other parties did not stay true to their part of the bargain. This was reflected in Kenya's reaction to Uganda's decision on the pipeline route, where Kenya decided to stop construction of the SGR in Kisumu, rather than extending it to the border with Uganda at Malaba, as previously agreed. This delay is also partly because Uganda has not made any real progress on the construction of the SGR, while Kenya has done a significant part of its construction,[112] with the Mombasa-Nairobi stretch already operational.[113]

Except for the relationship between Kenya and Uganda, which was slightly frosty two years into NCIP, it is difficult to estimate how relationships between Rwanda and Kenya, or Rwanda and Uganda, fared. This is mainly for two reasons. First, Kenya and Rwanda do not share a border, so common infrastructure projects between the two were purely incidental to common projects between Kenya and Uganda. Second, and this is a combination of many factors, the NCIP seemed, right from inception, a 'two bull' affair between Kenya and Uganda, with Rwanda being brought on board later in the day. While Rwanda would have agreed to NCIP decisions, its implementation of those decisions was entirely dependent on the other two states. It does not bode well that at the time of writing, there is tension between Rwanda and Uganda,[114] which shows that the NCIP was not as strong as it needed to be if it were to succeed.

[111] Both Duncan Karari and Sam Tulya-Muhika allude to this.

[112] This appears to be a cat and mouse game between the two countries, with Uganda now threatening to construct an SGR in consort with Tanzania, and up to Dar es Salaam if Kenya does not complete the Kisumu-Malaba leg. See A Olingo, 'Uganda May Join Dar as Kenya Weighs Options of Extending SGR to Malaba', *The East African*, www.theeastafrican.co.ke/business/Uganda-ditch-Kenya-SGR-route-Tanzania/2560-3935306-phdp9p/index.html (accessed 25 November 2017).

[113] B Duggan and I Muktar, 'Nairobi to Mombasa High-Speed Railway Opens', *CNN Marketplace Africa*, http://edition.cnn.com/2017/05/31/africa/kenya-nairobi-railway/index.html (accessed 25 November 2017).

[114] Discussed in ch 4, section IV.

The factors discussed above combined to bring a relatively quick end to what seemed like an effort, albeit rather ad hoc, to fast track the integration of the EAC. As discussed below, changing relationships between the three states had a clear effect on the relationships at the regional level.

ii. Extra-NCIP Relations

The NCIP did not only affect relations between participating states, but also affected (and was affected by) relations with the other EAC states, especially Tanzania. As already seen with the oil pipeline story above, the bloc had become so divided that Uganda's perceived betrayal of Kenya was the single act that restored cooperation:

> There were some successes in NCIP, such as the infrastructure projects they undertook, but the exclusion of other partners, the EAC (secretariat) and us (the East African Business Council – EABC), was not a good thing. We were told we are part of the EAC structure, so we had no business in the NCIP. This does not make sense, and we told them, 'we are not coming to compete with you; we are coming to complement what you are doing. We will give you recommendations that will work best for the private sector.' Most of them were not receptive. It was a structure that did not work well for the larger EAC. In fact, the fact that Uganda went into a partnership with Tanzania on the pipeline saved the EAC.[115]

The last part of this quotation is loaded with an indication that the rift that was growing between NCIP and non-NCIP states was so deep, it took the externalisation of a perceived NCIP project to attempt to salvage the situation. As discussed above,[116] Tanzania was consistently against the initiative, criticising it for replicating EAC projects and running contrary to EAC structures, decisions and expected practices. However, other factors affected the region's dynamics and are worth noting.

As variously noted in this chapter, the NCIP was an expensive venture. Even before focusing on the costs of the projects they intended to undertake, the sheer cost of administering the initiative was astronomical, and this had a direct impact on the EAC.[117] Naturally, Tanzania, which already hosts the EAC Secretariat, the EALA and the EACJ, felt like it was shouldering the burden of running the EAC, since the three states were diverting thinly spread resources to run a parallel structure. The perception appears to be that Burundi is 'allowed' to get away with much of the same behaviour because of its internal challenges. While discussing Tanzania's and Burundi's reluctance to implement EAC decisions, Awinja suggests that Burundi's challenges are more understandable:

> We understand Burundi from the perspective that it is not as developed as the other countries. The reason Tanzania is mentioned a lot in terms of failing to implement

---

[115] Interview with Awinja (n 88).
[116] Section II.D.
[117] Interview with Awinja (n 88).

some of the commitments or dragging its feet is that Tanzania is one of the original members of the EAC. In addition, Tanzania has not had any conflict. It is a stable country and has the resources, so it is the willingness that is missing. Tanzania is blamed a lot [more], although on many issues you will find Tanzania and Burundi have not implemented. Burundi sometimes does not implement because of lack of resources. They *may* be willing, but may not have the resources so they drag their feet. They are a young member of the EAC, and even when they joined, their contribution was paid by Rwanda for a number of years. They only started paying their own contribution after some time. Burundi is not blamed a lot; we look at it as a young state, although they are on the same level within the EAC and they should contribute the same amount.[118]

Even after the NCIP's apparent collapse, its effects are still leading to strained relationships between the EAC Partner States. For example, relations between Kenya and Uganda still struggle[119] following the decision to construct the oil pipeline from Western Uganda through Tanzania. This has been escalated by the possibility that Uganda will abandon the northern route for the construction of a railway to the coast in favour of a railway along the proposed pipeline in Tanzania.[120] These events do not only affect ties between Kenya and Uganda because through Uganda's preference for Tanzania, a subtle animosity has developed between Kenya and Tanzania.

In 2017, these simmering tensions escalated, with Tanzania seizing and burning 6,400 chicks that had been imported from Kenya on SPS grounds.[121] In the same week, Tanzanian authorities auctioned 1,300 heads of cattle from Kenya and 6,600 from Uganda.[122] Herding communities across the borders of the three countries historically graze their livestock on either side of the border as the seasons dictate,[123] so it is rather curious that Tanzania should find an issue with this *now*. Even more curious, however, is the specific mention of 'Kenya's cows' by the Tanzanian President, although the cattle from Kenya were barely a third of the cattle from Uganda. It seems to suggest that while Uganda may 'offend' Tanzania in greater terms than Kenya, Kenya's offence is larger. The livestock wars have not been the first of Tanzania's actions against Kenya or Kenyan owned businesses, with the most noticeable having been Tanzania's

---

[118] ibid.

[119] W Maina, 'Time for EAC to Lower its Sights; Throw Out Federation Dream', *The East African*, www.theeastafrican.co.ke/oped/comment/EAC-political-federation/434750-3948146-w43lh8z/index.html (accessed 27 November 2017).

[120] A Olingo, 'Uganda May Join Dar as Kenya Weighs Options of Extending SGR to Malaba', *The East African*, www.theeastafrican.co.ke/business/Uganda-ditch-Kenya-SGR-route-Tanzania/2560-3935306-phdp9p/index.html (accessed 27 November 2017).

[121] 'Tanzania Police Burn 6,400 Chicks to Death', *The East African*, www.theeastafrican.co.ke/scienceandhealth/Tanzania-police-burn-6400-chicks-alive/3073694-4166372-q3dus0/index.html (accessed 27 November 2017).

[122] 'Magufuli: Tanzania is Not a Grazing Land for Kenya's Cows', *The East African*, www.theeastafrican.co.ke/news/Magufuli-Kenya-cattle-diplomacy/2558-4177942-fkjac7z/index.html (accessed 27 November 2017).

[123] ibid.

banning of the *East African* newspaper in 2015,[124] an indication that something has been brewing between the two for a while.

At the time of writing, the full extent of the fallout from the NCIP is still being uncovered. This section has attempted to discuss the evolution of relationships between the NCIP states, and between the NCIP states and the rest of the EAC. Conspicuously absent from much of this discussion is the nature of relations with regard to Burundi and South Sudan. This is so for reasons specific to each of the two states. South Sudan is the subject of the next section, while Burundi's absence in the discussion is a reflection of the situation in the EAC today. Out of five interviews conducted for this book, Burundi is mentioned in only one,[125] and even then, in response to a question about Burundi's conspicuous absence. Awinja's response quoted above[126] reflects the 'Burundi is a young state with its own issues, so it can be excused for its shortcomings' attitude with which Burundi is treated in the bloc. Put another way, if Kenya is the big brother of the region, Burundi is the little brother.

C. Relations between the EAC and Third Parties

i. South Sudan

The Republic of South Sudan is the newest member of the EAC, having acceded to the EAC Treaty on 15 April 2016, although it had been a participant in the NCIP since 28 August 2013. South Sudan had applied to join the EAC as early as November 2011,[127] and eventually, the directive to start negotiations for South Sudan's accession was given in November of 2012.[128] Negotiations were due to commence in January 2014,[129] (just five months after South Sudan had been an NCIP Participating State), but war broke out in South Sudan in December of 2013, delaying the process until May 2015.

It would not be too far-fetched to suggest that South Sudan's participation in the NCIP had a role in fast tracking its admission to the EAC. Even with the political challenges South Sudan faced during the negotiations, Uganda had recommended that South Sudan's membership be fast-tracked so that

---

[124] 'Tanzania Bans 'The East African' Over Coverage of Govt, Registration', *The East African*, www.theeastafrican.co.ke/news/Tanzania-now-bans--The-EastAfrican--/2558-2600522-ydbvagz/index.html (last accessed 27 November 2017).

[125] Lilian Awinja.

[126] Interview with Awinja (n 88).

[127] EAC Secretariat, *Report of the 13th Summit of the Heads of State*, EAC/SHS 13/2011, Paragraph 7.1.

[128] EAC Secretariat, *Report of the 14th Summit of the Heads of State*, EAC/SHS 14/2012, and EAC/SHS 14/Directive 01.

[129] EAC Secretariat, *Report of the 15th Summit of the Heads of State*, EAC/SHS 15/2013, Paragraph 5.2.

South Sudan could become an EAC member by April 2014.[130] It would have been beneficial to the NCIP, if for nothing more than practicality, for South Sudan to join the EAC as quickly as possible. While to some extent this was achieved, other events in the bloc brought the curtain down on the NCIP, just days after South Sudan joined the EAC.

ii. *The European Union*

The main contemporary tie between the EAC and the EU relates to the Economic Partnership Agreement (EPA) between the two blocs, which has proved, so far, quite controversial. While the agreement was agreed upon by five of the EAC Partner States,[131] only two, Kenya and Rwanda have signed the agreement with the EU.[132] To drag an already long drawn out process even further, the bloc has agreed that Partner States that have not signed yet should not do so pending clarification of contentious issues, which have been highlighted in the agreement. The report from the 18th summit of the Heads of State of EAC States, held on 20 May 2017, contains the following decision:

The Summit-

(a) Took note that the remaining Partner States that have not signed the EU-EAC Economic Partnership Agreement are not in a position to do so pending clarification on issues they have identified in the agreement (*EAC/SHS 18/Decision 03*);

(b) Decided that due to the above action, Kenya should not be disadvantaged since she has already signed the agreement (*EAC/SHS 18/Decision 04*);

(c) Decided that the President of Uganda, as the new Chair of the Summit, was mandated within one month to reach out to the European Union (EU) to communicate the EAC circumstances (*EAC/SHS 18/Decision 05*);

(d) Decided that in the event that an acceptable way forward is not reached with the EU within the next six months, the chairperson was authorised to explore the use of variable geometry in implementation of the EPA by EAC Partner States working with the Council of Ministers (*EAC/SHS 18/Decision 06*);

(e) Decided that the EU sanctions on Burundi should be discussed alongside the EPA discussions (*EAC/SHS 18/Decision 07*)

These decisions have far-reaching implications for the EAC, and some of them might be related to the NCIP. The first observation from this state of affairs is the fact that the only states that have signed the EPA are both NCIP Participating States. This could signal the willingness of both to liberalise trade between them and third parties (the EU, at least) regardless of the factors causing hesitation

---

[130] F Oluoch, 'S. Sudan's Push to Join EAC Gains Momentum', *The East African*, www.theeastafrican.co.ke/news/S--Sudan-s-push-to-join-EAC-gains-momentum/2558-2946330-his9dpz/index.html (accessed 28 November 2017).

[131] Negotiations were conducted before South Sudan acceded to the EAC Treaty (EAC Secretariat, *Report of the 18th Summit of the Heads of State*, EAC/SHS 18/2017 Paragraph 4.0/iv).

[132] EAC Secretariat, *Report of the 14th Summit of the Heads of State*, EAC/SHS 18/2017 Paragraph 2(e).

in their counterparts. It is important to make a brief note of the most salient of these factors at this point.

There are three main reasons for the delay in signing the EPA, especially on the part of Burundi, Tanzania and Uganda. Burundi was concerned that the EU had unilaterally suspended direct partnership with it, which needed to be addressed.[133] Uganda's concerns were just as political, even though that conclusion may be speculative. While Uganda has no concern with the EPA itself, it insists that the EAC should sign the agreement as a bloc (rather than as individual states).[134] This may be considered a safety valve for Uganda, so that in the event that the EAC collapses, it has the option of not being bound by the EPA, if remaining bound would be disadvantageous to it.

Tulya-Muhika, however, believes it is based on the differences in development in the region. Kenya is classed as a developing country, and therefore does not qualify for the EU's 'Everything but Arms' trade arrangement. He suggests that this disqualification is what drove Kenya to sign the EPA, since it would otherwise lose access to the EU market. Uganda, however, insists that a different classification should be carried out that covers the whole bloc, since the agreement binds all the members of the bloc in equal measure, regardless of whether they are developing or least developed countries.[135]

Tanzania's concerns were more related to the content of the EPA itself. At the 18th summit, it expressed worry about the effects of the EPA on EAC industrialisation, agriculture, tax revenues, engagement with third parties, cooperation with other Africa-Caribbean-Pacific Group of States (ACP) Countries, balance of trade and the impact of the departure of the United Kingdom from the European Union (Brexit).[136] These concerns are more technical than those raised by Uganda and Burundi, and it is possible that they could lead to a stalemate or a reopening of negotiations between the two blocs.

While it remains to be seen how the concerns raised by the EAC and the EAC Partner States will affect the EPA or relations with the EU, these concerns reveal the nature of interests in the bloc. Some Partner States are interested in attracting more trade and accessing more markets, while others are more concerned about self-preservation and some do not even seem sure they have the opportunity to be players in the process. These differences are both the basis and the result of the EAC's variable geometry, which has been discussed in other chapters of this study. Indeed, the EAC's most recent decision on the EPA is that Partner States who wish to do so should be able to commence engagements with the EU with a view to starting the EU-EAC-EPA implementation under the principle of variable geometry.[137]

---

[133] Report of the 18th summit of Heads of State, ibid, Paragraph 4.0/ii.
[134] Paragraph 4.0/i ibid.
[135] Interview with Sam Tulya-Muhika.
[136] Paragraph 4.0/iii, Report of the 18th summit of EAC Heads of State.
[137] Paragraph 9, Communique of the 21st Ordinary summit of the EAC Heads of State, 27 February 2021.

IV. SUMMARY

This chapter has attempted to document the EAC's boldest attempt to implement variable geometry. The ad hoc nature of the NCIP is a principal challenge, which makes documenting even its most significant achievements a complex affair. During its brief existence, the NCIP promised changes in the landscape of East African integration – changes which, as this chapter has shown, might have been more ambitious than expected. The next two chapters look beyond the EAC to study the use – historical and theoretical – of flexible integration on a broader scale. Chapter seven traces the history of the Africa Continental Free Trade Area (AfCFTA), demonstrating how the incremental approach to integration led to the establishment of the largest free trade area in history so far. Chapter eight is a more theoretical review of flexibility in multilateral trade, with consideration of the reasons flexible approaches have not been widely adopted.

7

The Africa Continental Free Trade Area

THE AFRICA CONTINENTAL Free Trade Area (AfCFTA) was established on 21 March 2018, at a meeting of the African Union (AU) Heads of States in Kigali, Rwanda. It arose out of a desire to implement the Decision of the Assembly of the Heads of State and Government of the African Union,[1] made in January 2012, to establish a continent-wide trade bloc. In spite of this apparently recent development, integration of African economies across the continent is not as new as the AfCFTA would lead one to believe. It can, as this chapter shows, be traced as far back as the early post-independence days.

This chapter studies the Agreement establishing the AfCFTA and explores the history of the treaty and the events leading up to its signing. It highlights the role of flexible integration in the AfCFTA, linking it with the AU's vision of an African Economic Community (AEC). This is done, as with other parts of this study, through the lens of pan-Africanism, showing how the push for African unity has been a major factor in the integration of African economies.

I. A BRIEF HISTORY OF THE AfCFTA

African integration first came up at the dawn of independence, fuelled by African leaders' desire to stem the adverse effects of Africa's balkanisation. The political and economic reactions to these adverse effects triggered the establishment of a number of intergovernmental agencies operating in the field of integration, to enable African countries to speak with one voice and to ease the constraints linked to the limited size of national markets.[2] This 'integration rush' became centralised at continental level in the 1980s, with the Lagos Plan of Action[3] and the Final Act of Lagos. This was followed in 1991 by the signing of the Abuja Treaty Establishing the African Economic Community, and in 2000 by

---

[1] Assembly/AU/Dec. 394(XVIII).

[2] R N'Guettia Kouassi, 'The Itinerary of the African Integration Process: An Overview of the Historical Landmarks' (2007) 1(2) *African Integration Review* 1–23 1.

[3] Lagos Plan of Action for the Economic Development of Africa, 1980–2000.

the Constitutive Act of the African Union, respectively. It was under the auspices of the AU that the AfCFTA was established.

This section traces the history of the AfCFTA in two parts. The first stage considers the early post-independence efforts at establishing a continent-wide union in the form of the Organisation of African Unity (OAU). This is followed by a study of the post-1980 period and the effect of the Lagos Plan of Action and the Final Act of Lagos. This necessitates an evaluation of efforts across the continent leading up to the 1991 Abuja Treaty, focusing on the growth of flexible integration as a principle of integration. The post-1980 period will be examined for political, economic and other factors that laid the ground for the signing of the Kigali Treaty Establishing the AfCFTA, and the factors that may have delayed the integration process. Each of these stages will highlight the role, whether express or implied, of flexible integration across the African continent and in the regional blocs.[4]

A study of the history of integration in Africa would be incomplete without a brief note on the role of the United Nations Economic Commission for Africa (UNECA) in Africa's regional integration. UNECA was established by the United Nation's (UN) Economic and Social Council (ECOSOC) in 1958 as one of the UN's five regional commissions. UNECA's mandate is to promote the economic and social development of its Member States, foster intra-regional integration, and to promote international cooperation for Africa's development. It comprises of 54 African states, and plays a dual role as a regional arm of the UN and as a key component of the African institutional landscape.[5] As the following sections show, UNECA was not only the earliest effort at bringing the continent together for economic or trade purposes but is also the most consistently existing institution. In addition, it has played a direct role in the development of Africa's trade policies, especially as far as regional integration and trade are concerned. For the purposes of this book and this chapter, the most important was the establishment of Multinational Programming and Operational Centres discussed in section I.B below.

Another prominent factor that stands out in this section is pan-Africanism and its role in continental integration. While it is possible to write a volume on the subject and still not be exhaustive, it is a central theme in almost any study of African integration from 1960 to the modern day. As discussed in chapters one and two,[6] pan-Africanism is the belief in a shared heritage among Black Africans, and seeks to unite Africans, both in Africa and in the diaspora. Pan-Africanism drives the efforts to unify the continent, and this chapter

---

[4] It has been proposed that the story of African integration can be further divided into five stages. See CC Ajibo, CM Nwankwo and EO Ekhator, 'Regional Economic Communities as the Building Blocs of the African Continental Free Trade Area Agreement' (2021) 18(4) *Transnational Dispute Management*.

[5] UNECA, *Overview*, at the UNECA website, www.uneca.org/pages/overview (accessed 24 November 2018).

[6] Chapter 2, section III.

demonstrates that integration in Africa is an attempt to return to pre-colonial, borderless times.

A. Faltering, Learning and Unlearning: 1960–1980

Most African states gained independence in the 1960s. As demonstrated from the history of the EAC,[7] integration between African economies predates the independence of African states. Indeed, the oldest known customs union – the Southern African Customs Union (SACU) – is in Africa. Even with this colourful history, the main concern of this chapter is the integration of independent African states, which was, in large part, kick-started with the inception of the OAU.

At independence, African leaders advocated for a politically and economically united Africa. When the OAU was founded, Kwame Nkrumah famously inspired the unity of African states:

> Here is a challenge which destiny has thrown out to the leaders of Africa. It is for us to grasp that golden opportunity to prove that the genius of African people can surmount the separatist tendencies in sovereign nationhood by coming together speedily, for the sake of Africa's greater glory and infinite well-being, into a Union of African States.[8]

In spite of good intentions, Africa's commitment to integration appears to have been more ambitious than rational, more rhetoric than real. African integration ideals were based on lofty transcontinental ambitions and evocative political slogans and were not tailored to the day-to-day practical realities of the continent's economic and political life.[9] At independence, most African countries lacked large internal markets, human, social, technical or material capital, or the physical or institutional infrastructure for industrialisation, even though they had an abundance of raw materials.[10] As Nkrumah's statement and the failure to take advantage of the continent's potential show, regionalism in Africa was an expression of continental identity and coherence, which distinguished the region's integration from other regions of the developing world.[11]

At its formation in May 1963, the OAU was to be universal, with the main aim being to bring all states together rather than to establish stringent conditions

---

[7] Chapter 4, section I of this book highlights the early history of the EAC.

[8] K Kimbugwe, N Perdikis et al, *Economic Development Through Regional Trade: A Role for the New East African Community?* (Basingstoke, Palgrave Macmillan, 2012) 35.

[9] ibid.

[10] K Abraham, *The Challenges and Prospects of Pan-African Economic Integration*, a paper presented at the Conference on Economic Integration and Trans-Boundary Resources, organised by the Ethiopian International Institute for Peace and Development, Addis Ababa, June 2000.

[11] C McCarthy, 'Regional Integration: Part of the Solution or Part of the Problem', in S Ellis and J Currey (eds), *Africa Now: People, Policies and Institutions* (London, Heinemann, 1996) 211–231.

of membership. It represented an amalgam of lessons learnt from earlier efforts at integration and cooperation and it would supersede all other groupings. The effort was a curious hotchpotch of principles and purposes, which combined conservative statements designed to protect the status quo in intra-African relations with radical commitments towards the outside world.[12]

The OAU had an elaborate administrative structure. At the apex was the Assembly of Heads of State and Government, which was charged with discussing matters of common concern to Africa with a view to coordinating and harmonising the general acts of all the Union's organs and any specialised agencies.[13] Decision-making at this level was by resolution, which required a two-thirds majority in a one-member one-vote system.[14] Next to the Assembly was the Council of Ministers, which, responsible to the Assembly, was entrusted with preparing conferences for the Assembly. The Council was also responsible for the implementation of the decisions of the Assembly, as well as coordination of inter-African cooperation in accordance with the instructions of the Assembly.[15] The day-to-day running of the OAU was coordinated by the Secretariat, under the leadership of the Secretary General,[16] while the Commission of Mediation, Conciliation and Arbitration was charged with dispute settlement.[17]

Although the Assembly established a Specialised Economic and Social Commission,[18] there is little else to show an effort to integrate the continent's economies. The OAU was formed, among other things, to coordinate and harmonise general policies in economic cooperation among Member States[19] but it did not fully pursue economic integration at a continental level. The commission it established was tasked to investigate the prospects for the establishment of a free trade area in Africa, an African payments union, and the coordination of transport and telecommunications. This commission, like the others established by the OAU, was not an effective body due either to the complexity of its topic, internal division, and/or the reluctance of Member States to utilise the commissions instead of other organisations.[20] This was due to four main challenges, which subsequently raised several questions for continental integration.[21]

The first challenge was a question of structure: should the main purpose of an organisation be to work directly for political unity either at regional or continental level, or rather to encourage such unity indirectly by facilitating joint

---

[12] C Hoskyns, 'Pan-Africanism and Integration', in A Hazlewood (ed), *African Integration and Disintegration: Case Studies in Economic and Political Union* (Oxford, Oxford University Press, 1967) 366–7.

[13] Article VIII of the OAU Charter.

[14] ibid, Art X.

[15] ibid, Art XII.

[16] ibid, Art XVIII.

[17] ibid, Art XIX.

[18] ibid, Art XX.1, and Hoskyns, 'Pan-Africanism and Integration' (n 12) 387.

[19] OAU Charter, Art II.2(b).

[20] T Mays and M Delancey, *Historical Dictionary of International Organisations in Sub-Saharan Africa,* 2nd edn (London, The Scarecrow Press, 2002) 162.

[21] Hoskyns, 'Pan-Africanism and Integration' (n 12) 360.

action on common problems? In either case, what powers should be given to the organisation and at what stage should any surrender of sovereignty be considered? This dilemma is similar to the one attributed to Bela Balassa in chapter two, in which regional integration and regional cooperation can be mixed up.[22] The second challenge relates to the creation of smaller, geographically-based regional blocs. While it seemed like a pragmatic approach, it was unclear whether they should be encouraged, permitted, or opposed. Indeed, Kwame Nkrumah cautioned against regionalism:

> Only on a continental basis shall we be able to plan the proper utilisation of all our resources for the full development of our continent … By belonging to different economic zones, how will we break down the currency and trading barriers between African States, and how will the economically stronger amongst us be able to assist the weaker and less developed states? … It has been suggested that our approach to unity should be gradual, that it should go piece-meal. This point of view conceives of Africa as a static entity with 'frozen' problems which can be eliminated one by one and when all have been cleared, then we can come together and say: 'now all is well. Let us now unite.' This view takes no account of external pressures. Nor does it take cognisance of the danger that delay can deepen our isolations and exclusiveness; that it can enlarge our differences and set us drifting further and further apart into the net of neo-colonialism, so that our union will become nothing but a fading hope, and the great design of Africa's full redemption will be lost, perhaps forever.[23]

While, as this chapter shows, the incremental approach was eventually adopted, the limited success of continental integration appears to vindicate Nkrumah and his warnings. Understandably, his proposals were radical at the time, and might still be difficult to pursue today given the even wider differences that he correctly predicted.

The third challenge relates to the nature of blocs to be created. Should they be intergovernmental in nature, operating purely between governments, or should they be more fundamental, linking people and other parties more closely? While this has been discussed in chapter two,[24] it has also been cited as one of the issues the EAC has had to grapple with in its integration, since there appears to be more collaboration at state level, and less integration of societies across borders.[25] The final challenge is a central theme in this book, and relates to what method of integration should be used. In the interests of continental unity, is it better to form 'partial' or 'universal' organisations? Is it better to form an organisation consisting of a nucleus of ideologically similar states (likely to reach an agreement and act) while hoping that other states will be attracted and

---

[22] Chapter 2, section I, and B Balassa, 'The Theory of Economic Integration: An Introduction', in *The Theory of Economic Integration* (London, Routledge, 2012) 1.

[23] K Nkrumah, 'Speech at the First Organisation of African Unity Summit', 24 May 1963, in *African Union*, 'Speeches and Statements Made at the First Organisation of African Unity (OAU) Summit' 44–53, 50–51.

[24] Chapter 2, section II.C.

[25] Interview with Duncan Karari, Communications and Brand Manager (East Africa), Deutsche Gesellschaft für Internationale Zusammenarbeit (GIZ) GmbH, May 2017.

join, or is it better to form from the beginning an organisation that includes all shades of opinion, even though the compromises this involves may jeopardise effective action?

These questions are reminiscent of Nkrumah's 1963 speech, and represent the challenges African states faced soon after independence as they grappled with forging a new identity in the wake of a new pan-Africanism. Indeed, some of these questions are still valid today, and form part of the questions this book raises. For example, the question of whether to form 'partial' or 'universal' organisations indirectly considers flexible integration based on the multi-speed approach considered in chapter three.[26] In response to these questions, Catherine Hoskyns unwittingly made a correct prediction of the future of integration in Africa:

> The advantages and disadvantages of universal and partial organisation have not really been resolved, and the future is likely to see a continuing swing from one to the other. One of the reasons for this fluidity would seem to be the fact that Africa, unlike either the Americas or Europe, has no states that are unquestionably more powerful and dominant than the others. Political influence thus depends on an ever-shifting pattern of alliance, prestige, and national interest, which in turn radically affects the type of organisation required at any one time. For the immediate future, however, it seems likely that the OAU will remain as a universal cover organisation, while groupings that are in reality partial, exist within it.[27]

Although this was written 14 years before the Lagos Plan of Action and the Final Act of Lagos (1980), Hoskyns' predictions are nearly square with the propositions of these two documents. As discussed in chapter five, variable geometry in the EAC was adopted from the continental context, where it was intended that regional blocs would form the constitutive elements of the African Economic Community (AEC).[28] This theory is worth unpicking a bit further, especially for how it relates to the history of continental integration in Africa.

Hoskyns predicted that Africa would see a continuing swing from 'partial' to 'universal' organisation in its attempts to integrate. While this is true, for the most part, it is due to various factors, which are discussed below. Africa's integration history is a smorgasbord of blocs, each with a 'unique' approach to integration. In the 1960s, integration was principally driven by political motivation and interests, especially the need to attain the independence of African states. This was characterised by continent-wide integration, specifically, the OAU. By the mid-1970s, however, integration became increasingly regionalised, with more than 20 economic cooperation organisations on the continent.[29] At the same time, African states were pursuing continental cooperation at the OAU level, which, for the fledgling states they were, inevitably presented

---

[26] Chapter 3, Section III.A.i.

[27] Hoskyns, 'Pan-Africanism and Integration' (n 12) 369.

[28] Chapter 5, section I on Variable Geometry in the EAC.

[29] A Adedeji, 'The need for Concrete Action', in African Association for Public Administration and Management, *Regional Cooperation in Africa: Problems and Prospects* (Addis Ababa, 1977) 10.

several challenges and slowed down integration on both the 'partial' and 'universal' planes.

There are several possible explanations for the relatively slow progress of integration across the continent in the 1960s and 1970s. The principal factor is, of course, that economic integration was not the main aim of the process. The main driving force behind African integration in the early days was the desire to band together to win independence,[30] followed by, in the early days of the OAU, the aforementioned surge of pan-Africanism, which was not grounded on much more than sentiment and catchy political rhetoric. Even where there was the will to pursue integration beyond colourful speeches, integration was hampered by the age-old problems facing African economies, including small markets, dealing in primary products, transport problems, and a heavy dependence on Europe.[31]

Perhaps the most significant reason for the slow process of integration at the continental level was in the form of strained and in fact opposing political interests, as has variously been the case in the EAC. Continental priorities remained political, and as national/internal interests and responsibilities increased, they were often at odds with those of other states. As S.K.B Asante and David Chanaiwa noted:

> The new African leaders became divided into pro-East and pro-West blocks, and further into revolutionaries, progressives, reactionaries, capitalists, socialists, traditionalists and 'middle-of-the-roaders ...' The overriding aim of pan-African conferences during the 1960s was to intensify the political struggle for independence ... , and consequently, economic development, although of vital importance, did not constitute the principal policy objective. Leaders became preoccupied with immediate territorial problems [such as] the unification of ethnic and regional groups, the consolidation of their own parties and power over the masses and against opposition leaders, the fight against poverty, disease and ignorance, as well as defence and security of their nations against the Cold War and internal *coups d'état*.[32]

It would appear, therefore, wrong to have expected the newly formed OAU to lead to an economically integrated continent. While its formation was a partial success for the integrationist aspect of pan-Africanism, it fell short of the expectations of the old and radical pan-Africanists led by Kwame Nkrumah. The OAU concentrated on the liberation aspects of pan-Africanism, while many independent states concentrated on internal developments and strengthening their ties with their former colonial powers.

With the deposition of Nkrumah, the integration aspect of pan-Africanism lost its momentum throughout the second half of the 1960s. It was replaced by

---

[30] Hoskyns, 'Pan-Africanism and Integration' (n 12).

[31] ibid 383–384.

[32] SKB Asante and D Chanaiwa, 'Pan-Africanism and Regional Integration', in A Mazrui and C Wondji (eds), *General History of Africa, Volume VIII – Africa Since 1935* (Oxford, UNESCO/Heinemann Educational, 1993) 724–743, 726–727.

movements for the formation of regional and inter-state groupings.[33] By 1977, there were over 20 inter-governmental, multi-sectoral economic cooperation organisations in Africa, and about 100 single multinational organisations that were meant to promote technical and economic cooperation.[34] Many of these were established in the 1960s, which were the halcyon years of African integration. This period, however, was also characterised by the decline of several regional groupings, including the EAC (1966 and 1977), and the Customs Union of West Africa (1966).[35] By the 1970s, it was clear that African integration efforts were in serious trouble.[36]

With the exception of the EAC, whose members attained independence as an economic community, there was little success with integration of early post-independence African states. The initiatives among French-speaking West African countries, including the West African Customs Union (WACU) and the Customs Union of West African States[37] both failed. The Economic Community of West Africa was formed in 1973 and quickly replaced by the Economic Community of West African States (ECOWAS) in 1975,[38] which survives at the time of writing. Several others did not make it past the 1970s, and the story was only gloomier in English-speaking parts of the continent. No regional economies were established in Anglophone West Africa during the early years of independence, with the few joint institutions being disbanded. These included the British West African Currency Board, the West African Court of Appeal, the West African Cocoa Research Institute and West African Airways Corporation, all of which had been established by the British.[39]

Significant, of course, was the decline of the EAC. While it was arguably the most sophisticated regional cooperative arrangement in the Global South at independence, it experienced such acute tensions that the level of economic integration had declined. As reported in Chapter four, at independence, external trade, fiscal and monetary policy, transport and communication infrastructure, and university education were all regional rather than national. These links were systematically dismantled and all the high hopes that the East African region would evolve into a full federation under one government evaporated.[40]

---

[33] ibid 728.

[34] Adedeji, 'The need for Concrete Action' (n 29).

[35] Union Douanière et Economique de L'Afrique de l'Ouest (UDEAO) was an initiative among the French-speaking west African countries.

[36] Asante and Chanaiwa, 'Pan-Africanism and Regional Integration' (n 32) 728.

[37] WACU was formed in 1959, and included Benin, Burkina Faso, Ivory Coast, Mali, Mauritania, Niger and Senegal. It disintegrated and was replaced in 1966, with the same membership, by the West African Economic and Customs Union (WAECU). WAECU lacked vigour and was replaced in 1970 by the West African Economic Community (WAEC), which was replaced in 1994 by the West African Economic and Monetary Union (WAEMU).

[38] ECOWAS brings together Benin, Burkina Faso, Cape Verde, Cote d'Ivoire, The Gambia, Ghana, Guinea, Guinea Bissau, Liberia, Mali, Niger, Nigeria, Senegal, Sierra Leone and Togo. It is aimed at both economic and political cooperation between the Member States (ECOWAS, *History*, available at www.ecowas.int/about-ecowas/history/, last accessed 13 December 2018).

[39] Asante and Chanaiwa, 'Pan-Africanism and Regional Integration' (n 32) 728–730.

[40] A more detailed review of this decline is done in ch 4, sections I and II.

A common thread running throughout early integration efforts (both regional and continental) is the effect of inward-looking policies. It is important to consider their origin and the effect they had on integration. Colonialism left behind a patchwork of sovereign states, which were themselves artificial entities. They were anxious to encourage national integration, and so their new leaders were compelled to look inward and prioritise the political, economic and social developments of their own polities. For most, if not all of them, the immediate concern was to build viable nation states based on their own traditions and customs. To the extent that national consolidation received high priority, cooperation with other African countries would have to be secondary. Since cooperation necessarily implied long-term commitment, there was reluctance to take decisions that restrained national sovereignty in certain key areas.[41]

This 'policy space' argument is an important consideration for integration purposes. Policy space is the scope for domestic policies, especially in the areas of trade, investment and industrial development, which might be framed by international disciplines, commitments and global market considerations.[42] For young African states in the 1960s–1970s, this was particularly important, mainly because they needed to establish their own domestic policies and structures. This would often require opposition to the integration of policies. African states were not willing to sacrifice perceived national interests on the regional altar. They entered into agreements to liberate trade or allocate industries on a regional basis only when these integrative objectives were not in conflict with considerations of national security, prestige, or economic advantage.[43] This convergence was, understandably, a rare occurrence.

By the 1970s, a more honest admission of the shortcomings and challenges of integration was apparent, and with this, efforts were made to achieve a more realistic form of integration. Leaders like Julius Nyerere preferred incremental regionalism, so Africa was faced with a choice between continuing to support an inherited structure of dependence and beginning to break away from this structure in part through regional economic integration.[44] With the rise of the new international economic order (NIEO),[45] there was a resurgence of efforts to negotiate as a bloc, but these often failed. As a result, African leaders decided it was time to go back to the drawing board and launched the Lagos

---

[41] Asante and Chanaiwa, 'Pan-Africanism and Regional Integration' (n 32) 731

[42] Paragraph 8, UNCTAD, *Draft Sao Paulo Consensus*, TD/L.380 16 June 2004.

[43] Asante and Chanaiwa, 'Pan-Africanism and Regional Integration' (n 32) 731–732.

[44] ibid 735.

[45] In 1974, the United Nations (UN) proclaimed a determination to establish the NIEO. It was based on equity, sovereign equality, interdependence, common interest and cooperation among all states, irrespective of their economic and social systems. The NIEO's aim was to correct inequalities and redress existing injustices, make it possible to eliminate the widening gap between the developed and the developing countries, and ensure steady economic and social development, peace and justice for present and future generations. See the UN General Assembly Resolution 3201 (UNGA Res 3201 (S-VI)): Declaration on the Establishment of a New International Economic Order, UN Doc A/RES/3201(S-VI).

Plan of Action.[46] This ushered in the next phase to be studied in this chapter: the period from 1980 to 2000.

B. The Post-Lagos Surge: 1980–2018

While the efforts of the first two decades of African integration did not yield much, the second phase started with a new passion for continental integration. This phase was kicked off with the launch of the Lagos Plan of Action (LPA) and the Final Act of Lagos (FAL) in 1980. These two were adopted by the Assembly of Heads of State and Government of the OAU at the Second Extraordinary Session devoted to Africa's economic problems.[47] The LPA was based on the need, among other things, to 'pursue efforts towards African economic integration with renewed determination in order to create a continent-wide framework for the much needed economic co-operation for development based on self-reliance'.[48] This reflected an admission of the failures of the OAU in the past with regard to economic integration.

This newfound fervour was still driven by pan-Africanist ideology. Pan-Africanism was now seen to be an important element in reducing dependence and in helping to improve the bargaining position of African countries, thus contributing to their development potential.[49] Apart from the more orthodox benefits promised by regional groupings in the shape of expanded trade and investment, economic integration in this period was vigorously advocated as a means of reducing external vulnerability. It was hoped that regional economic integration would break the dependent relationship by helping each member nation to export manufactured goods, and eventually, capital goods to their neighbours. The underlying premise was the desire by African states and leaders to determine, as far as possible, their own economic policies based on their national aspirations, natural resources and political ideologies outside the influence of developed countries.[50]

The 1980 strategy recommended several measures for expanding intra-African trade. These included the reduction or elimination of trade barriers by laying the ground for regionalisation and the establishment of preferential trade areas and institutions.[51] They came with a 1985 deadline, and the plan was to progressively reduce and eventually eliminate inter-sub-regional trade barriers.[52] This wording is indicative of a slightly protracted process, which, while it has been alluded to in chapter five,[53] should be discussed briefly here.

---

[46] Asante and Chanaiwa, 'Pan-Africanism and Regional Integration' (n 32) 735.

[47] Paragraph 15, Lagos Plan of Action, 1980–2000.

[48] ibid, para 14(vi).

[49] Asante and Chanaiwa, 'Pan-Africanism and Regional Integration' (n 32) 735–736.

[50] ibid.

[51] Paragraph 250 of the LPA.

[52] ibid, para 250 (i)(b).

[53] Chapter 5, section I.

The years leading up to the LPA saw a redirection of integration efforts from a concerted, continent-wide effort to an incremental, region-based process of integration. Early in the 1960s, UNECA realised that the most viable approach to regional integration was one that was gradual and embraced narrower geographical areas as opposed to an all-embracing continental arrangement. The African region was therefore subdivided into Multilateral Programming and Operational Centres (MULPOCs) along four sub-regions: Eastern and Southern, Central, West, and North Africa, each with sub-regional offices. Their main role was to provide backstop services that would facilitate collective decisions and actions at the grassroots level by undertaking relevant studies, participating in the programming and implementation of multinational projects and providing technical assistance on a continuous basis.[54] In 1977, these were reconfigured to separate Southern Africa from East Africa, and to account for Indian Ocean Island states. The current configuration of the MULPOCs includes North Africa, West Africa, Central Africa (formerly Great Lakes Community), East Africa and Indian Ocean Islands, and Southern Africa.[55] These are represented in Table 7.1 below.

Table 7.1 Multilateral Programming and Operational Centres and Their Membership

MULPOC	North Africa	West Africa	Central Africa	East Africa and Indian Ocean Islands	Southern Africa
Member States	• Algeria • Egypt • Libya • Mauritania • Morocco • Sudan • Tunisia	• Benin • Burkina Faso • Cape Verde • Cote d'Ivoire • The Gambia • Ghana • Guinea • Guinea-Bissau • Liberia • Mali • Niger • Nigeria • Senegal • Sierra Leone • Togo	• Cameroon • Central African Republic • Chad • Congo • Democratic Republic of Congo • Equatorial Guinea • Gabon • Sao Tome and Principe	• Burundi • Comoros • Eritrea • Ethiopia • Kenya • Madagascar • Rwanda • Seychelles • Somalia • South Sudan • Tanzania • Uganda	• Angola • Botswana • Lesotho • Malawi • Mauritius • Mozambique • Namibia • South Africa • Swaziland • Zambia • Zimbabwe

(continued)

[54] A Adedeji, 'Comparative Strategies of Economic Decolonisation in Africa', in A Mazrui and C Wondji (eds), *General History of Africa VIII: Africa Since 1935* (Paris, United Nations Educational Scientific and Cultural Organization, 1999) 393–431 409.

[55] UNECA, *MULPOCs, (Multinational Programming and Operational Centres) – Strengthening ECA's Sub-regional Presence*, UNECA website, at www.uneca.org/cfm1997/pages/mulpocs-multinational-programming-and-operational-centres-strengthening-ecas (accessed 24 November 2018).

Table 7.1 *(Continued)*

MULPOC	North Africa	West Africa	Central Africa	East Africa and Indian Ocean Islands	Southern Africa
Blocs/ IGOs[56]	• UMA[57] • CEN-SAD[58] • COMESA	• ECOWAS • WAEMU[59] • MRU[60]	• ECCAS[61] • CEMAC[62]	• EAC • COMESA • IGAD[63] • CEPGL[64] • IOC[65]	• SADC • SACU • COMESA

The basis of the MULPOCs is easier to understand by returning to pre-independence and even pre-colonial Africa. The partition of Africa and the granting of political independence occurred with complete disregard for history, culture, economic and political viability.[66] At independence, Africa was a patch-work of a large number of miniscule states, each gaining independence at a different time and often, on different terms. In addition, the nature of the colonial legacy was such that contiguous political units existed as separate and isolated entities with minimum structural links between them. African states were consciously structured to produce primarily for, and trade exclusively with, their respective colonial powers. Under the circumstances, the pursuit of national goals of economic decolonisation was seen to be dependent on a strategy of regional economic integration and the establishment of multi-national institutions to promote development and undertake joint cooperative efforts.[67] This should have led to an increase in intraregional trade and less dependence on western markets which, in any case, benefited their former colonial masters more. In this regard, pan-Africanism was framed as a positive 'us and them' strategy, where strengthening the 'us' was intended to make the African states less reliant on a pre-independence 'them'.

In Africa today, there are several regional blocs composed of the countries in each of these MULPOCs. While, as discussed elsewhere, overlapping

---

[56] The blocs and IGOs (Intergovernmental Organisations) in this table are gleaned from their respective MULPOC pages on the UNECA website.

[57] Arab Maghreb Union.

[58] Community of Sahel-Sahara States.

[59] West African Economic and Monetary Union.

[60] Manu River Union.

[61] Economic Community of Central African States.

[62] Central African Economic and Monetary Community.

[63] Intergovernmental Authority on Development.

[64] Economic Community of Great Lakes Communities.

[65] Indian Ocean Commission.

[66] Adedeji, 'The need for Concrete Action' (n 29) 407–408.

[67] ibid.

membership is common,[68] the strategy appears to have worked. For example, UNECA, using the Eastern and Southern African MULPOC, established the Eastern and Southern African Preferential Trade Area,[69] which is the predecessor institution to COMESA.[70] To further integrate their economies, COMESA, the EAC and SADC signed a tripartite treaty in 2017 creating a free trade area between the three blocs, and bringing together 22 countries.[71]

The COMESA-EAC-SADC Tripartite Free Trade Area (TFTA) is an umbrella organisation consisting of three regional economic communities, and brings together 26 Member States. The main objective of the TFTA is to contribute to the broader objective of the African Union in accelerating economic integration of the continent and achieving sustainable economic development.[72] Although it is signed and must be ratified by all Member States, the TFTA Treaty was negotiated between the three trading blocs and they are considered members of the TFTA along with the states in those blocs. Twenty-two out of the 26 Member States have signed the Treaty, and it should come into force when it has been ratified by 14 of the Member States. By June 2021, only ten countries had ratified the Treaty. These are Botswana, Burundi, Egypt, Eswatini, Kenya, Namibia, Rwanda, South Africa, Uganda, and Zambia.[73] As an 'intermediate' bloc, the argument can be made that the TFTA is a continental equivalent of the NCIP in the sense that it is likely to be abandoned in favour of continent-wide integration under the AfCFTA.

The TFTA is based on a commitment to championing and expediting the continental integration process under the Abuja Treaty,[74] and aims to build upon the success and best practices achieved in trade liberalisation within the three RECs.[75] In some ways, the TFTA has been a stepping-stone between existing regional blocs and the establishment of the AfCFTA, by being Africa's first attempt at creating a free trade area between existing regional blocs. Indeed, it has been hailed as a basis for negotiating and eventually signing the AfCFTA Treaty,[76] as stated by the UNECA Executive Secretary, Vera Songwe:

> The negotiated AfCFTA text, the ideas put on paper and signed by our Heads of State in March germinated from the good work of the Tripartite (TFTA) negotiators.

---

[68] For example, ch 2, section III.B discusses the overlapping membership as a factor slowing down integration in Africa.

[69] Adedeji, 'The need for Concrete Action' (n 29) 413.

[70] Preamble to the Treaty Establishing the Common Market for Eastern and Southern Africa.

[71] The Agreement Establishing a Tripartite Free Trade Area between COMESA, EAC and SADC, signed May 2017 (the TFTA Treaty).

[72] EAC Website, *COMESA-EAC-SADC Tripartite*, www.eac.int/tripartite (accessed 4 January 2019).

[73] M Gakunga, *COMESA-EAC-SADC Tripartite Leadership Changes Hands*, June 2021, www.comesa.int/comesa-eac-sadc-tripartite-leadership-changes-hands/.

[74] The Abuja Treaty Establishing the African Economic Area.

[75] Preamble to the TFTA Treaty.

[76] Trade Law Centre, *South Africa on Ratification of the COMESA-EAC-SADC Tripartite Free Trade Area*, www.tralac.org/news/article/13158-south-africa-on-ratification-of-the-comesa-eac-sadc-tripartite-free-trade-area-tfta.html (accessed 24 November 2018).

The shape and structure of the AfCFTA and many of its solutions, from non-tariff barriers to trade remedies, were formed here in the Tripartite negotiations.[77]

This progression is relevant because, as shown in chapter five, the AEC and the LPA are the source of the EAC's variable geometry.[78] The Abuja Treaty provides for a multi-centric approach to economic integration on the African continent, and it was anticipated that this incremental integration would use the MULPOCs and their respective regions as building blocks for the AEC, or the AfCFTA, as we have it today. Evidence for this is first provided in Paragraph 250 of the LPA, and in Paragraph II.B.1 of the FAL. Paragraph 250 reads, in relevant part:

> In so far as intra-African trade expansion – which is meant to constitute the mainstay for the present strategy – is concerned, the following measures are recommended:

> (i)   Reduction or elimination of trade barriers;
>   (a)   Interested countries, within the framework of their respective MULPOCs, should commence negotiations among themselves as soon as possible, with a view to establishing appropriate preferential trade areas or similar institutions.
>   (b)   In anticipation of establishing preferential trade areas or institutions, inter-sub-regional negotiations should commence with a view to progressively reducing and eventually eliminating inter-sub-regional trade barriers.
>   (c)   Existing economic integration groupings which have advanced beyond the level of preferential trade area arrangements should be assisted in achieving more advanced cooperation arrangements among themselves.
>   [...]
> (iv)   *The above measures, including those for the establishment of sub-regional arrangements and the strengthening of existing ones, are meant to converge on the establishment of an African Common Market* (emphasis added).

The wording of this paragraph points to several things. The first, which is one of the bases of flexible integration, is that integration activities in Africa are always voluntary and highly dependent on political will. The wording of Paragraph 250(i)(a), in opening with the words 'interested countries' signifies that only those countries that would be keen to integrate should be expected to do so. In addition, no set timelines are provided for this, with the OAU (as it then was) choosing instead to commence negotiations 'as soon as possible'. Arguably, this language forms the basis of the 'different speeds' aspect of the EAC's variable geometry discussed in chapter three.[79] The second thing to note is, as has been argued in this chapter and in chapter five, the MULPOCs were intended

---

[77] UNECA, *Synergies between the AfCFTA and TFTA will Benefit Africa's Traders and Consumers, Says ECA Chief*, www.uneca.org/stories/synergies-between-afcfta-and-tripartite-fta-will-benefit-africa%E2%80%99s-traders-and-consumers-says (accessed 30 November 2018.

[78] Chapter 5, section I.

[79] Chapter 3, section I.F of this book.

as building blocks for the integration of the continent's economies. This would be done by two methods – the encouragement of intra-regional trade,[80] and the deepening of integration between already existing regional groupings.[81]

These aspirations and plans are further codified in Paragraph II.B.1 of the FAL. This Paragraph laid the roadmap for the establishment of an African economic community by the year 2000,[82] using three approaches. The first approach was to strengthen the existing regional economic communities and establish other economic groupings in other regions of Africa, in order to cover the continent as a whole (Central Africa, Eastern Africa, Southern Africa, Northern Africa).[83] This was to be done, as expected, in the arena of the MULPOCs, as discussed above.

The second approach would aim to strengthen sectoral integration at the continental level, and particularly in the fields of agriculture, food, transport and communications, industry and energy.[84] So far, this approach appears to have yielded little, even though the AEC has existed, at least in treaty form, since 1990. The reasons for this slow progress are discussed below.[85] The third approach was through the promotion of coordination and harmonisation among the existing and future economic groupings for a gradual establishment of an African Common Market.[86] This is a classic example of Ernst B Haas' *disjointed incrementalism* discussed in chapter two of this book.[87]

These provisions emphasise two points about Africa's integration story. The first, and perhaps more important one, was the renewed zeal for the establishment of a continental common market. This was partly achieved by signing the Abuja Treaty in 1990 to establish the AEC. The second point is, of course, the admission that the best way to achieve continental integration is through flexible methods of integration. As paragraph 250 above demonstrates, the MULPOCs were considered essential for continental integration, and have guided this process, leading up to the signing of the more recent Kigali Treaty.

The AEC is an important predecessor of the AfCFTA. Established 10 years after the LPA and FAL, it too, adopted the incrementalist approach. Article 6 of the Abuja Treaty provides for a gradual establishment in six stages, and lasting up to 34 years.[88] The first stage requires strengthening of existing regional economic communities and the establishment of new ones in regions where they do not exist.[89] The second would be a consolidation of tariff and non-tariff barriers to trade, customs duties and internal taxes and their gradual removal or

---

[80] Paragraph 250(i)(b) of the LPA.
[81] ibid, para 250(i)(c).
[82] Paragraph II.A of the FAL.
[83] ibid, para II.B(1)(a).
[84] ibid, para II.B(1)(b).
[85] Section I.B.i below.
[86] Paragraph II.B(1)(c) of the FAL.
[87] Chapter 2, section II.C.
[88] Article 6(1) of the Abuja Treaty Establishing the African Economic Community.
[89] ibid, Art 6(2)(a).

harmonisation, as appropriate, for intra-community trade.[90] In the third stage, each regional economic community is expected to be a customs union[91] in order to pave the way for the fourth stage, in which a customs union would be established at the continental level.[92] The fifth stage would be the establishment of an African Common Market,[93] and finally, the sixth stage would be a consolidation of the common market by implementing a raft of harmonised policies and rules across various sectors continent-wide.[94]

From this process, then, the establishment of the TFTA and the AfCFTA are concurrent building blocks towards the establishment of the African Common Market. The AU Decision to operationalise the continental free trade area[95] envisioned the TFTA as part of the process towards the establishment of the AfCFTA. Paragraph 4 of this decision reads as follows:

> The Assembly decides that the CFTA should be operationalised by the indicative date of 2017, based on the framework, Roadmap and Architecture, with the following appropriate milestones:
>
> i) Finalisation of the East African Community (EAC) – the Common Market for Eastern and Southern Africa (COMESA – Southern African Development Community (SADC) Tripartite initiative by 2014;
> ii) Completion of FTA(s) by Non-Tripartite RECs,[96] through parallel arrangement(s) similar to the EAC-COMESA-SADC Tripartite Initiative or reflecting the preferences of their Member States, between 2012 and 2014;
> iii) Consolidation of the Tripartite and other regional FTAs into a Continental Free Trade Area (CFTA) initiative between 2015 and 2016;
> iv) Establishment of the Continental Free Trade Area (CFTA) by 2017 with the option to review the target date according to progress made.

This timeline has, however, been changed by the signing of the AfCFTA Treaty before the establishment of the FTAs mentioned in Paragraph (ii) above. Section III below discusses why the process was accelerated, even though the AfCFTA Treaty was signed in March 2018, a few months later than planned. And even with the establishment of the AfCFTA, the TFTA continues to take shape, with some sectoral negotiations still going on. For example, in November 2018, it was scheduled to hold a validation workshop on its Transport and Transit Facilitation Programme, for cross-border road transport agreements, model laws and regulations in Eastern and Southern Africa.[97]

---

[90] ibid, Art 6(2)(b).

[91] ibid, Art 6(2)(c).

[92] ibid, Art 6(2)(d).

[93] ibid, Art 6(2)(e).

[94] ibid, Art 6(2)(f).

[95] African Union, *AU Decision on Boosting Intra-African Trade and Fast Tracking the Continental Free Trade Area*, Assembly/AU/Dec.394(XVIII).

[96] Regional Economic Communities recognised by the African Union (Article 1(t) of the AfCFTA Treaty).

[97] EAC, *Tripartite Transport and Transit Facilitation Programme* – Press Release, www.eac.int/press-releases/150-infrastructure/1244-tripartite-transport-and-transit-facilitation-programme (accessed 29 November 2018).

Where, then, does this period (1980–2018) fit in with the story of integration in Africa, especially in light of pan-Africanism? The first thing to note is the renewed zeal for a unified continent, illustrated by the establishment of both the African Economic Community (AEC) and the African Union (AU). The reasons for this resurgence are discussed below.[98] The second is the incremental approach leading up to the establishment of the African Common Market. This stage saw the establishment of new regional blocs and the strengthening of existing ones, including the COMESA, the EAC, SADC and eventually, the TFTA. The third and final stage starts with the establishment of the AfCFTA, and signifies a return to pan-African ideals by skipping the rest of the scheduled incremental integration by the signing of a continental treaty. This stage should culminate in the establishment of the African Common Market (ACM) between 2028 and 2034.[99] From 1980, this process has followed the path illustrated in Figure 7.1 below.

Figure 7.1 Progression of Integration in Africa[100]

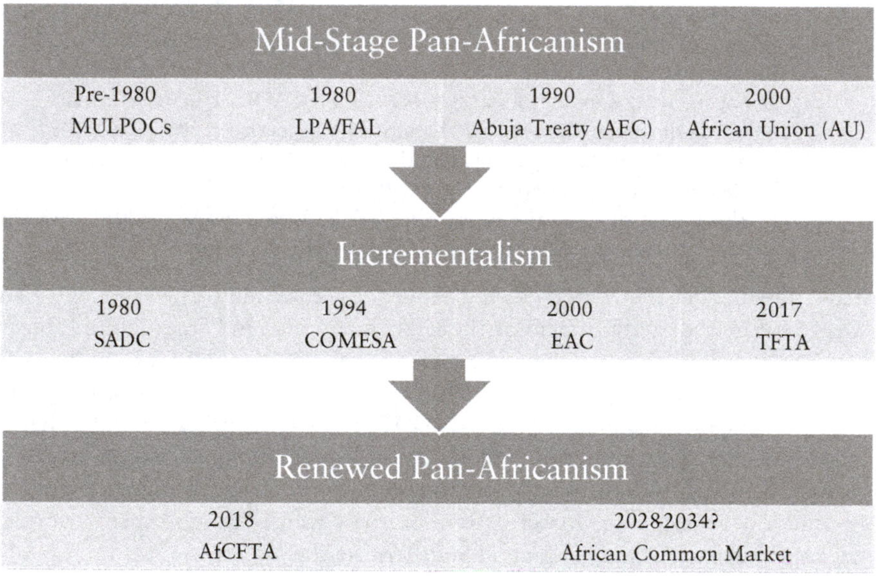

Mid-Stage Pan-Africanism			
Pre-1980	1980	1990	2000
MULPOCs	LPA/FAL	Abuja Treaty (AEC)	African Union (AU)

Incrementalism			
1980	1994	2000	2017
SADC	COMESA	EAC	TFTA

Renewed Pan-Africanism	
2018	2028-2034?
AfCFTA	African Common Market

---

[98] Section II.A.

[99] Article 6(1) provides for a transition period not exceeding 34 years, while Art 6(6) provides that the cumulative transitional period (including extensions) shall not exceed 40 years from the date of entry into force of the treaty. The treaty entered into force on 12 May 1994, and therefore 34 years would be in 2028, and 40 years would be 2034 (African Union, *Treaty Establishing the African Economic Community*, https://au.int/en/treaties/treaty-establishing-african-economic-community (accessed 4 January 2019)).

[100] This figure only uses the example of the three blocs making up the TFTA. Other blocs that would be considered in the Incrementalism phase are ECOWAS and the Economic Community of Central African States (ECCAS).

The TFTA therefore did lay the ground and provide inspiration for the negotiation and establishment of a continental bloc, thereby leading to a rebirth of pan-Africanism. It is a combination of the third and fourth stages envisioned by Article 6(2) of the Abuja Treaty, while the AfCFTA dispenses with the incremental approach, opting, instead, to combine 54 of Africa's 55 countries in one ambitious integration project. The framers of the Abuja Treaty were realistic enough to set a timeline of 34–40 years for the establishment of a continent-wide common market, with the first steps towards continental integration expected 23–29 years after the Abuja Treaty. The AfCFTA was established 24 years after the Abuja Treaty came into force. While this looks like the process is moving smoothly, it has not been without its challenges. The slow pace of integration in Africa has been dealt with at length in chapter two,[101] but some reasons are unique to the MULPOC and LPA process, and should be considered.

i. Challenges to a Renewed Zeal

Despite the establishment of MULPOC-based regional blocs and dozens of intergovernmental, multi-sectoral economic organisations aimed at technical and economic cooperation the process of integration has remained slow. Some of the reasons for this are similar to the reasons for slow integration in Africa, which have been discussed in this and previous chapters.[102] This section focuses on those peculiar to the continent-wide experience with particular regard to the MULPOCs.

The main constraint to the MULPOCs resulted from an insufficient appreciation of what continental economic integration might involve. Adedeji questions the motives and methods that lay behind the underlying push towards integration in Africa:

> Intra-African penetration has been constrained by, first and foremost, the inadequacies in understanding the objectives and modalities of economic cooperation. Far too often, assumptions which are obtained in advanced countries, but which are untrue as far as developing African countries are concerned, have been brought to bear on the formation and operation of economic groupings in Africa.[103]

This paragraph is packed with reasons for the slow integration in Africa even in the context of the MULPOCs, and these should be dealt with in some detail. Adedeji's starting point is the inadequacies in understanding the objectives and modalities of economic cooperation. The post-1980s efforts were not immune from the 'catchy rhetoric and colourful speeches' trap that plagued the continent

---

[101] Chapter 2, section III.B studies why integration has not been successful in African regional economic blocs.

[102] Section I.A of this chapter, and ch 2, section III.B, for example.

[103] Adedeji, 'The need for Concrete Action' (n 29) 413.

in the 1960s. While the attraction of an integrated continent was easy to see, it was not often considered what integration meant in practice, weighed against the continent's capacities. Integration aspirations did not account for the meagre resources available to national governments of African states, many of which were plagued by civil wars and other political challenges in the early 1980s. The LPA, for example, though it is admittedly no more than a strategy, proposed a path of integration that is considerably ambitious, such as requiring that all MULPOCs establish appropriate preferential trade areas within four years.

While this might have been feasible for the smaller groups, it would inevitably pose a challenge for the bigger, and often diverse, groups. This can be demonstrated by a quick look at the EAC (initially three members, now expanded to six) and ECOWAS, which started out with 15 countries. Admittedly, both blocs struggled through the early years of their existence, but while the EAC seems to have bounced back more than 20 years after its 1977 collapse, ECOWAS appears to have stalled. It has existed in its current constitution since 1975, and only notified the WTO as being a customs union in 2005,[104] five years later than the EAC.[105]

The African process of integration is often based on the wrong assumptions that cannot be applied to the African setting. Chapters two and six criticise the adoption of one-size-fits-all policies, which are often taken without the necessary adjustments for the African context.[106] Akin to Ombeni Mwasha's sub-optimal conditions for integration,[107] Adedeji argues that the conditions obtaining in Africa are characterised by an inadequate supply of entrepreneurs, a scarcity of skilled manpower, and a limited knowledge about the supply of raw materials or their sources. Other traits he describes are limits in technology, inter-industry integration, and domestic markets.[108]

Given these conditions, the objectives, principles and methods of integration should account for the unique conditions of the African states seeking to integrate. Variable geometry is a form of flexible regional economic integration unique to Africa, which has been adopted out of these unique conditions.[109] This would limit the direct transfer of integration ideals from industrialised states to African states as if the two settings were identical. Similarly, integration goals should bear in mind the needs of the African markets, and aim at lowering

---

[104] WTO-RTAIS, *Regional Trade Agreements – ECOWAS*, http://rtais.wto.org/UI/PublicShow MemberRTAIDCard.aspx?rtaid=36 (accessed 17 December 2018).

[105] WTO-RTAIS, *Regional Trade Agreements, EAC*, http://rtais.wto.org/UI/PublicShowMember RTAIDCard.aspx?rtaid=94 (accessed 17 December 2018).

[106] Chapter 2, section III.B and ch 6, section II.B.i.

[107] ibid, and ON Mwasha, 'The Benefits of Regional Economic Integration for Developing Countries in Africa: A Case of East African Community (EAC)' (2008) 11(1) *Korea Review of International Studies* 69–92, 70.

[108] Adedeji, 'The need for Concrete Action' (n 29) 415.

[109] See ch 5 and section IV below.

the costs of goods and services, first for internal markets, and when capacity has been improved sufficiently, for export to other regions.

Another challenge that has hampered the achievement of the Lagos goals, and nearly incapacitated the function of the MULPOCs, is the struggle to reach acceptable formulae and procedures for sharing the costs and benefits of economic cooperation. Of particular importance is the concern of participating states over the possibility of loss of income from export and import taxes because of trade liberalisation measures implicit in common market arrangements. This problem is closely linked with considerations of equity and balance within economic groupings where certain countries have progressed at slower rates than they would have done outside the groupings.[110] This is reminiscent of the East African experience as early as 1960, before the first customs union collapsed. At the time, both Tanzania and Uganda were dissatisfied with the operation of the common market, because Kenya appeared to benefit from the process more than the other two did.[111] As will be argued below,[112] such considerations are no doubt the reason for the inclusion of variable geometry in both the EAC Treaty and the AfCFTA Treaty.

Another reason for the slow progress of integration in Africa post-1980 is the reluctance of states to yield policy space (especially with regard to crucial areas of economic policy) to regional integration initiatives. This is similar to the hesitations of the post-independence governments discussed in the previous section. Another challenge is the inadequacy of infrastructure and institutional frameworks to promote economic cooperation. Ill-equipped transport links and clearing services make it nearly impossible for seamless trade to happen across regions. Further challenges present themselves in the form of political differences, especially between socialist and capitalist states, and general ambivalence in attitudes towards economic cooperation.[113] As chapters five and six have shown, these differences led to the adoption of flexible regional economic integration and the establishment of NCIP in the EAC.[114]

While these may have been bumps on the road to the African Common Market, they have not presented, thus far, a fatal blow to the aspirations of African leaders to integrate the continent. As mentioned above, the LPA and the Abuja Treaty paved the way for the strengthening of the MULPOCs, in the hope that they could then make continental integration seamless. Indeed, this was attempted with the TFTA, an effort that appears to have slowed down in favour of AfCFTA. The next section explores, in part, why the incremental approach has been set aside in favour of the more 'deep-end' approach followed by AfCFTA.

---

[110] ibid.
[111] See ch 4, section I, on the early beginnings of the EAC.
[112] Sections III and IV.
[113] Adedeji, 'The need for Concrete Action' (n 29) 415–416.
[114] Chapter 5, section II, and ch 6, section II.

II. AfCFTA: OBJECTIVES, PRINCIPLES AND ENABLING FACTORS

The AfCFTA Treaty follows the path envisioned by the LPA and FAL 38 years earlier. It acknowledges the Regional Economic Communities (RECs) as building blocks towards the establishment of a continental FTA.[115] Further, it recognises the existing blocs that constitute these building blocks. These include UMA, COMESA, CEN-SAD, EAC, ECCAS, ECOWAS, IGAD and SADC.[116] All of these groups, their Member States and respective MULPOCs have been presented in Table 7.1 above. The AfCFTA has, as its primary objective, the creation of a single market for goods and services, facilitated by the movement of persons in order to deepen the economic integration of the African continent.[117] This involves the creation of a liberalised market for goods and services through successive rounds of negotiations,[118] and enabling the movement of capital and natural persons.[119] It is anticipated, in keeping with the LPA and the Abuja Treaty, that the AfCFTA will lay the foundation for the establishment of a Continental Customs Union,[120] and, eventually, a common market.[121]

This new initiative, like others on the African continent, waxes lyrical about promoting and attaining sustainable and inclusive socio-economic development, gender equality and structural transformation of the State Parties,[122] while enhancing the competitiveness of their economies within the continent and the global market.[123] Like many before it, the AfCFTA aims to promote industrial development through diversification and regional value chain development, agricultural development and food security.[124] Crucially, and this is a unique objective, it seeks to resolve the challenges of multiple and overlapping memberships and expedite the regional and continental integration processes.[125] The reasons why this last objective is important have been previously discussed in chapter two.[126]

While the general objectives impose responsibilities on the bloc as a whole, the specific objectives impose some responsibilities on State Parties. These include a progressive elimination of tariffs and non-tariff barriers to trade in goods, the progressive liberalisation of trade in services, as well as cooperation

---

[115] Preamble to the Treaty Establishing the Africa Continental Free Trade Area.
[116] ibid, Art 1(t).
[117] ibid, Art 3(a).
[118] ibid, Art 3(b).
[119] ibid, Art 3(c).
[120] ibid, Art 3(d).
[121] Article 4(2)(h) of the Abuja Treaty establishing the African Economic Area.
[122] Article 3(e) of the Treaty Establishing the Africa Continental Free Trade Area.
[123] ibid, Art 3(f).
[124] ibid, Art 3(g).
[125] ibid, Art 3(h).
[126] Chapter 2, section III.B.

on investment, intellectual property rights and competition policy. States are also enjoined to cooperate on all trade-related matters, on customs matters, and on the implementation of trade facilitation measures. Together, they are expected to establish a mechanism for the settlement of disputes concerning their rights and obligations, as well as an institutional framework for the implementation and administration of the AfCFTA.[127]

Of particular interest to this chapter are the principles by which AfCFTA has elected to be governed. These are contained in Article 5 of the Treaty, and include, most relevantly, the following:

> ...
> (b) RECS' Free Trade Areas (FTAs) as building blocks for the AfCFTA;
> (c) Variable geometry
> (d) Flexibility and special and differential treatment;
> ...
> (k) Consensus in decision-making; and
> (l) Best practices in the RECs, in the State Parties and International Conventions binding the African Union.

The first three principles are relevant for more obvious reasons. This is a book about flexible regional economic integration, and it has found that the EAC's variable geometry has its origins in the LPA and the FAL, which are precursors to the AfCFTA. This chapter, especially, has discussed at considerable length the role of the MULPOCs and their respective RECs as a foundation for continental integration. As discussed in chapter three, flexible regional economic integration works in multiple ways. The EAC's variable geometry is just one of those, in which state parties to a treaty are able to implement treaty provisions at different speeds and can select the subject matter or provisions that apply to them.

This chapter has also shown that the establishment of the AfCFTA has applied a different form of flexible regional economic integration, by following an incremental path to integration, represented by Article 5(b) above. In addition, the AfCFTA treaty adopts variable geometry in, presumably, the same way as the EAC does. 'Presumably', because as section IV below discusses, the AfCFTA Treaty does not provide a definition for variable geometry. In adopting variable geometry in the same way as the EAC has defined it, the AfCFTA completes the evolution of flexible regional economic integration in Africa. It starts as an idea at the continental level (LPA and FAL), gets clarified and defined at the EAC, and returns to the continental level to be applied.[128]

The fourth principle, referring to consensus in decision-making, plays a slightly less obvious role although it has been discussed in other chapters.[129]

---

[127] ibid, Art 4.
[128] This argument is pursued further in section III. below.
[129] Chapter 3, section IV and ch 6, section II.A.

Flexible integration does not bar the operation of consensus in regional decision-making. The fact that AfCFTA has adopted this as a principle in addition to the articles on decision-making[130] reflects its intention to clarify that consensus and flexible integration are not mutually exclusive. It shows that while there will be various avenues of flexibility in the implementation of the Treaty and other future agreements, the decisions at continental level will be agreed upon by all the State Parties, and will be binding on them.

The final principle, relating to best practices, is less familiar and is relevant mainly for its first part: 'best practices in the RECs'. Of all the RECs and MULPOCs that constitute the AfCFTA, the EAC has been the most explicit and in fact the most practical about the use of variable geometry. The TFTA expressly provided for variable geometry,[131] but at the time of writing, it has not been fully operationalised, and so implementation of variable geometry could not be observed.

This section now considers the factors that have contributed to the establishment of the AfCFTA, highlighting why the incremental approach has been abandoned in favour of more pan-Africanist ideals.

A. AfCFTA: A Long Time Coming, But Why *Now*?

The AfCFTA was established, principally, to promote intra-African trade as a fundamental factor for the sustainable economic development, employment generation and effective integration of Africa into the global economy.[132] While this seems like a tired song that has been sung by the upper echelons of Africa's leadership for decades, the AfCFTA is the first time considerable progress has been made towards the achievement of continent-wide economic integration. The main difference now, it would seem, is the presence of a widespread political will among the current leaders of the State Parties.

As has been discussed variously in this book, one of the main reasons for the slow progress of integration in Africa has been the reluctance to make extraterritorial commitments that could potentially run counter to national interests. The rhetoric has shifted from inward-looking policy to more collaborative efforts, and this can be shown by the growth of regional groups in each of the MULPOCs, and crucially, the establishment of the TFTA. Indeed, the TFTA has been credited as a stepping stone to the establishment of the AfCFTA.[133]

Closely related to this is the fact that on the continental plane, priorities have changed in ways that can facilitate closer economic cooperation. It goes without

---

[130] Article 14 of the AfCFTA Treaty.

[131] Article 6(b) of the Agreement Establishing a Tripartite Free Trade Area Among COMESA, the EAC and SADC.

[132] Paragraph 2, African Union Decision on Boosting Intra-African Trade and Fast Tracking the Continental Free Trade Area, Assembly/AU/Dec.394(XVIII).

[133] Section I.B above, and Vera Songwe, n 77.

saying that in contemporary Africa, all African states have long gained their independence. While many, if not most of them have major internal political challenges, they do not need the support or advocacy of a pan-African bloc to push for their liberation. They have reached a stage where it is easier for them to focus their energies on closer cooperation in ways that benefit their economies. Economic development is now a principal policy objective.[134] The AfCFTA is, then, an appropriate forum for this goal at this point in Africa's history.

As priorities have evolved, so too has the readiness to put into action what has been known since independence: that to compete favourably in global trade, African states would have to trade together. Achieving this necessitates integration for two reasons. In the first place, it is anticipated that continent-wide integration will boost intra-African trade,[135] which will have positive implications for the states involved. Second, as a 54-member trading bloc, the AfCFTA should have access to a better bargaining position in global trade negotiations than the current fragmented position affords African states.[136] This would be in keeping with the proposition that integration results in an improvement of terms of trade, since members of the bloc may be able to exploit their influence on those terms more effectively than if they imposed tariffs separately.[137]

Another factor that has facilitated the establishment of the AfCFTA is the fact that broadly speaking, there has been a convergence of political and economic thinking across Africa. Unlike the early post-independence days that were marked by ideological divergencies,[138] African states today are increasingly similar. Although it might be just in name, most African states have adopted some form or other of capitalism. This has led to an increase in both domestic and foreign investment, which in turn, has spurred production and productivity. Eventually, the need for wider markets becomes obvious, and the most convenient source for such markets will be by trading on preferential terms with other African states.

The creation of the AfCFTA has been precipitated by the realisation that African states can pursue integration in spite of their differences. The abandonment of the incremental approach in favour of a continent-wide agreement demonstrates their acceptance that policy space can be accommodated, especially through flexible integration. The previous section has discussed the inclusion of

---

[134] Section I.A above cites Asante and Chanaiwa, who, in explaining the slow economic integration of the 1960s, argue that economic development did not constitute a principal policy objective for African states.

[135] Preamble to the AfCFTA Treaty; and the Preamble and Art 2(2) of the AfCFTA Protocol on Trade in Goods; and the Preamble and Art 18(3) of the AfCFTA Protocol on Trade in Services.

[136] Paragraph 2 of the AU Decision on Boosting Intra-African Trade and Fast Tracking the Continental Free Trade Area, and Art 3(f) of the AfCFTA Treaty.

[137] Chapter 2, section II.D.iii, and P Robson, *The Economics of International Integration*, 4th edn (London, Routledge, 1998) 40–41.

[138] Section I.A and Asante and Chanaiwa, 'Pan-Africanism and Regional Integration' (n 32) 726–727

various forms of flexible integration in the AfCFTA treaty, which are, no doubt, geared towards accommodating differences in capacity or the political will to integrate. Favouring a single continent-wide treaty over the gradual integration of regions envisioned by the Abuja Treaty shows that African states today are more willing to set aside their differences and work towards a unified economic bloc.

Similarly, the success of some regional groups has provided the much-needed evidence that supranational cooperation can be effective and beneficial. The AfCFTA treaty acknowledges the RECs as building blocs (sic) towards the establishment of the AfCFTA.[139] As if to prove the 'avant-garde' argument in chapter three,[140] this initiative plans to rely on the RECs and their success in order to facilitate continental integration.[141] In the 'avant-garde' argument, a subgroup (or REC in the AfCFTA context) forms an avant-garde, which creates a leadership trail, with deeper integration spreading to the other members that may not have started out at the same level of integration.[142]

The establishment of the AfCFTA has revealed the realisation, or rather, the admission that a specific agreement on trade is necessary. This has paved the way for discussions and action on the achievement of Paragraph 250 of the LPA and the timelines set in the Abuja Treaty. The AfCFTA was established due to a determination to strengthen the economic relationship and to build upon rights and obligations under the AU Treaty, the Abuja Treaty, and at the WTO.[143] The AU Decision on Boosting Intra-African Trade and Fast Tracking the CFTA,[144] for example, recognised the necessity of intra-African trade and laid down timelines and strategies for the operationalisation of the CFTA.[145] These have been discussed above,[146] and show a clear intention to foster closer cooperation on trade. This is a starkly different approach to integration from the approaches used in the past, in which regional integration in Africa was either for political objectives, as with the OAU, or was a mixture of aims and objectives that was too diverse to be realistically achieved. As discussed in chapter three, one of the reasons for the existence of flexible regional economic integration is the need to accommodate the various integration objectives in many African blocs.[147]

A reason given for the slow progress of economic integration in Africa was the inadequacies in understanding the objectives and modalities of economic integration. However, there appears to be some improvement of this situation in

---

[139] Preamble of the AfCFTA Treaty.

[140] Chapter 3, sections I.C and I.D.

[141] Article 5(b) and (l) of the AfCFTA Treaty.

[142] F Dehousse, W Coussens and G Grevi, *Integrating Europe: Multiple Speeds – One Direction?* EPC Working Paper No. 9, April 2004.

[143] Preamble to the AfCFTA Treaty.

[144] Assembly/AU/Dec.394(XVIII).

[145] ibid, paras 2, 3 and 4.

[146] Section I.B.

[147] Chapter 3, section IV.A.

Africa today. For instance, some previous agreements were adaptations of other agreements elsewhere, as was the case with the TFTA, much of which is based on the EAC and COMESA Treaties. On the other hand, a quick read of the AfCFTA Treaty reveals it is mostly unique in that it fits the context of trade on the continent, and has been designed to fit those unique needs.

AfCFTA is the world's biggest REC by state parties, and there was a need to make it robust and to accommodate the diversity of the parties. This would naturally require a good grasp of the continent's affairs, as well as creativity in tackling the continent's economic and trade needs. This appears to have been achieved, as 54 (out of 55) states have signed the Treaty, and 34 had ratified it by December 2020.[148] It is increasingly clear that the AfCFTA has taken into account Africa's specific trade and economic situation, and is therefore tailored to the continent.[149] This would, it is hoped, make it immune from the criticism of one-size-fits-all efforts.

One of the biggest peculiarities of the AfCFTA Treaty is the position of the RECs. While this has been discussed above, the AfCFTA's desire to resolve the challenges of overlapping memberships and expedite the regional and continental integration process[150] is important. No treaty before the AfCFTA has attempted to resolve this challenge, which as has been variously noted, is a recurrent challenge to the process of integration, both at the regional and continental level. This recognition is a sign that African states are ready to make a real commitment on the matter, to the point that they are willing to enter an agreement on its resolution.

The AfCFTA recognises the need to establish clear, transparent, predictable and mutually advantageous rules to govern trade and related matters by, among other means, the reduction of multiple and overlapping trade regimes. This should lead to policy coherence, including relations with third parties.[151] The main challenge is that it is not clear how this will be done, especially in light of other provisions that reflect an aim to preserve and build on, if not strengthen, the existing RECs.

There are, of course, several possible explanations for the readiness of African states to attempt a continent-wide integration. Some of these have not be dealt with in detail, but deserve mention. They relate to other areas

---

[148] African Union, *Statement by the Secretary-General of the AfCFTA Secretariat, H.E. Wamkele Mene, at the 13th Extraordinary Session of the Assembly of Heads of State and Government on AfCFTA*, https://au.int/en/speeches/20201205/statement-he-wamkele-mene-13th-extraordinary-session-assembly. By the end of July 2021, 37 states had deposited their instruments of ratification, with a further three completing their domestic processes of ratification but pending deposit. See TRALAC, *Status of AfCFTA Ratification*, www.tralac.org/resources/infographic/13795-status-of-afcfta-ratification.html.

[149] TRALAC, *The African Continental Free Trade Area – A TRALAC Guide*, 3rd edn, August 2018.

[150] Article 3(h) of the AfCFTA Treaty.

[151] Preamble to the AfCFTA Treaty.

of cooperation, especially in security/political stability and infrastructure. Admittedly, several African states still face challenges in both areas, but the case can be made, and successfully so, that most of the upheavals of the 60s and 70s have been set aside. Even where unrest or disquiet remains, it does not appear to have been a hindrance for African states in joining AfCFTA. There are also several explanations for the improvements in infrastructure, and in some limited cases, this can be attributed to the regional collaboration in the existing RECs.

All these factors appear to have collaborated in getting the wheels turning in favour of AfCFTA. It is still too early to authoritatively comment on the success of this new initiative, since at the time of writing it has only been in place for a few months. While it is now in force following the requisite number of ratifications, operationalisation was delayed in 2020 by the Covid-19 pandemic.[152] The next section attempts to draw some parallels between the AfCFTA and the EAC, especially with regard to the use of flexible integration.

III. THE EAC AND AfCFTA: MOTHER AND CHILD, OR EGG AND FOWL?

The EAC and its Partner States are, respectively, a building block (in the context of the MULPOCs) and parties to the AfCFTA. This section briefly compares intra-EAC relations with EAC Partner State relations at the continental level, by comparing the states that were quick to ratify the AfCFTA, and drawing parallels between these states and their counterparts in the EAC. It studies those relations in three stages. The first stage summarises the relationship between the flexibility in the two blocs, simultaneously laying the ground for the final section of this chapter.[153] The second stage considers EAC states' responses to the AfCFTA, and whether this is comparable to intra-EAC relations. The final stage draws parallels between the EAC and the AfCFTA, proposing future studies of states that were quick to ratify the AfCFTA and the EAC Partner States that had a positive response to the new initiative.

A. The Egg and Fowl Debate

Chapter five discusses the double-edged context in which Article 7(1)(e) of the EAC Treaty was conceived,[154] tracing the origin of variable geometry in the EAC

---

[152] African Union, *Decision on the Start of Trading Under the African Continental Free Trade Area (AfCFTA)*, 5 December 2020, Ext/Assembly/Dec.1(XIII).
[153] The final section questions whether the AfCFTA is a threat to or holds promise for flexible integration.
[154] Chapter 5, section I.A.

Treaty back to the LPA. The conclusion in that chapter led to the question as to whether variable geometry was designed with the idea that the EAC and other blocs would be components of the planned African Common Market. Both that chapter and this one have found this to be the case. It is worth emphasising, however, that before the EAC Treaty, this principle of flexibility was not referred to as variable geometry.

As a concept, flexibility in international economic treaties has existed for some time. It has been applied in the EAC from as far back as the 1960s,[155] and even during the negotiations to re-establish the EAC in the 1990s.[156] Even then, it only took on the name 'variable geometry' in the 1997 EAC Development Strategy, and subsequently, in the 1999 EAC Treaty. The current definition of the EAC consolidates AEC aspects of flexibility into what is now called variable geometry.[157] The nomenclature and definition have been copied, verbatim, in the TFTA Treaty,[158] and although the AfCFTA Treaty does not provide a definition for the principle, it is adopted under the same name. This might point to the fact that in the African context, variable geometry is now perceived as codified and not needing definition in new treaties.

Both the EAC and AfCFTA apply flexibility as a principle of integration, with the minor difference that at the continent-wide level, the 'smaller units' are not only states, but also include existing and future RECs and the MULPOCs. The AfCFTA has gone further to provide for multiple aspects of flexibility, such as special and differential treatment, which enjoins State Parties to provide flexibilities to other State Parties at different levels of economic development or that have individual specificities.[159]

The relationship between flexibility in the EAC Treaty and flexibility in the AfCFTA Treaty is therefore similar to the chicken-and-egg riddle, albeit with a simpler conclusion. This is that the continent-wide context is the birthplace of expressly agreed flexibility in Africa, while the EAC is where this flexibility was expressly accepted, defined and christened 'variable geometry', a principle that is, arguably, so widely recognised it no longer needs definition.

B. The EAC and AfCFTA: Friend or Foe?

How then, does the EAC regard the AfCFTA? The answer to this can be deduced from the practice of the EAC Partner States in the months following

---

[155] Chapter 4, section II.B.ii discusses the flexibility of the East African Development Bank.
[156] Chapter 5, section I.B.
[157] Chapter 5, section I.C.
[158] Articles 1 and 6(b) of the TFTA Treaty.
[159] Article 5(d), TFTA Treaty, Art 6, TFTA Protocol on Trade in Goods, and Art 7 of the TFTA Protocol on Trade in Services.

the establishment of the AfCFTA. Kenya, Rwanda, South Sudan, Tanzania and Uganda signed the AfCFTA Treaty on 21 March 2018,[160] although they had differing rates of ratification. Burundi signed the AfCFTA Treaty on 2 July 2018,[161] nearly four months after it was launched, and received parliamentary approval for ratification on 6 July 2021.[162] Three of the Partner States that initially signed the Treaty had deposited instruments of ratification within the first year. These are, unsurprisingly for this study, Kenya (10 May 2018), Rwanda (26 May 2018) and Uganda (9 Feb 2019). This is so because as chapters two, five and six have shown, they have consistently been fast movers in the EAC. It does not appear to be the case that they have signed and ratified the AfCFTA Treaty as a part of their collaboration, which was the main focus of this study. However, given the nature of relations between them, which has been reported in various chapters,[163] this relatively fast-paced adoption of the AfCFTA is not surprising.

Similarly, the reluctance of Burundi – which signed the AfCFTA Treaty three months after the rest – as well as Tanzania, and South Sudan's non-ratification are also fairly predictable. Burundi and Tanzania are generally less integrationist, while South Sudan is currently grappling with endless internal strife, so the process of ratifying a trade treaty might not be its highest priority. This is understandable, as internal priorities can be a bar to regional cooperation.

Another aspect of the EAC-AfCFTA relationship that calls for more detailed observation as it unfolds, is the place of the TFTA in this entire process. As reported above, negotiations on some aspects of the TFTA are still ongoing between the EAC, COMESA and SADC, while, at the same time, EAC states are taking part in AfCFTA negotiations and seeking to open their economies to even wider markets.

It is still too early to make any conclusions on these questions, but already, there are some challenges to the AfCFTA, which may have an effect on the TFTA. The main challenge results from the state of relationships between the EAC states. *The East African* reports that rising trading tensions between some of the EAC Partner States have resulted in declines in intra-regional trade, with the bloc trading at just half its potential. This, along with growing nationalist and protectionist stances could weaken the implementation of the AfCFTA.[164]

---

[160] African Union, *Interactive Map*, https://treaties.au.int/.

[161] ibid.

[162] TRALAC, *Status of AfCFTA Ratification*, www.tralac.org/resources/infographic/13795-status-of-afcfta-ratification.html.

[163] Chapter 5 and ch 6, especially section I.B.

[164] See ch 4, section IV and IR Mugisha, 'Nationalism in the Region Could Derail Continental Trade Bloc', *The East African*, www.theeastafrican.co.ke/business/Nationalism-in-EAC-could-derail-continental-trade-bloc/2560-4870596-td2h1x/index.html (accessed 30 November 2018.

Chapter four discusses the growing acrimony between EAC Partner States, which threatens the integration process between them.[165] If this trend continues, the AfCFTA could see a failure of the incremental approach to integration, especially since the EAC has negotiated and continues to negotiate trade under the TFTA as a bloc. It is unlikely that a collapse of the EAC would favour deeper integration at the continental level, at least for EAC Partner States. This is mainly because the slower integration in the EAC appears to be more the result of inward-looking policies – or more likely, practices – than due to a shift in its integration focus.

C. AfCFTA: The EAC Supersized?

One question remains unanswered in this section. Is the AfCFTA just a bigger version of the EAC? In many ways, it is. It is a trade bloc based on similar principles and objectives as the EAC, and has, as an element of the plan for its growth, the EAC as a constitutive part. Like the EAC, it has been born out of similar challenges across generations, which have slowed down the process of its establishment. To counter some of these challenges, it has adopted the EAC's model of flexible integration – variable geometry – in the hope that this will encourage states that are parties, or wish to become so, to liberalise their economies and implement Treaty provisions at their own pace. As with the EAC, the AfCFTA appears to have both 'fast movers' and more cautious states.

By July 2021, 37 out of the 54 Partner States of the AfCFTA had ratified the AfCFTA Treaty.[166] While a study of the similarities between the EAC and non-EAC states that have signed and ratified the AfCFTA would no doubt be interesting, it would be outside the scope of this book to consider them in detail. It would be useful to assess the non-EAC states in terms of their openness to integration, their implementation of existing treaty provisions, their economic and political systems, and their involvement in their respective RECs.

If they were found to be similar to the three EAC states that have ratified, then a correlation between the EAC integration and the AfCFTA could be inferred. An enquiry of this nature would not be complete without a comparison of Burundi, Tanzania and South Sudan on the one hand and the non-EAC states that have not ratified the AfCFTA Treaty on the other. Similarities in such a comparison could go a long way in predicting the success or failure of the AfCFTA, based on the experiences of the EAC. This is not to suggest that correlation necessarily results in replication, but it can guide a process that is at its own beginning.

---

[165] Chapter 4, section IV.
[166] TRALAC, *Status of AfCFTA Ratification* (n 162).

IV. SUMMARY: IS THE AFCFTA A CASE FOR
OR AGAINST FLEXIBLE INTEGRATION?

A multitude of words could be employed in answering this question, and the result would be the same: in its current form, the AfCFTA is a win for flexible integration. The AfCFTA is not just a case for variable geometry; in Africa, it is at once the origin and the culmination of the principle. It laid the ground for incremental integration, developed the principles upon which it was based, and encouraged their implementation through the MULPOCs. The EAC may have put this principle and its name in a treaty before anyone else, but the AfCFTA – or its predecessors at least – has every right to boast about its evolution and development. The first MULPOCs were proposed by UNECA as early as the 1960s, leading to the development of a principle, which in the opinion of the AfCFTA, needs no introduction.

The evolution of integration in Africa has shown the post-independence optimism of early, pan-Africanist leaders committed to securing the independence of African states still under colonialism, and the realisation that specific collaboration on trade was necessary for continental unity. It has revealed the admission that a continent-wide project of integration would be too ambitious, and the resultant resort to an incremental approach. There is a new wave of pan-Africanism in Africa, which is more focused on economic integration, and has taken account of the lessons of the past, choosing to apply flexible regional economic integration in various forms in an attempt to exorcise the ghosts of the past.

It remains to be seen whether the form of flexible regional economic integration applied in Africa has been effective. It has been applied as an incremental approach to create the AfCFTA, by relying on the MULPOCs and the blocs created within them. Flexible regional economic integration is also being relied on, in multiple forms, to ensure the success of the bloc going forward. The effectiveness of this strategy will undoubtedly make a rich area for study in the future. For now, scholars must wait with bated breath as African countries slowly but steadily implement the AfCFTA Treaty. It provides fertile ground for the growth of African theories of integration, as well as the place of regional economic integration in the achievement of the pan-African ideal: a united Africa sharing a common identity.

8

Beyond the Regions: Flexibility in Multilateral Trade

FLEXIBLE ECONOMIC INTEGRATION has not only developed within the context of regional integration. The GATT/WTO employed a variant of flexible integration in a bid to accommodate the varied political views and to narrow the divide between developed and developing nations. Flexibility was the desirable middle ground between two extremes: absolute consistency on the one hand, and broad statements of principle on the other.[1] It was favoured by the EU and developing countries, and as the scope of the GATT trading system began to expand in the 1960s and 1970s, countries opted out of agreements they considered too intrusive. This trend was, however, stopped in its tracks by the Tokyo Round's 'fast track' and the Uruguay Round's 'single undertaking'. The WTO Doha Round attempted to continue this trend, seeking to secure a single undertaking, albeit with an 'early harvest' scheme that allows the implementation of agreements as they are agreed upon.[2] However, following the Nairobi Ministerial Conference in 2015, the Doha Round has unofficially been declared 'dead' since negotiations have all but stalled.

This chapter starts by considering the limited use of flexible integration in multilateral trade, before questioning why flexibility has not been widely adopted at the WTO. It does not purport to offer any answers, and is aimed at highlighting some of the questions that might need to be answered before the world moves to the next phase of multilateral trade integration.

I. THE WTO TODAY – A SINGLE UNDERTAKING?

In addition to the special and differential treatment discussed in chapter three,[3] the argument can be made that there is some flexibility in multilateral trade under the WTO. The literature and practice reveal that in spite of the WTO's single undertaking, there have been attempts at flexibility with varying degrees

---

[1] See C VanGrasstek and P Sauvé, 'The Consistency of WTO Rules: Can the Single Undertaking be Squared With Variable Geometry?', (2006) 9(4) *Journal of International Economic Law* 837, 838.

[2] Paragraph 47, Doha Ministerial Declaration of 2001.

[3] Chapter 3, section I.A.

of success. These are discussed in some detail in chapter three,[4] but some can be summarised here.

A. Inconsistent Commitments

Craig VanGrasstek and Pierre Sauvé define the 'consistency of WTO commitments' as the extent to which the obligations established in WTO agreements are given equal effect, both in principle and in practice by the membership.[5] They argue that this utopian position is unattainable, since the WTO does not write and enforce 'the rules', but instead makes 'rules about rules'. A perfectly consistent system would therefore be one in which the text of the WTO agreements was reproduced verbatim in *all* countries' laws, while in a perfectly inconsistent system, all countries' legal obligations would be unique enactments. The WTO is therefore a hybrid of the two extremes since it goes beyond a set of 'best-endeavours clauses' but does not establish a set of uniform codes among all WTO Members.

While this tension is arguably rooted in the nature of international law, with monist states more likely to favour consistent rules and dualist states more likely to support a flexible approach, it goes a bit further than that. For example, the US typically expects a consistent outcome from negotiations, and expects other countries to support the same level of consistency, while the EU is more closely aligned to a variable geometry in which not all countries adhere to the same agreements or arrangements. Beyond this, developing countries are more likely to argue that countries of unequal economic status should not be made subject to equal legal commitments.[6] This extends beyond the monist-dualist debate to include considerations about states' individual or even collective abilities to liberalise their trade. With the broadening mandate of the world trading system, inconsistent commitments have become more difficult to sustain, whether because they would be considered too intrusive, or simply because, as with the Information Technology Agreement (ITA – discussed below), some states do not consider some commitments relevant to them. The result is, more often than not, an inconsistent regime that affords Members some flexibility.

B. Transitional Arrangements

Writing in the context of intellectual property rights (IPRs), Frederick M Abbott argues that the TRIPS Agreement recognised differential interests in technology

---

[4] Chapter 3, section IV.
[5] VanGrasstek and Sauvé, 'The Consistency of WTO Rules (n 1) 841.
[6] ibid 839.

needs through the incorporation of transitional arrangements.[7] These differential interests can be dealt with in a number of ways, including exceptions in the grant of IPRs, variations in the terms of the grant of IPRs, and variations in the scope of regulatory authority with respect to the use of IPRs.[8] Abbot argues in favour of a flexible IPR regime while showing how it has been applied in the TRIPs Agreement, although it has not been expressly referred to as a flexible integration model. This need for differentiated integration is steeped in the intrinsic differences between WTO Members, and consequently, the variable geometry model of flexibility would be appropriate in the TRIPS context.

This approach is perhaps even more apparent in GATT Article XXXVI and the 'Enabling Clause.'[9] Under these provisions, developed Members may accord differential and more favourable treatment to developing countries without according such treatment to other Members,[10] which is a clear exception to the non-discrimination principle of MFN. The non-expectation of reciprocity,[11] adds a further dimension to the flexibility afforded to developing countries in multilateral trade.

C. The Plurilateral Agreements

Lloyd writes that at the WTO, variable geometry strategies were used during the GATT negotiations, though not under that name. During the Tokyo Round, there were irreconcilable differences among the contracting parties in the negotiations that prevented agreement among *all* of them. The resultant Tokyo Round Codes were stand-alone agreements with their own signatories and institutional procedures.[12] Those codes were opt-in agreements, and reciprocity applied only to other code signatories, not on an MFN basis. Five of the codes (technical barriers, anti-dumping, subsidies, customs valuation and import licencing) were renegotiated in the Uruguay Round to become part of the 'single undertaking' binding on all Members of the WTO as part of the Marrakesh Agreement. The other four (government procurement, bovine meat, civil aircraft and dairy) were given the designation of 'plurilateral agreements' to distinguish them from the multilateral agreements in the WTO.[13] The terms of a plurilateral agreement

---

[7] FM Abbott, 'Toward a New Era of Objective Assessment in the Field of TRIPS and Variable Geometry for the Preservation of Multilateralism', (2005) 8(1) *Journal of International Economic Law* 77 99.

[8] ibid 98.

[9] Decision of the GATT Contracting Parties of 28 November 1979 on Differential and More Favourable Treatment, Reciprocity and Fuller Participation of Developing Countries.

[10] ibid, para 1, and GATT Article XXXVI.8.

[11] Decision of the GATT (n 9) para 5, Enabling Clause.

[12] P Lloyd, 'The Variable Geometry Approach to International Economic Integration', (2009) 1(1) *International Journal of Business and Development Studies* 51–66, 55.

[13] The Dairy and Bovine Meat Agreements were terminated at the end of 1997 (World Trade Organisation, *Understanding the WTO: The Agreements – Plurilaterals: Of Minority Interest*, at www.wto.org/english/thewto_e/whatis_e/tif_e/agrm10_e.htm (accessed 7 April 2016).

are binding only on those Members that sign the agreement, and reciprocity is extended only to Members of the plurilateral agreement. These types of agreement are similar to Stubb's variable geometry and à la carte flexibility discussed in chapter three.

D. The Critical Mass Approach

Lloyd also writes about the 'critical mass' approach adopted in the negotiation of the Information Technology Agreement (ITA) and services agreements negotiated between the Uruguay and Doha rounds. This and other Doha Development Round agreements are opt-in agreements with the added feature that participants form a sufficient mass to bring the agreements into force. The ITA required signature by 90 per cent of the WTO Members for it to come into force, but even if the rest of the Members do not sign it, the terms are applied on an MFN basis and do not discriminate against non-signatories. This makes it a multilateral agreement, even though it is outside the single undertaking. It exists on a 'phased-in' basis and therefore fits the bill of a 'multi-speed' agreement.

Mary Footer proposes that a similar approach should be adopted for decision-making at the WTO. Under her approach, Members would agree to refrain from blocking consensus where a 'critical mass' of them support a proposed change.[14] The critical mass would be assessed on the basis of an overwhelming majority of Members in the forum adopting the decision (as with the ITA above), and/or taking account of their overall trade weight, such as 90 per cent of total share of world trade, or a combination of both factors.[15] Arguably, these propositions would relate to decision-making, which is not usually in the realm of flexible integration. Flexible integration is more commonly associated with the implementation of decisions/treaty provisions that have been agreed to by all the parties. While the à la carte method of flexible integration is based on decision making – by parties deciding what agreements or what parts of agreements they want to be bound by – the 'critical mass' approach would fall short of flexible integration because it still results in an agreement that is equally binding on all the parties.

E. 'Trade And –'

The general exceptions to MFN created under GATT Article XX might inadvertently be the most prominent form of multilateral flexibility in place

---

[14] M Footer, 'An Institutional and Normative Analysis of the World Trade Organisation', vol 46, in *Legal Aspects of International Organisation* (Leiden, Martinus Nijhoff Publishers, 2006) 161.
[15] JH Jackson, 'The WTO 'Constitution' and Proposed Reforms: Seven 'Mantras' Revisited' (2001) 4(1) *Journal of International Economic Law* 67–78, 74–75.

today. As discussed below,[16] the pursuit of sustainable development as part of multilateral trade regulation led to the recognition that Members needed the flexibility to pursue environmental and other policies in relation to trade in goods. Article XX seeks to create the all-important balance between multilateral trade liberalisation on the one hand and the need for policy space to impose trade measures that achieve justifiable non-trade concerns on the other.[17] This trend carries on in the application of other WTO agreements that give effect to the general exceptions in Article XX, namely the TBT and SPS Agreements.

While they may not immediately be recognisable as flexibility, these exceptions give Members the right to do as they individually need in order to achieve non-trade goals. Section II.B shows that the ever increasing realisation that global trade is connected to health, the environment, labour standards and so forth is part of the basis for multilateral trade rules as we have them today. Without the flexibility to protect these 'other' interests, world trade would pose a danger to human life, and yet, that policy space has to be balanced against the goals of multilateral trade liberalisation that form the basis of global cooperation.

II. WHY HAS FLEXIBILITY BEEN AVOIDED?

This section attempts to highlight why, in spite of the possibilities and realities in the preceding section, flexibility has not been considered an option in multilateral trade. It considers five main factors that underpin the multilateral trade system, and shows how these factors run contrary to the possibility of a flexible approach to world trade. These factors are the reasons for the rules, the single undertaking, the sovereignty debate, the role of the regions and practicality.

A. The Reason for the Rules

In order to understand why the multilateral trade system avoids flexibility, it is important to understand, first and foremost, why WTO law is the way it is. Peter Van den Bossche and Werner Zdouc advance four reasons for the rules regulating international trade.[18] First, countries must be restrained from adopting trade-restrictive measures, both in their own interest and in the interest of the

---

[16] Section II.A.

[17] See G Marceau and J Wyatt, 'The WTO's Efforts to Balance Economic Development and Environmental Protection: a Short Review of Appellate Body Jurisprudence' (2013) 1(1) *Latin American Journal of International Trade Law*.

[18] See P Van den Bossche and W Zdouc, *The Law and Policy of the World Trade Organisation – Text, Cases and Materials*, 4th edn (Cambridge, Cambridge University Press, 2017) 34–37.

world economy. This flows from the various theories explored in chapter two, as it is accepted that trade liberalisation (and consequently, economic integration) is beneficial for development, economic growth, and access to goods and services.[19] Given the reciprocal nature of trade concessions, flexibility is likely to limit, rather than encourage the removal of trade restrictions.

The second reason for the rules is that traders need a level of security and predictability as they engage in cross-border trade. Clear rules enable them to anticipate how countries will respond to their trade, and what protections they can expect for themselves and other traders in those countries. A system of flexibility would, even if predictable, increase the costs to traders and consequently, consumers as traders would need to comply with different rules in different jurisdictions. This challenge has been considered in chapter three.[20]

A third justification for rules on trade is, arguably, a function of an increasingly comprehensive globalisation. Along with trade, there is a need to protect important societal values and interests such as public health, sustainable use of the environment, consumer safety, cultural identity, and minimum labour standards. Given the interconnected nature of the world today, the protection of these is no longer a truly domestic matter, and international trade rules can more easily be relied on to promote these values. This happens along two planes. In the first instance, these interests are increasingly appreciated for their global nature, with the result that only a global approach to protecting them will be effective. The Covid-19 pandemic and the global climate crisis are clear examples of this. Second, clear trade rules specify what states can and cannot do to protect these interests, which links back to the second reason for the rules mentioned above. The general exceptions to MFN in GATT Article XX are an example of such limits. Unbridled flexibility could leave the door open for states to restrict trade under the guise of protecting these interests. Conversely, an opt-in or opt-out approach could limit the protection of these interests as states would be able to choose which ones to protect, and to what level.

The final reason for the state of the rules is the need to achieve a greater measure of equity in international economic relations. The WTO attempts to do this by treating each Member as an equal partner, regardless of their size, development level or share of world trade. With decisions being made by universal consensus, this means that even the world's smallest or least wealthy nation can prevent a decision which would be adverse to its interests. The apparent collapse of the Doha Round is a result of this set up, with lower income countries not reaching common ground with the higher income countries on development-related

---

[19] See ch 2, section II.
[20] Chapter 3, section V.

aspects of trade. A flexible trade regime, while desirable for its equalisation effects, could be abused as has been alleged in the case of the EU.[21]

B. The Rule about the Rules

In addition to these reasons for the existence of the rules, it is important to consider how the nature of the resultant rules runs contrary to the possibility of flexibility. This requires an enquiry into two peculiarities of the multilateral trading system: the single undertaking and the collaborative nature of the WTO. Both of these are provided for in Article II of the Marrakesh Agreement Establishing the WTO. This sub-section focuses on the single undertaking, and the next explores the collaborative nature of the WTO.

Under Article II.2 of the Marrakesh Agreement, the Multilateral Trade Agreements, which are annexed to the Treaty, form part of the Marrakesh Agreement and are binding on all Members. Consequently, consent to the Marrakesh Agreement meant consent to 17 additional agreements[22] negotiated as part of the Uruguay Round. This all-or-nothing requirement means that an à la carte approach is restricted to the Plurilateral Trade Agreements,[23] a practice that extends to accession.[24]

The single undertaking is a direct result of the justifications for international trade rules discussed above. The commitment to trade liberalisation would need to be 'total' in order for it to be effective in curbing trade-restrictive measures. Similarly, the security and predictability of the system is heavily reliant on the uniform application of rules, so that traders can expect the same or similar rules, or adherence to the same rules regardless of the jurisdiction. This same logic can be applied to the protection of societal values and interests and the regulation of such protection, since all Members can expect the same rules to apply to all of them on the same issues. The single undertaking also facilitates the creation of equitable international economic relations by ensuring that all parties are bound by all the same rules.

While it is possible to protect these interests in a regime that allows for flexibility, that is much easier in a 'few-countries, many-issues' setting that the regions provide.[25] With 164 Members[26] and more than 2000 rules to administer,[27] the WTO is manifestly a 'many-countries, many-issues' setting.

---

[21] See ch 3, section III.C.i.

[22] Annexes 1, 2 and 3 to the Agreement Establishing the World Trade Organisation.

[23] Annex 4 to the Agreement Establishing the World Trade Organisation.

[24] Article XII of the Agreement Establishing the World Trade Organisation.

[25] See ch 3, sections I–III for a detailed discussion of the nature of flexible integration.

[26] The World Trade Organisations, *Understanding the WTO: Members and Observers*, www.wto.org/english/thewto_e/whatis_e/tif_e/org6_e.htm.

[27] RB Stewart and M Ratton, S Badin, 'The World Trade Organisation and Global Administrative Law', in C Joerges and E-U Petersmann (eds), *Constitutionalism, Multilevel Trade Governance and International Economic Law* (Oxford, Hart Publishing, 2011 457.

C. The Sovereignty Debate

As with all issues in public international law, the multilateral trading system is founded on the sovereignty of its members. Sovereignty embraces

> notions (*inter alia*) of monopoly of power within a nation-state, equality of nations, freedom of the nation from external interference (force or otherwise), theory of consent as a basis of any higher (international) norm, source of stability in world international relations, enhanced opportunity for market economies, controls over movement across borders, [and] freedom to make foreign policy choices.[28]

Sovereignty formed the early basis of international legal personality, with only states able to participate in international law. This has evolved over the years, so that organisations and institutions can have personality conferred upon them. The legal personality of the WTO created by Article VIII of the Marrakesh Agreement is a relevant example here. Even then, the idea that there is no higher power than the nation-state endures, negating the idea that there is a higher power – whether international or foreign – unless consented to by the nation state. Treaties almost always imply, in a broad sense, satisfactory consent of the nation-states which accept the treaty.[29]

In an increasingly globalised world, notions of sovereignty can be controversial, counter-productive, or even obsolete. New forms of production and instant communication 'have resulted in greatly enhanced interdependency, which often renders the older concepts of "sovereignty" or "interdependence" fictional'.[30] With the emergence of cross-border institutions and structures – whether public or private – to accommodate or regulate the changes due to globalisation, traditional conceptions of sovereignty are often at odds with the concept of the international institution.

Sovereignty has had its benefits, not least of all as a basis for the development of international law:

> Sovereignty has been a source of stability for more than two centuries. It has fostered world order by establishing legal protections against external intervention and by offering a diplomatic foundation for the negotiation of international treaties, the formation of international organisations, and the development of international law. It has also provided a stable framework within which representative government and market economies could emerge in many nations.[31]

Is it time to thank sovereignty for its service, and move on to the next phase of public international law? Arguably, we already have, at least in some areas

---

[28] JH Jackson, *Sovereignty, the WTO Law and Changing Fundamentals of International Law* (Cambridge, Cambridge University Press, 2006) 214.

[29] ibid 58.

[30] ibid 60.

[31] RN Haass, *Sovereignty: Existing Rights, Evolving Responsibilities*, remarks at the School of Foreign Service and the Mortara Centre for International Studies, Georgetown University, 14 January 2003.

of international cooperation, especially regional integration. The EAC learnt from its history and with the current treaty, ensured the establishment of a central, if partially supranational, authority.[32] The EU with its Commission, Parliament and Court has conferred competence over some matters to the bloc, so that nations are bound by regional law and decisions.[33] In both, the principle of subsidiarity facilitates regional integration while recognising the constituent status of the states. On the contrary, the absence of a central, supranational authority appears to have limited the progress of MERCOSUR, and was a clear factor in the short-lived existence of the NCIP.

But why would this be important, or even necessary? For integration to succeed, whether regional or indeed multilateral, a truly central, supranational authority is essential.[34] Can the WTO be said to be one such authority? There is no simple answer to this question, and while an exhaustive discussion would exceed the scope of this book, some important considerations cannot be avoided. Babatunde Fagbayibo offers a useful definition of supranationalism:

> Supranationalism is a politico-legal concept which embodies but is not limited to the following core elements: decisional autonomy (in particular the rule of the voting majority as opposed to consensus), the binding effect of the laws of international organisations (where member states are precluded from enacting contradictory laws), the institutional autonomy of an organisation from its member states, and the direct binding effect of laws emanating from regional organisations on natural and legal persons in member states. Essentially, supranationalism implies the existence of an organisation capable of exercising authoritative powers over its member states.[35]

For an institution to be truly supranational, it would need to enjoy a vertical relationship with its members, so that, for example, its decisions and rules are automatically binding on the members. Some aspects of both the EAC[36] and the EU[37] fit this bill. This relationship is not express in the WTO, except for the requirement for each Member to ensure the conformity of its laws, regulations and administrative procedures with its obligations as provided in the multilateral trade agreements.[38]

For an institution to be supranational, its members would need to confer upon it the competence to make decisions that would be binding on them without need for further action on the member's part. Naturally, this could lead into a lengthy debate on the relationship between international law and domestic law.

---

[32] See ch 4 for a history of the EAC.

[33] Articles 4 and 5 of the Treaty on European Union (TEU) and Title I, Treaty on the Functioning of the European Union (TFEU). See also ch 3, section III.C.i.

[34] See ch 2, section 2.2.3, and ch 6 for illustrations of this argument.

[35] B Fagbayibo, 'Common Problems Affecting Supranational Attempts in Africa: An Analytical Overview' (2013) 16(1) *PER/PELJ* 31–69, 33.

[36] Article 8(4), Treaty Establishing the East African Community. See also ch 4, section III.A.

[37] Article 2, TFEU. See also ch 3, section III.C.i.

[38] Article XVI.4 of the Marrakesh Agreement Establishing the WTO.

This adds multiple layers of complexity to the status of the WTO as an institution and how it relates to its members. From the structure in Article IV and the decision-making rules in Article IX of the Marrakesh Agreement, it is safe to treat the WTO as an inter-governmental body, administered by the Members to provide an arena for the regulation of trade. It is not fully autonomous, in the sense that it can only execute what the Members have agreed upon – a process that can be convoluted at times. It is, essentially, a negotiating forum, where Members can attempt to establish new rules, with the additional benefit of a relatively robust dispute settlement mechanism.

This is by no means the first time the supranationality of the WTO is being proposed or debated, especially in the context of state sovereignty. John H Jackson,[39] Christian Joerges, Ernst-Ulrich Petersmann and others[40] have grappled with this debate, and so a detailed review is not necessary. The summary of what is admitted by those and other works is that while the WTO's current structure has worked thus far, the time is ripe to adjust the sails. The move to a more autonomous, even supranational body would be a great start, but in the multilateral arena, that is unlikely to be easy in light of sovereignty and the different legal systems involved. The current 'compromise' preserves sovereignty interests and balances the multiple legal systems by having a set of rigid rules in the form of the single undertaking and justified by the ideals in section II.A above. The downside of this, however, is that the rigid rules have made further multilateral integration a complex affair, mainly because of increasingly divergent state interests. Aside from the ITA discussed in section I above, no new multilateral treaties have been successfully negotiated at the WTO since the Uruguay round. Even then, the ITA is not in force because it has not been signed by 90 per cent of WTO Members as required.

Of course, agreements for the sake of agreements, or integration for the sake of integration would not be ideal. This is therefore not to make the blanket argument that the lack of new agreements is a bad thing. However, given the unclear fate of the Doha Round 20 years since it started, it is reasonable to suggest that attempts to reach further agreement have been unsuccessful. As Jackson suggests:

> Some of these issues have led to a worry that the decision-making processes are inhibiting the ability of the organisation to achieve its goals and, some would say, may be leading to paralysis (a criticism particularly addressed to the 'consensus' process of decision making). Obviously, these circumstances reflect some of the policy tensions between outmoded ideas of international law (such as 'sovereignty,' 'consent theory' and 'equality of nations') ....[41]

---

[39] Jackson, *Sovereignty, the WTO Law and Changing Fundamentals of International Law* (n 28).

[40] Joerges and Petersmann, *Constitutionalism, Multilevel Trade Governance and International Economic Law* (n 27).

[41] Jackson, *Sovereignty, the WTO Law and Changing Fundamentals of International Law* (n 28) 83.

A suggestion that dispenses with sovereignty does not require a reinvention of the wheel; it requires a reinvention of the whole cart. As it is now, the cart and its wheels appear to be functional to a degree, but even though they were launched in 1995, they were designed and partially constructed in 1947 in a centuries-old paradigm of international law. Section III below questions the possibility of approaches to decision making which, while preserving the much-cherished sovereignty, will attempt to pave the way for new agreements and even negotiation possibilities in multilateral trade.

D. The Ironic Role of Regional Trade Agreements (RTAs)

As explained in chapter two, more than half of world trade was taking place on preferential terms by 2011.[42] By 2021, there were 568 regional agreements notified to the WTO, of which 350 were in force.[43] The graph below, based on data from the WTO's Regional Trade Agreements Database, is useful for illustrating an important trend.

Graph 8.1 RTAs currently in force (by year of entry into force), 1948–2021[44]

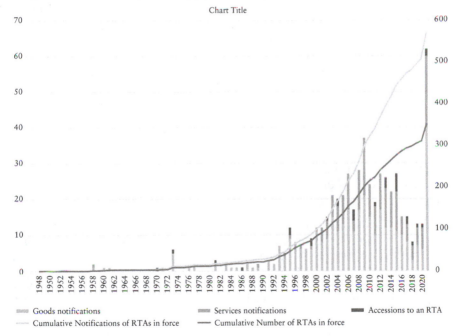

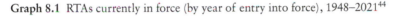

---

[42] Chapter 2, section I.
[43] The WTO, Regional Trade Agreements Information System (RTA-IS), available at http://rtais.wto.org/UI/charts.aspx.
[44] Graph based on data downloaded from WTO RTA-IS, ibid.

One of the most noticeable things about this trend is the increase in RTAs since the establishment of the WTO. Between 1958 and 1994, cumulative notifications of RTAs in force rose from two to 45, while the RTAs in force rose from one to 39. Between 1995 and 2021, however, these numbers grew to 568 and 350 respectively. Even accounting for the fact that there was no WTO to notify before 1995 (which would incorrectly disregard the existence of GATT as an institution), the sharp rise post-1995 is eye-catching. It cannot be attributed to the 'non-existence' of GATT Article XXIV, because that has been in place since 1947, although it was 11 years before the first RTA was notified. The argument can be advanced that the sharp rise in regional arrangements is due to a reluctance to further liberalise trade at the multilateral level, causing states to shift their attention to regional, plurilateral and bilateral arrangements.

The cause of the explosion notwithstanding, the present discussion is concerned more with the effect of that explosion. The shift in trade from the multilateral arena to the regional plane[45] has meant a shift in the venue of rule-making. Since 1995, more than 500 new RTAs have been notified to the WTO, with each of those establishing a new set of rules between the parties. While RTAs have been touted as building blocks towards the multilateral liberalisation of trade,[46] they can also be an impediment, especially where regional cooperation is pursued more for political reasons.[47] Given the benefits of regional cooperation, including the improvement of negotiating positions and the relative ease of reform and agreement in comparison to multilateralism, RTAs offer a more attractive incentive for states than the WTO does. When these factors meet with an easier, quicker and altogether more practical process of negotiation and implementation, the WTO's relevance appears to fade.

This argument can be made for multilateral cooperation in general, but is enlightening for the discussion on flexibility. It is easier to pursue flexibility in a few-country, many issue setting than in a setting with 164 states. Combined with the cardinal nature of consensus in decision making at the WTO, further agreement, whether on the flexibility of liberalisation or any other pursuits at the multilateral level, is difficult to achieve. To quote Thomas Cottier and Marina Foltea:

> It is evident that any progress will be difficult to achieve under the present consensus-based decision-making procedures as long as individual Members choose to protect treaty-making powers, taking into account potential distorting effects. Likewise, consensus renders the operation of procedural devices equally difficult .... The cyclical proliferation of RTAs in relation to the multilateral trade negotiations shows that WTO Members revert to preferential or regional agreements to the extent that policy

---

[45] 'Regional' in this context is not strictly geographic, and includes preferential trade arrangements between states and customs unions that do not share a border. See ch 2, section I.

[46] See ch 2, section II.B.

[47] For a review of this argument from a political economy perspective, see C Damro, 'The Political Economy of Regional Trade Agreements', in L Bartels and F Ortino (eds), *Regional Trade Agreements and the WTO Legal System* (Oxford, Oxford University Press, 2006).

goals cannot be sufficiently and promptly achieved in WTO negotiations based upon MFN and formal equality of States.[48]

The issues surrounding decision-making in the WTO, especially the lack of consensus in voting practice, do not need repeating here. RTAs offer an arena where these impediments are less likely. It might be time, as Cottier and Foltea propose, to reform the decision-making process at the WTO, as this might be key to preserving the multilateral trading system and create some balance between global and regional integration.[49] This would also allow for the adoption of new options for the implementation of multilateral decisions, including a flexible approach.

The principal irony about the role of the RTAs is that theory and experience point to their use in facilitating wider and deeper integration.[50] Whether they are leading to more trade liberalisation or a disintegration of multilateralism can be an endless debate. The other irony is that indirectly, RTAs have created an environment in which multilateral integration has been flexible. If we treat each RTA as a bilateral or plurilateral agreement with varying degrees of integration and commitment, whether on similar or different issues, we can begin to view the WTO in much the same way as we view the EU with its parallel arrangements. The infamous 'spaghetti bowl' might indeed be little more than a series of agreements between WTO Members and occasionally, non-Members, that take trade liberalisation between themselves further than the WTO has hitherto allowed. The main effect of this is the erosion of the MFN standard – strictly speaking – except that this process is reasonably envisioned as an exception to MFN by GATT Article XXIV.

E. The Fragility of Practicality

This chapter has highlighted the practical difficulties involved in decision-making and administration of the multilateral trading system. This argument is often intertwined with the attachment to sovereignty discussed above, but is more closely related to the size of the WTO. At 164 Members, adopting flexibility in the way the reasons have is likely to be difficult. Indeed, by 2003, it was clear that decision-making was a titanic venture:

> ... The WTO will likely suffer from slow and cumbersome policy-making and management – an organisation with more than 120 member countries cannot be run by a 'committee of the whole'. Mass management simply does not lend itself to operational efficiency or serious policy discussion.[51]

---

[48] T Cottier and M Foltea, 'Constitutional Functions of the WTO and RTAs', in L Bartels and F Ortino (eds), *Regional Trade Agreements and the WTO Legal System* (Oxford, Oxford University Press, 2006) 73.

[49] ibid.

[50] See ch 2, section II.C and ch 3, sections III and IV.

[51] Cottier and Foltea, 'Constitutional Functions of the WTO and RTAs' (n 48) 74.

Flexibility in a setting this large could result in disintegration, as exemplified by the role of the regions above, although it remains a possibility that it could lead to deeper and closer multilateral integration based on the experience of the regions. For example, is it multilateral disintegration if states are more closely integrated in the regions? On the face of it, yes, especially where the states trade more within the region than outside the region. However, regions, like the states that constitute them, are not capable of being self-sufficient, and must therefore continue to trade with each other or with other states. This has led to a more recent rise in 'interregionalism' – cooperation between regions as exemplified by the TFTA and the various EU Economic Partnership Agreements.[52]

One possible solution to this dilemma is to accept the reality of this delicate situation and consider flexibility that takes account of two possible planes. The first is likely to be easier as it can be based on already existing regions, whether in the classic WTO negotiation sense or using trade blocs. A MULPOC-style process of differentiated integration[53] can then be pursued in a coordinated effort to achieve multilateral trade goals. The second approach is not entirely new either, and has some evidence to support its viability. This approach would base flexibility on producers, so that treaties and decisions that affect specific producers can take effect when accepted by an agreed threshold, even as high as 'all producers'. Admittedly, this will present complexity given the range of products and services the multilateral trading system is concerned with, but this might be an alternative to, for example, a stalemate already referred to in this chapter. The Information Technology Agreement (ITA), reached in 1996, will come into force when it is signed by 90 per cent of WTO Members, and will apply on an MFN basis. By mid-2021, only 81 Members (43.4 per cent), representing 97 per cent of world trade in information technology products, had signed.[54] A flexible system that allowed implementation of a treaty upon signature by Members representing 90 per cent of trade in the product covered by the treaty would resolve the issues currently hampering the ITA.

The practical implementation of flexibility on the multilateral plane is bound to form the basis of intense debate until we take the audacious step in a more flexible direction. In the same way the current system emerged out of the post-World War Two desire to establish a regulated system of trade liberalisation, it is time to accept that the system as it is has served its purpose, and needs to be reformulated.

---

[52] For an extensive coverage of interregionalism, see C Gammage, *North-South Regional Trade Agreements as Legal Regimes: A Critical Assessment of the EU-SADC Economic Partnership Agreement* (Cheltenham, Edward Elgar, 2017).

[53] See ch 7, section I.

[54] The WTO, *The Information Technology Agreement – An Explanation*, www.wto.org/english/tratop_e/inftec_e/itaintro_e.htm.

III. THE BIG QUESTION: HOW?

The question of how we make the move to a more flexible multilateral trading system is ripe for research and can form the basis of multiple volumes. This question gives rise to two further immediate questions, neither of which can be sufficiently answered in this chapter. The first question is a matter of practicality and implementation: what form would multilateral flexibility take? This would involve a consideration of the legal implications of multilateral flexibility, a matter that will no doubt befuddle us for a while. The second, too, is a matter of practicality, which might benefit from wider discussion involving political scientists and diplomats. This one concerns how we go about convincing the states and the traders they represent that flexibility is a more feasible option. This section briefly considers these questions in turn, highlighting some of the further issues and questions that might arise from their exploration.

A. How Would Multilateral Flexibility Look?

This book has made the case for regulated flexible integration. In keeping with this theme, the question of how we can adopt flexible methods of trade liberalisation in the WTO elicits the need for prior agreement – if this can be secured under current procedures. Prior agreement on flexibility is essential as shown by the EAC, TFTA, AfCFTA and the EU, and by its absence in the WTO. It is an established principle of public international law that states would only be bound by what they agree to, and so an agreement to this effect is inescapable. This agreement would need to be robust enough to preserve the principal aims of the liberalisation project without inordinately limiting the possibility of further integration of the world's economies. Chapter 9 proposes an amendment to the EAC's Article 7(1)(e), although the equivalent flexibility provisions on the multilateral plane would need to be more detailed, and potentially the basis of a separate treaty.

What kind of flexibility would be suitable for multilateral adoption? This book has explored several forms, from the African conceptualisation of variable geometry to the EU's parallel arrangements. Incremental integration as with Africa's MULPOCs, the EAC's attempt at variable geometry embodied in the NCIP, the EU's web of flexibility demonstrated by enhanced cooperation, parallel agreements and opt outs, and the multiple methods studied in chapter three are only some of the possibilities that can be transposed to the WTO project. The question, therefore, of which would be most appropriate is not one that can be answered in a few pages without the need for a detailed evaluation of a myriad of factors. Section II above has grappled with some of these considerations, and even then, has barely scratched the surface of how much needs to be considered.

A reformation or perhaps reformulation of the WTO might be essential for the adoption of flexibility in the multilateral arena. It is clear that the need for a central authority, if possible with supranational status, is essential for the effective coordination of differentiated integration. In its current form, with states making the rules and implementing them in keeping with Westphalian sovereignty, flexibility is likely to remain unattractive. If it is adopted in the current set up, it is likely to suffer the same fate as the NCIP did, especially if there is no mechanism to regulate its operation, down to the detail of what areas of cooperation can be undertaken flexibly.

One possible approach, for example, could be to treat the regions as integrative building blocks for the next phase of liberalisation and integration. Each region would represent its constituents at the global level, ensuring a coordinated pursuit of global integration goals. If this sounds familiar, that is because it is based on the MULPOCs. A next generation WTO could have the AfCFTA, ASEAN, CARICOM, EU, MERCOSUR, NAFTA, etc. as members representing the states that make them up. In a world that increasingly recognises the international legal personality of these and other institutions, this should not be such a wild idea. Indeed, the WTO itself and most – if not all – of these institutions are vested with the personality that enables them to enter into binding agreements with other institutions.

Would this approach require an erosion of the highly cherished sovereignty? Possibly, but not necessarily. The institutions at the global level would have the mandate conferred upon them by the states they represent in much the same way the states represent their citizens at the regional and global level. Naturally, this will prompt questions on decision-making at regional level, including whether a decision is valid if it is not made by consensus. These are questions that might never fully be resolved in a world with billions of people having quite diverse views and interests.

Another approach would be the aforementioned alignment along the lines of products or sectors. However, this would be even more complex given the number of products traded in the world today, which are only likely to increase. In addition, this might be reminiscent of the plurilateral agreements in Annex 4 of the Marrakesh Agreement, some of which are not in force anymore.

B. How do we Sell Multilateral Flexibility?

The practical challenges around popularising multilateral flexibility can seem daunting, but not from the perspective of showing its benefits. These have been widely written about for years, as chapter three and indeed this chapter have shown. The bigger question, I suspect, is along the lines of 'how do we make the switch?' This is a different question from the first in that it relates to the task of convincing states to reconsider the meaning and role of sovereignty, the nature of the rules, the place of the regions, and perhaps most importantly, the reason for the rules. The previous section considered how the reasons for the rules have been a bar to the adoption of flexibility in multilateral trade. Overcoming this calls for a slightly philosophical review, even briefly, of the multilateral trading system.

At the core of all rules is a justification, an aim or objective that the rules seek to achieve. Let us, for the present discussion, call this 'the why'. Why do we have the rules we have today? This has been summarised in section II above, but the discussion can be taken a bit further. Why do we trade? This too, has been answered, fairly extensively, in chapter two. But is 'the why' still the same? The rules we have today are based in part on negotiations in a post-World War Two world. Even if we shorten their age by using the Uruguay Round as the baseline, they have been in place long enough for world trade to have undergone considerable change. The reasons we traded in 1945–47 (or 1986–94) directly influenced the rules we have today. Is the world the same as it was 75 or even 28 years ago? The answer is emphatically in the negative, even if we considered only the developments and advancements in communications. If the reasons for trade and the context in which we trade have evolved, what reason do we have to still be trading on the same old terms?

Any good law must be dynamic and able to change with the times. And as the law changes, so must the institution that law relates to. As Jackson has succinctly put it:

> Perhaps the most significant lesson is that human institutions inevitably evolve and change, and concepts which ignore that, such as concepts which try to cling to 'original intent of the draftspersons' or some inclination to disparage or deny the validity of some of these evolutions and changes, could be damaging to the broader purposes of the institutions. Governments (or societies) which consent to become members of institutions must do so with the realisation that institutional structures will not be frozen in time, and that such consent will certainly bring some surprises to the constituencies concerned.[55]

The non-static nature of international trade does not, perhaps, require much debate anymore. The real debate appears to extend beyond multilateral trade to challenge our understanding of public international law and globalisation in broader terms. To quote Stewart and Badin:

> The current reality requires a reframing of the inter-state paradigm of traditional international law to a more pluralistic and cosmopolitan framework. At the same time, we believe that the divisions and differences in regimes, interests and values are too wide and deep to support at this point a constitutionalist paradigm for global governance. Current conditions, however, are compatible with and indeed call for

---

[55] Jackson, *Sovereignty, the WTO Law and Changing Fundamentals of International Law* (n 28) 82.

development of a global administrative law, which can be applied to particular global regulatory bodies and their relations with domestic administrations to enhance regulatory governance without positing all-encompassing global legal order.[56]

This is the heart of the complexity we now face. How do we establish more central structures for the administration of trade, while accounting for the incredibly varied interests, and facilitating confluence? How do we do this without eroding the position of the state as a sovereign entity?

[56] Stewart and Badin, 'The World Trade Organisation (n 27) 458.

9

Flexibility: Looking Ahead

FLEXIBLE REGIONAL ECONOMIC integration is an essential part of the African integration story. It is both a natural consequence and a cause of the path that integration has taken in Africa. As a result of the impediments to regional economic integration in Africa, recourse to flexible forms of integration has been inevitable in order to counter those challenges. Integration in Africa has been, by design, based on a gradual approach, which is a variant of flexible regional economic integration.

The EAC's flexible integration is at the same time affected by, and has an effect on, the pace of regional economic integration in Africa. Flexibility is at the centre of the relationship between the EAC and African integration efforts in two ways. First, the EAC was envisioned as one of the multilateral programming and operational Centres (MULPOCs) in the Lagos Plan of Action (LPA). It was meant to be a building bloc towards a continent-wide common market. An extension of this centrality is the fact that the EAC's variable geometry has been traced back to the LPA. Second, due to the relative success of the EAC, especially its collaboration with the Southern African Development Community (SADC) and the Common Market for East and Southern Africa (COMESA) in establishing the Tripartite Free Trade Area (TFTA), African integration has been reignited. This has led directly to the establishment of the African Continental Free Trade Area (AfCFTA) – an essential step towards the establishment of the African Common Market (ACM).

Africa's chequered integration history has brought the need for flexibility to the fore. This is mainly due to the differences the integrating states possess: differences in history, economic systems, political ambitions, economic size, wealth, resource endowment, infrastructural development, export capacity, technical and skill bases, and varied levels of political stability. All these factors have in the past contributed to a slow pace of integration in Africa, often crippling blocs and even leading to their disintegration. This has been the case twice in the EAC, and with finality in the West African Customs Union (WACU) and the Customs Union of West African States. Largely, the African Economic Community (AEC) did not progress according to plan because of these differences. This caused the regional blocs to recognise and accept these differences, and create a way to pursue common goals in spite of the differences. It is out of this recognition that variable geometry was born.

Variable geometry altered the direction of integration in Africa. Although it was not called variable geometry or even flexible regional economic integration in 1980, the incremental approach adopted by the LPA demonstrates a clear intention to take advantage of the diversity of African states and regions in unifying the continent. Through the MULPOCs, African states sought to integrate their economies first at regional level, and then at the continental level, in order to establish the ACM.

What then, is the effect of the use of flexible regional economic integration on regional integration in the EAC and Africa? Observation has been easier at the continental level, with a nearly 40-year long period to be observed. The flexible approach to integration has enabled continental integration by creating an environment that encouraged the establishment of the AfCFTA. While it might have taken longer than anticipated, and not been as smooth or successful in all regions as planned, the MULPOCs have delivered Africa's first solid treaty for economic integration. Although the Abuja Treaty Establishing the AEC laid out a roadmap for African economic integration, it did not purport to establish a continental bloc. This is only done by the establishment of the AfCFTA.

In the EAC, the result has been mixed. While it was hoped that the establishment of the Northern Corridor Integration Projects (NCIP) would fast-track the EAC's integration process and lead to a federation, insufficient planning, the non-existence of structures, and conflicts between the cooperating states led to a quick expiry of the initiative. Additionally, the establishment of the NCIP threatened the existence of the EAC, as it only highlighted and even exacerbated the differences between NCIP states and non-NCIP states. In its brief existence, it both managed to widen the rift that led to its establishment, and build a bridge over that rift, leading to its own decline. As shown in chapter six, the conflicts between Uganda and Kenya over the construction of an oil pipeline, which led Uganda to agree to construct the pipeline through Tanzania, may have been the one NCIP conflict that saved the EAC. The application of variable geometry did not, therefore have the anticipated result. The short conclusion, explained in chapter six, is that it was only a firework: loud and bright, but short-lived.

One question lingers unanswered, even though unasked in this book. Is flexible regional economic integration inherently pan-African? The answer is a resounding yes. Whether considered from the Afrocentric or Eurocentric perspective of pan-Africanism, or even deeper, to the more encompassing concept of 'Ubuntu', flexible regional economic integration is a reflection of the unity engendered by pan-Africanism. It is based on the recognition, espoused by Mwalimu Julius Nyerere's definition, that even though they may be so different as to not speak the same language, in relation to the rest of the world, Africans are one. The differences they may have, whether merely ideological, as an acquisition of a diverse education, or more fundamental, such as culture or even natural resource endowment, should not get in the way of the desire to find common ground, unify, and improve the lives of those on the continent.

Flexibility is part of the nature of the African. It is an admission that one's weaknesses may need to be accommodated by the strengths of one's neighbour, and that the favour may need to be returned in another form. It is a recognition that stripped down to the core of our nature as humans, there is no possibility of uniformity, and that uniqueness cannot be avoided on the national, regional and continental planes. Unity, on the other hand, is always desirable. To quote my mother tongue, Rukiga (and I suspect any African reader would claim I am quoting theirs):

'*Agatereine nigo gaat'eigufa.*' ('Only the united teeth will crush the bone.')

and

'*Engar' ibiri zinaabisana.*' ('Two hands wash each other.')

Both of these proverbs, which are taught to many Africans in our infancy, reveal a philosophy that is at the core of this thesis: difference is the essence of cooperation. The teeth in the human mouth are unique in design and purpose, but insufficient on their own. The opposing nature of our hands is necessary for their function in concert. Biting and chewing food are essential to our sustenance, but just as the incisors can only bite, or canines tear through flesh and the molars crush what we chew, no single type of tooth can serve all these functions without the others. The incisors slice food into smaller sizes and this is passed on to the molars to be ground further before we swallow it and benefit from it. Our fingers, palms, and thumbs rub and scrub the ones on the other hand in a way made possible only by the differences they possess, as are other basic motor abilities like lifting things, or the more complex activities like operating machinery.

Cooperation, by its nature, is reliant on difference. International trade, as explained in chapter two, is based on difference. Comparative advantage, even just by its name, denotes difference, and yet it forms the incontrovertible basis for trade. For generations, humanity has attempted to disregard or indeed remove the differences on which our economic interactions are based, usually by the device of harmonising economic policy. Both flexible regional economic integration and pan-Africanism show that this should not be the case. The uniqueness of nations is where the wealth of the aggregate lies. This is not to disregard differences which may well be irreconcilable, but to encourage an adoption of the pan-African perspective, that in spite of those differences, and for the greater good, an agreeable way forward should be found. The best way to do this, I propose, is through a carefully planned flexible regime with clear parameters.

The ideal flexible integration process would, as proposed in chapter three, retain a common goal, with clear, non-derogable objectives, to which all integrating parties must aspire. These would form the basis of the agreement, and the nature of flexibility to be applied should be included in the agreement, as the EAC, TFTA and AfCFTA have done. Unlike the two blocs, however, integrating states should specify the circumstances under which flexibility would be resorted to, and the modalities for its application. This could include matters such as whether there will be a time limit on its application, in order to prevent parties from taking a back seat indefinitely, and whether the other parties would need to consent to the application of flexibility. It would also be beneficial to clarify what form of flexible regional economic integration is to be applied, and to which aspects of the integration process it should be applied. Indeed, if I was asked to redraft the EAC Treaty's Article 7(1)(e), it would take the following form:

Article Seven – Operational Principles

1. The principles that shall govern the practical achievement of the objectives of the community shall include:

    ...

    (e) Flexible regional economic integration, which is a method of preferential trade in which parties to an agreement are allowed to implement treaty provisions at different speeds and in smaller groups in order to facilitate continued integration.

2. The principle of flexible regional economic integration shall not be applied to the following Chapters of this Treaty:

    (a) Chapter 2: Establishment and Principles of the East African Community.
    (b) Chapter 3: Establishment of the Organs of the Community
    (c) Chapter 4: The Summit
    (d) Chapter 5: The Council
    (e) Chapter 6: The Coordination Committee
    (f) Chapter 7: Sectoral Committees
    (g) Chapter 8: The East African Court of Justice
    (h) Chapter nine: The East African Legislative Assembly
    (i) Chapter ten: The Secretariat and Staff of the Community.
    (j) Chapter twenty eight: Financial Provisions
    (k) Chapter twenty nine: General, Transitional and Final Provisions

3. The principle of flexible regional economic integration shall be applied:

    (a) Where a Partner State provides evidence that the implementation of a Community Decision would expose it to economic or other risk.
    (b) Where, in the opinion of the Partner States, it would be expedient to do so.
    (c) In all cases, with the consent of all Partner States.

4. The principle of flexible regional economic integration shall only be applied as a temporary or transitional measure. Where time limits have been specified, they shall not amount to more than ten years, including any extensions.

5. The principle of flexible regional economic integration shall apply in the following forms:

    (a) Time flexibility, in which agreed variations in time limits for implementation of Community Decisions are applied;

    (b) Scope flexibility, in which cooperation on agreed areas of cooperation is delayed for one or more Partner States. Such delay must be preceded by a notification of intention to delay, which clearly sets out:

        i.   The areas of cooperation to be affected by the delay, and
        ii. The proposed length of the delay.

        The delay shall be allowed subject to the consent of all Partner States, and shall not be inordinately extended.

    (c) For the avoidance of doubt, the Community shall not allow subject matter or à la carte flexibility, in which Partner States would elect to permanently abstain from the implementation of Community decisions.

The importance of water-tight legislative drafting cannot be overstated. If the EAC had more detailed provisions on its variable geometry, and those provisions had been properly followed, the NCIP would not have been necessary, and closer cooperation between Kenya, Rwanda and Uganda might have taken a different path. The disgruntlement that led to the birth of the NCIP would have been addressed within EAC structures, so that proposals for fast-tracking integration are made at the Community level. Burundi and Tanzania would then be able to rely on the flexibility provisions, indicating the reasons for their abstention, and if these were found satisfactory, they would be excluded from the fast-tracking projects. This alone would have solved most, if not all of NCIP's problems.

First, what would have been NCIP activities would instead be EAC activities, meaning they could be monitored, implemented, regulated, and managed by EAC structures. This would have prevented the ad hoc nature the NCIP adopted, and centralise power and accountability structures. Second, since they would have remained EAC activities, they would have been funded by the bloc, eliminating the NCIP's funding issue. Third, the projects undertaken under a clear, albeit flexible mandate would have more readily received the political and other backing of the states that did not participate in them from the start. The NCIP presented itself as a self-sufficient, exclusive club, which alienated non-participating states. This could have been avoided if, for example, the standard gauge railway project (SGR) had been undertaken as a region, with plans to connect it to Tanzania and Burundi at a specified time in the future.

Properly applied, flexible regional economic integration could provide a solution to one of the biggest challenges facing integration in Africa: the 'replacement syndrome'. With flexibility, African blocs would avoid the countless stalemates they have encountered since independence, and rather than abandon old blocs to start new ones, they would stick to existing structures and make the necessary adjustments for the integration process to continue on areas of cooperation where implementation is not in dispute.

As chapter four has shown, the EAC appears to be on the cusp of another collapse, just over twenty years into the current integration effort. Whether it makes it past the current tensions is a function of many factors, but one thing remains certain: ambition does not always match reality. The drafters of the EAC Treaty took the bold step to include variable geometry in the Treaty. This was noble and admirable, but as the NCIP has demonstrated, and as this book has argued, merely providing for flexibility is not enough. The application of that flexibility must also be clearly provided for. It is not too late to make the necessary amendments to the EAC, TFTA and AfCFTA Treaties in order to create a clear path for the application of variable geometry.

Beyond the regional context, it is increasingly clear that flexibility would be a desirable alternative to the current all-or-nothing, consensus-based approach adopted under the WTO. Underpinned by existing notions of sovereignty, the shift to a more flexible approach to multilateral trade liberalisation is bound to be slow until new conceptualisations of public international law become mainstream. One such conceptualisation is one that this book has latently explored: the pan-Africanist understanding of public international law. This is an approach to international cooperation that takes cognisance of the wealth of the diversity we collectively have. It is an interpretation of 'the why' in chapter eight that does not see players as competitors but as collaborators. Public international law – especially international economic law – should be about sharing the resources available to man. Indeed, the reconceptualisation of sovereignty considered in chapter eight is consistent with the pan-African notion of human (and international) unity. Viewed through the pan-African lens, sovereignty is not eroded by closer international cooperation, even if that cooperation results in a shift of the centre of authority from the national to the supranational. This is based on the recognition that a united collective is more beneficial than its constituent elements.

There are still more questions than answers on multilateral flexibility. How would it work? What are the legal implications? Would it result in disintegration instead? Is it possible to have flexibility without a supranational WTO? Is a truly neutral and impartial supranational WTO possible in the current international geo-political setting? Is flexibility the only way out of the current slowdown in multilateral trade law-making? Would flexibility be the easy way out; a cop out? Given the hundreds of regional trade agreements in force, is it time to trade in the case-knife we're now using for a 'case-knife'?[1] Has the role of the WTO changed so much, that rather than attempt to integrate states, we should focus

---

[1] See ch 3, section II, n 33.

on integrating regions, both within themselves and with each other? Is multilateral disintegration a bad thing if it leads to more effective trade liberalisation, albeit by a different route?

These and many more questions will, no doubt, occupy our minds for years to come, and therein lies part of the problem. We have contemplated multilateral flexibility for many years, but its pursuit remains elusive. We have fallen in what could be termed the 'readiness trap'. There is merit to making big changes when we are ready for them and fully understand the implications, but that does not appear consistent with the adventurous spirit of humanity. Sometimes, as was the case in 1945–47 when GATT was first negotiated and agreed, we have to adopt changes, even if it takes us decades to figure out how to properly operate with those changes. In other words, if GATT 1947 had not been adopted in spite of the failure of the International Trade Organisation (ITO), we might never have had the WTO we have today.

GATT 1947 was negotiated with the aim of:

> Raising standards of living, ensuring full employment and a large and steadily growing volume of real income and effective demand, developing the full use of the resources of the world and expanding the production and exchange of goods ... [and] contributing to these objectives by reciprocal and mutually advantageous arrangements directed to the substantial reduction of tariffs and other barriers to trade, and to the elimination of discriminatory treatment in international commerce.[2]

While these objectives have not been fully achieved, significant progress has been made. Is it time to revisit these aims, and reframe 'the why'? It might be beneficial to resort to a philosopher of old, Thales of Miletus, to whom the Ionian Enchantment can be traced. As described by physicists Brian Cox and Jeff Forshaw:

> This poetic term describes the belief that the complexity of the world can be explained by a small number of simple natural laws because at its heart, it is orderly and simple .... The scientist's job is to strip away the complexity we see around us and to uncover this underlying simplicity. When the process works out, and the simplicity and unity of the world are revealed, we experience the Ionian Enchantment. Imagine for a moment cradling a snowflake in the palm of your hand. It is an elegant and beautiful structure, possessed of a jagged crystalline symmetry. No two snowflakes are alike, and at first sight, this chaotic state of affairs seems to defy a simple explanation. Science has taught us that the apparent complexity of snowflakes hides an exquisite underlying simplicity; each is a configuration of billions of molecules of water, H_2O. There is nothing more to a snowflake than that, and yet an overwhelming complex of structure and form emerges when those H_2O molecules get together in the atmosphere of our planet on a cold winter's night.[3]

---

[2] Preamble to GATT 1947, and reproduced, with some modification in the Preamble to the Marrakesh Agreement Establishing the WTO.

[3] B Cox and J Forshaw, *Why Does E=mc2 (And Why Should We Care?)* (Boston, Da Capo Press, 2009) 78.

What is the 'H$_2$O' of international trade? What is at the core of the multilateral trading system? Unlike the water molecules that make up a snowflake, it is possible for the law to change as society evolves. Is the objective above still the same today? If the answer to this question is no, then the biggest lesson the multilateral system can learn from the African integration experience, is that change is not a bad thing. That might seem like a surprising conclusion, given this book's emphasis on flexibility, but change is a fundamental implication of flexibility. Flexibility does not hold onto principles that may stand in the way of achieving the goals of cooperation, even if those goals were premised on those principles. As warned in chapter eight, the WTO today is at risk of not achieving its aims due to the static nature of the laws we rely on to regulate the ever-evolving international trading landscape. Do we have the flexibility and the courage to change them?

Bibliography

BOOKS

African Union, *Echo*, 2013.

Anyang' Nyong'o, P, *Regional Integration in Africa: Unfinished Agenda* (Nairobi, African Academy of Sciences, 1990).

Balassa, B, *The Theory of Economic Integration* (London, Routledge, 2012, 1st published 1961)

Cox, B and Forshaw, J, *Why Does E=mc² (And Why Should We Care?)* (Boston, Da Capo Press, 2009).

Gammage, C, *North-South Regional Trade Agreements as Legal Regimes: A Critical Assessment of the EU-SADC Economic Partnership Agreement* (Cheltenham, Edward Elgar, 2017).

Gathii, JT *African Regional Trade Agreements as Legal Regimes*, (Cambridge, Cambridge University Press, 2011).

Genn, H, Partington, M and Wheeler, S, *Law in the Real World: Improving Our Understanding of How Law Works* (London, The Nuffield Foundation, 2006).

Haas, E, *The Uniting of Europe* (Stanford, Stanford University Press, 1958).

Hazlewood, A, *Economic Integration: The East African Experience* (1975, Heinemann Educational Books, London.

Heckscher, EF and Ohlin, B, *Heckscher-Ohlin Trade Theory* (trans and ed H Flam and MJ Flanders, 1991, Cambridge, Mass, MIT Press, 1991).

Jackson, JH, *Sovereignty, the WTO Law and Changing Fundamentals of International Law* (Cambridge University Press, Cambridge, 2006).

Kahnert, F et al, *Economic Integration Among Developing Countries* (Paris, OECD Development Centre, 1969).

Kimbugwe, K, Perdikis, N et al, *Economic Development Through Regional Trade: A Role for the New East African Community?* (Palgrave Macmillan, Basingstoke, 2012).

Krugman, PR, Obstfeld, M and Melitz, MJ, *International Economics: Theory and Policy*, 10th edn (Harlow, Pearson, 2015).

Lester, S, Mercurio, B and Davies A *World Trade Law: Text Materials and Commentary* (Oxford, Hart Publishing, 2012).

Lindberg, L and Scheingold, S, *Europe's Would-Be Polity: Patterns of Change in the European Community* (Englewood Cliffs, New Jersey, Prentice-Hall, 1970).

Markusen, JR, Melvin, JR, Kaempfer, WH and Maskus, KA, *International Trade: Theory and Evidence* (New York, McGraw Hill, 1995).

Mays, T and Delancey, M, *Historical Dictionary of International Organisations in Sub-Saharan Africa*, 2nd edn (London, The Scarecrow Press, 2002).

Mazrui, A and Wondji, C, *General History of Africa, Volume VIII – Africa Since 1935*, 1993, (Oxford, UNESCO/Heinemann Educational).

Mazrui, AA, *Africa's International Relations: The Diplomacy of Dependency and Change* (Boulder, Colorado, Westview, 1977).

Mikić, M, *International Trade*, (New York, St. Martin's Press, 1998).

Nakagawa, J, *International Harmonisation of Economic Regulation* (Oxford, Oxford University Press, 2001).

Nye, J, *Pan Africanism and East African Integration* (Oxford, Oxford University Press, 1966).

Pearce, D, Campbell, E and Harding, D, *Australian Law Schools: A Discipline Assessment for the Commonwealth Tertiary Education Commission* (Canberra, Australian Government Publishing Service, 1987).

Ricardo, D, *The Principles of Political Economy and Taxation* (Cambridge, Cambridge University Press, 1951).

Robson, P and Low, DA, *The Economies of Africa* (London, George Allen and Unwin, 1969).

Robson, P, *Economic Integration in Africa* (London, Allen and Unwin, 1968).

—— *The Economics of International Integration*, 4th edn (London, Routledge, 1998).

Tamanaha, BZ, *Realistic Socio-legal Theory: Pragmatism and a Social Theory of Law* (Oxford, Clarendon Press, 1997).

Van den Bossche, P and Zdouc, W, *The Law and Policy of the World Trade Organisation – Text, Cases and Materials*, 4th edn (Cambridge, Cambridge University Press, 2017).

Viner, J, *The Customs Union Issue* (London, Stevens & Sons, 1950).

Williams, M, *The Pan-African Movement*, in M Azevedo (ed), *Africana Studies: A Survey of Africa and the African Diaspora*, (Durham, Carolina Academic Press, 2005).

ARTICLES, BOOK CHAPTERS AND CONFERENCE PAPERS

Abbott, FM, 'Toward a New Era of Objective Assessment in the Field of TRIPS and Variable Geometry for the Preservation of Multilateralism' (2005) 8(1) *Journal of International Economic Law* 77.

Abraham, K, *The Challenges and Prospects of Pan-African Economic Integration*, A paper presented at the Conference on Economic Integration and Trans-Boundary Resources, organised by the Ethiopian International Institute for Peace and Development, Addis Ababa, June 2000.

Adedeji, A, 'Comparative Strategies of Economic Decolonisation in Africa', in A Mazrui and C Wondji (eds), *General History of Africa VIII: Africa Since 1935*, (Paris, United Nations Educational Scientific and Cultural Organization, 1999) 393–431.

—— 'The need for Concrete Action', in African Association for Public Administration and Management (ed), *Regional Cooperation in Africa: Problems and Prospects* (Addis Ababa, 1977).

—— *History and Prospects for Regional Integration in Africa*, Paper presented at the Third Meeting of the African Development Forum, UNECA, Addis Ababa, 5 March 2002.

Ajibo, CC, Nwankwo, CN and Ekhator, EO, 'Regional Economic Communities as the Building Blocs of the African Continental Free Trade Area Agreement' (2021) (18(4) *Transnational Dispute Management*.

Allen, JJ, 'The European Common Market and GATT – A Study in Compatibility' (1961) 26(3) *Law and Contemporary Problems* 559.

Asante, SKB and Chanaiwa, D, 'Pan-Africanism and Regional Integration', in A Mazrui and C Wondji (eds), *General History of Africa, Volume VIII – Africa Since 1935* (Oxford, UNESCO/ Heinemann Educational, 1993) 724–743.

Baldwin, J and Davis, G, 'Empirical Research in Law' ch 3 in P Cane, and M Tushnet, *The Oxford Handbook of Legal Studies* (Oxford, Oxford University Press, 2003).

Byé, M, 'Free Trade and Social Welfare, Comments on Mr. Heilperin's Article' [1958] *International Labour Review* 38–47

Cotterell, R *Socio-legal Studies, Law Schools, and Legal and Social Theory*, Paper presented at the 40th Anniversary Conference, Centre for Socio-Legal Studies, University of Oxford, 22 June 2012.

Cottier, T and Foltea, M, 'Constitutional Functions of the WTO and RTAs', in L Bartels and F Ortino (eds), *Regional Trade Agreements and the WTO Legal System* (Oxford, Oxford University Press, 2006).

Damro, C, 'The Political Economy of Regional Trade Agreements', in L Bartels and F Ortino (eds), *Regional Trade Agreements and the WTO Legal System* (Oxford, Oxford University Press, 2006).

De Melo, J, Panagariya, M and Rodrik, D, *The new Regionalism: A Country Perspective*, ch 6 in J De Melo and A Panagariya (eds), *New Dimensions in Regional Integration* (Cambridge, Centre for Economic Policy Research, 1993).

Deardorff, AV, *What do We (and Others) Mean by "The Terms of Trade"?*, Gerald R. Ford School of Public Policy, The University of Michigan, Discussion Paper No. 651, 23 May 2016.

Dehousse, F, Coussens, W and Grevi, G *Integrating Europe: Multiple Speeds – One Direction?* EPC Working Paper No. 9, April 2004.

DeRosa, DA, *Regional Integration Arrangements: Static Economic Theory, Quantitative Findings and Policy Guidelines*, Policy Research Working Paper No. WPS2007, 1998.

Elkan, W and Nulty, L, 'Economic Links in East Africa from 1945 to Independence', in DA Low and A Smith (eds), *History of East Africa, Volume III* (Oxford, Clarendon Press, 1976).

Ewald, W, 'Comparative Jurisprudence (I): What Was It Like to Try a Rat?' (1995) 143 *University of Pennsylvania Law Review* 1890.

Fagbayibo, B, 'Common Problems Affecting Supranational Attempts in Africa: An Analytical Overview' (2013) (16)1 *PER/PELJ* 31–69.

Gade, CBN, 'The Historical Development of the Written Discourses on Ubuntu' (2011) 30(3) *South African Journal of Philosophy* 303–329.

Goldstein, A and Quenan, C, 'Regionalism and Development in Latin America: What Implications for Sub-Saharan Africa?', in *Regional Integration in Africa*, 2002, African Development Bank and OECD, Paris, 47–76.

Haas, EB and Schmitter, PC, 'Economics and Differential Patterns of Political Integration: Projections about Unity in Latin America' (1964) 18(4) *International Organisation*.

Haas, EB, 'International Integration: The European and the Universal Process' (1961) 15(4) *International Organisation* 366–392

—— 'Turbulent Fields and the Theory of Regional Integration' (1976) (30) *International Organisation* 173–212.

Haass, RN, *Sovereignty: Existing Rights, Evolving Responsibilities,* remarks at the School of Foreign Service and the Mortara Centre for International Studies, Georgetown University, 14 January 2003.

Hawtrey, R, 'Review of 'The Theory of Customs Unions' by J.E. Meade' (1956) 66(262) *The Economic Journal* 337–339.

Hazlewood, A, 'Problems of Integration Among African States', in A Hazlewood (ed), *African Integration and Disintegration: Case Studies in Economic and Political Union* (Oxford, Oxford University Press, 1967).

Heilperin, MA, 'Free Trade and Social Welfare: Some Marginal Comments on the "Ohlin Report"' (1957) 75 *International Labour Review* 173.

Henderson, D, 'International Economic Integration: Progress, Prospects and Implications' (1992) 68(4) *International Affairs* 633–653.

Hoekman, BM and Mavroidis, PC, 'WTO: 'à la carte' or 'menu du jour'? Assessing the Case for More Plurilateral Agreements' (2015) 26(2) *The European Journal of International Law* 319.

Hoskyns, C, 'Pan-Africanism and Integration', in A Hazlewood (ed), *African Integration and Disintegration: Case Studies in Economic and Political Union* (Oxford, Oxford University Press, 1967).

Hosny, AS, 'Theories of Economic Integration: A Survey of the Economic and Political Literature' (2013) 2(5) *International Journal of Economy, Management and Social Sciences* 133–155.

Hutchinson, T and Duncan, N, 'Defining And Describing What We Do: Doctrinal Legal Research' (2012) 17(1) *Deakin Law Review* 83–119.

Iyoha, M, *Enhancing Africa's Trade: From Marginalization to an Export-Led Approach to Development*, African Development Bank, Economic Research Working Paper No 77 (August 2005).

Jackson, JH, 'The WTO 'Constitution' and Proposed Reforms: Seven 'Mantras' Revisited', (2001) 4(1) *Journal of International Economic Law* 67–78.

Karioki, JN, 'Tanzania and the Resurrection of Pan-Africanism' (1974) 4(4) *Review of Black Political Economy* 2–22.

Kaunda, D, 'Against All Odds: Mega-Railway Project Becomes a Reality', in *Uchukuzi* (Magazine by Kenya's Ministry of Transport and Infrastructure), Issue 1, June 2014, 6–8.

Koenig, N, *A differentiated View of Differentiated Integration,* Policy Paper 140, Jacques BelorInstitut, Berlin, 23 July 2015.

Laursen, F, 'Theoretical Perspectives on Comparative Regional Integration', in F Laursen (ed), *Comparative Regional Integration* (Aldershot, Ashgate, 2003) 3–28.

Leebron, D, 'Lying Down with Procrustes: An Analysis of Harmonisation Claims' in J Bhagwati and R Hudec (eds), *Fair Trade and Harmonisation, Vol 1: Economic Analysis* (MIT Press, Cambridge, Mass, 1996) 41–117.

Levy, PI, 'Do We Need an Undertaker for the Single Undertaking? Considering the Angles of Variable Geometry', in SJ Evenett and BM Hoekman (eds), *Economic Development and Multilateral Trade Cooperation* (Palgrave Macmillan/World Bank, 2005).

Lipsey, RG, 'The Theory of Customs Unions: Trade Diversion and Welfare' (1957) 24 *Economica* 40–46.

Lloyd, P, 'The Variable Geometry Approach to International Economic Integration' (2009) 1(1) *International Journal of Business and Development Studies* 51–66.

M'bayo, T, 'W.E.B. Du Bois, Marcus Garvey, and Pan-Africanism in Liberia, 1919–1924' (2004) 66(1) *Historian* 19–44.

Makalani, M, *Pan-Africanism, African Age: African and African Diasporan Transformations in the 20th Century,* available at http://exhibitions.nypl.org/africanaage/essay-pan-africanism.html (accessed 25 November 2018).

McCarthy, C, 'Regional Integration: Part of the Solution or Part of the Problem', in S Ellis and J Currey (eds), *Africa Now: People, Policies and Institutions* (London, Heinemann, 1996) 211–231.

Meade, JE, *The Theory of Customs Unions* (Amsterdam, North Holland, 1995) 67–82.

Mugomba, AT, 'Regional Organisations and African Underdevelopment: The Collapse of the East African Community' (1978) 16(1) *Journal of Modern African Studies* 261–272.

Mwasha, ON, 'The Benefits of Regional Economic Integration for Developing Countries in Africa: A Case of East African Community (EAC)' (2008) 11(1) *Korea Review of International Studies* 69–92, 70.

N'Guettia Kouassi, R, 'The Itinerary of the African Integration Process: An Overview of the Historical Landmarks' (2007) 1(2) *African Integration Review* 1–23.

Nantambu, K, 'Pan-Africanism Versus Pan-African Nationalism' (1998) 28(5) *Journal of Black Studies* 561–574.

Nyerere, J, 'Africa's Place in the World', in *Symposium on Africa* (Massachusetts, Wellesley College, 1960).

Nyirabu, M, *Deepening Regional Integration of the East African Community,* Workshop Report of 'Deepening Integration in the East African Community', Development Policy Management Forum, 8–9 September, Addis Ababa.

Okhonmina, S, 'The African Union: Pan-Africanist Aspirations and the Challenge of African Unity' (2009) 3(4) *Journal of Pan African Studies* 85–100.

Omenya, GO, *Coalition of the Willing as a Pathway to African Future Integration: Some Reflections on East Africa Regional Integration,* Paper presented at the 14th CODESRIA General Assembly, 8–15 June 2015, Dakar, Senegal.

Omutunde, J, 'Economic Integration in Africa: Enhancing Prospects for Success' (1991) 29(1) *Journal of Modern African Studies* 1–26.

Ong'wen, O, 'The Political Economy of Regional Trade Agreements in Africa' (2004) 7(6) *SEATINI Bulletin.*

Onyango Omenya, GO, *Coalition of the Willing as a Pathway to African Future Integration: Some Reflections on East Africa Regional Integration,* Paper presented at the 14th CODESRIA General Assembly, 8–15 June 2015, Dakar, Senegal.

Osagie, E, *African Economic Integration: Lessons from Outside Africa, in The Challenges of African Economic Integration*, selected papers for the 1992 Annual Conference of the Nigerian Economic Society, Ibadan.

Palmer, VV, 'From Lerotholi to Lando: Some Examples of Comparative Law Methodology' (2004) 4(2) *Global Jurist Frontiers*.

Patterson, WE, 'Does Germany Still Have a European Vocation?' (2010) 19 *German Politics* 1.

Philip, A, 'Social Aspects of European Economic Cooperation', [1957] *International Labour Review* 255.

Pound, R, 'Law in Books and Law in Context' (1910) 44 *American Law Review* 12.

Rafael Leal-Arcas, R, 'The Fragmentation of International Trade Law: Is Now the Time for Variable Geometry?' (2011) 12(2) *The Journal of World Investment and Trade* 145–195.

Rodney, W, *Pan-Africanism with Special Reference to the Caribbean*, Lecture given at Howard University, Washington DC, September 1975.

Röpke, W, ,Integration und Disintegration der Internationalen Wirtschaft', in W Röpke (ed), *Wirtschaftsfragen der Freien Welt* (Frankfurt, Erherd Festschrift, 1957) 500.

Rusuhuzwa, TK, *The Potential Implications of the Entry of the New Republic of South Sudan into the EAC*, 2014, African Research and Resources Foundation.

Schweiger, C, 'Poland, Variable Geometry and the Enlarged European Union' (2014) 66(3) *Europe-Asia Studies* 394–420, 396–397.

Sebalu, P, 'The East African Community' (1972) 16(3) *The Journal of African Law* 345–363.

Sinnot, R, *Integration Theory, Subsidiarity and the Internationalisation of Issues: The Implication for Legitimacy*, 1994, EUI Working Paper RSC No. 94/13.

Srinivasan, TN, Whalley, J and I Wooton, I, 'Measuring the Effects of Regionalism on Trade and Welfare', in K Anderson and R Blackhurst (eds), *Regional Integration and the Global Trading System* (New York, St. Martin's Press, 1993) 52–79.

Stewart, RB and Badin, MRS, 'The World Trade Organisation and Global Administrative Law', in C Joerges and E-Ulrich Petersmann (eds), *Constitutionalism, Multilevel Trade Governance and International Economic Law* (Oxford, Hart Publishing, 2011).

Stubb, AC-G 'A Categorisation of Differentiated Integration' (1996) 34(2) *Journal of Common Market Studies*.

United Nations Economic Commission for Africa (UNECA), *On the General Scheme for Coordinating and Harmonising Integration Activities in Africa (A Critique of the Principle of Variable Geometry)*, Seventh Joint ECA/UNDP/African IGOs/UN Specialised Agencies Meeting, Addis Ababa, 23–24 April 1993.

Vaitsos, CV, 'Crisis in Regional Economic Cooperation (Integration) Among Developing Countries: A Survey' (1978) 6 *World Development* 719.

VanGrasstek, C and Sauvé, P, 'The Consistency of WTO Rules: Can the Single Undertaking be Squared With Variable Geometry?' (2006) 9(4) *Journal of International Economic Law*.

Wallace, W, 'Exercising Power and Influence in the EU: The Roles of Member States', in S Bulmer and C Lequesne (eds), *The Member States of the European Union*, 2nd edn (Oxford, Oxford University Press, 2005).

REGIONAL REPORTS, DECLARATIONS AND DOCUMENTS

African Union, *AU Decision on Boosting Intra-African Trade and Fast Tracking the Continental Free Trade Area*, Assembly/AU/Dec.394(XVIII)

——— *Indication of Legal Instruments Signed at the 10th Extraordinary Session of the Assembly on the Launch of AfCFTA*.

Annex XXI to the Report on the 28th Meeting of the EAC Council of Ministers.

Communiqué by H.E. Uhuru Kenyatta, President of the Republic of Kenya, after a working visit to his counterpart, H.E. Yoweri Kaguta Museveni, President of the Republic of Uganda, on 24–25 June 2013, at State House, Entebbe, Uganda.

Decisions of the EAC Ministerial Council Meeting of 13 September 2008, *East African Community Gazette*, 30 December 2008, Arusha.

EACJ, *In the Matter of a Request by the Council of Ministers of the East African Community for an Advisory Opinion*, Application No. 1 of 2008.

EAC Council of Ministers, *Proposal for Requesting Advisory Opinion of the East African Court of Justice*, 13 September 2008.

EAC Secretariat, *Report of the 13th Summit of the Heads of State*, EAC/SHS 13/2011.

—— *The East African Community Trade Report 2006*.

—— *The East African Community Trade Report 2012*.

—— *Report of the 14th Summit of the Heads of State*, EAC/SHS 14/2012.

—— *Report of the 15th Summit of the Heads of State*, EAC/SHS 15/2013.

—— *Report of the 18th Summit of the Heads of State*, EAC/SHS 18/2017.

East African Community, *Outline of Issues for Possible Inclusion in the Proposed Treaty*, contained in Annex IX to the Report of the 8th Meeting of the PTCEAC (EAC/C8/1/97).

East African Cooperation Development Strategy 1997–2000 EAC/DS/4/97.

Joint Communiqué of the 13th Summit of the Northern Corridor Integration Projects, at the Munyonyo Commonwealth Resort, Kampala, Uganda, 23 April 2016.

Joint Communiqué of the 2nd Infrastructure Summit between the Republics of Kenya, Burundi, Rwanda, South Sudan and Uganda, at the White Sands Beach Resort and Spa, Mombasa, Kenya, 28 August 2013.

Joint Communiqué of the Integration Projects Summit between the Republics of Rwanda, Kenya, South Sudan and Uganda, at Urugwiro Village, Kigali, Rwanda, 28 October 2013.

Organisation of African Unity, *The Final Act of Lagos*, Annex 1 to the Lagos Plan of Action for the Economic Development of Africa, 1980–2000.

—— *The Lagos Plan of Action for the Economic Development of Africa*, 1980–2000.

Permanent Tripartite Commission for East African Cooperation (PTCEAC) Secretariat, *Synopsis on East African Cooperation*, April 1999, Arusha, Tanzania.

Report of the Third Meeting of the East African Cooperation Forum, Nairobi, Kenya, July 1992.

UNECA, *Approaches to African Economic Integration: Towards Cooperation in Economic Planning and an African Common Market*, 7 May 1963.

OTHER REPORTS, DECLARATIONS AND DOCUMENTS

Calabrese, L and Eberhard-Ruiz, A, What Types of Non-Tariff Barriers Affect the East African Community?, 2016, ODI Briefing, page 2, available at www.odi.org/sites/odi.org.uk/files/resource-documents/11110.pdf (accessed 23 November 2017).

Scollay, R, Prospects for Linking PTAs in the Asia-Pacific Region, in the Pacific Economic Cooperation Council (PECC)/ABAC Joint Study on FTAAP, 2007.

Sir Stephen Wall (Chair) et al, Flexibility and the Future of the European Union, Federal Trust Report on Flexible Integration in the European Union, October 2005.

—— The Doha Ministerial Declaration of 2001.

—— World Trade Report 2011, The WTO and Preferential Trade Agreements: From Co-existence to Coherence, 2011, WTO.

—— EAC Trade Policy Review, Report by the Secretariat, 17th October 2012, WT/TPR/S/271.

Trade Law Centre (TRALAC), The African Continental Free Trade Area – A TRALAC Guide, 3rd edn, August 2018.

United Nations Conference on Trade and Development (UNCTAD), Draft Sao Paulo Consensus, TD/L.380, 16 June 2004.

World Bank, Doing Business 2017: The EAC, Washington.

World Trade Organisation, EAC Trade Policy Review, Report by the Secretariat, 20th September 2006, WT/TPR/S/171.

WEBSITES AND OTHER INTERNET RESOURCES

African Union, *AU in a Nutshell*, https://au.int/en/history/oau-and-au (accessed 9 January 2019).

Asiimwe, D, *Uganda Joins Kenya, Rwanda in Abolishing Work Permits for Professionals*, The East African, 13 June 2015, www.theeastafrican.co.ke/news/Uganda-joins-Kenya--Rwanda-in-abolishing-work-permits/2558-2750958-om9sh7/index.html (accessed 10 February 2017).

Bagala, A, *Museveni, Nkurunziza in Strong Exchange*, The Daily Monitor, 14 December 2018, www.monitor.co.ug/News/National/Museveni--Nkurunziza-strong-exchange/688334-4894670-rl9ijuz/index.html (accessed 27 December 2018).

BBC News, *Burundi President Nkurunziza Faces Attempted Coup*, 13 May 2015, www.bbc.co.uk/news/world-africa-32724083 (accessed 27 December 2018).

——*Yoweri Museveni – Uganda's President Profiled*, 17 February 2016, www.bbc.co.uk/news/world-africa-12421747 (accessed 4 November 2016).

Butagira, T, *Government Suspends National ID Project Again*, The Daily Monitor, 26 August 2013, www.monitor.co.ug/News/National/Government-suspends-national-ID-project-again/688334-1966618-ko3qd7z/index.html (accessed 25 November 2017).

Duggan, B and Muktar, I, *Nairobi to Mombasa High-Speed Railway Opens*, CNN Marketplace Africa, 31 May 2017, http://edition.cnn.com/2017/05/31/africa/kenya-nairobi-railway/index.html (accessed 25 November 2017).

EAC Website, *COMESA-EAC-SADC Tripartite*, www.eac.int/tripartite (accessed 4 January 2019).

East African Community, *About the Treaty*, www.eac.int/treaty (accessed 12 October 2016).

—— *EAC Institutions*, www.eac.int/about/institutions (accessed 19 December 2016).

—— *Joint Communiqué from the 17th Ordinary Summit of the EAC Heads of State Summit*, March 2016, www.eac.int/news-and-media/statements/20160302/joint-communique-17th-ordinary-summit-east-african-community-heads-state (accessed 20 December 2016).

—— *Overview of the EAC*, www.eac.int/overview-of-eac (accessed 2 July 2018).

—— *History of the EAC*, available at www.eac.int/eac-history (accessed 20 December 2018).

East African Development Bank, *History*, www.eadb.org/about-us/history (accessed 20 December 2016).

Economic Community of West African States (ECOWAS), *History*, www.ecowas.int/about-ecowas/history/, (accessed 13 December 2018).

Filadoro, M, Flexibility in the EU External Relations With Other Regions: *The Cases of MERCOSUR, CAN, EFTA, ENP, Western Balkans and ACP*, Unpublished, www.ies.be/files/Filadoro-A2.pdf (accessed 18 March 2016).

Immigration Services Department of Tanzania, www.immigration.go.tz/module1.php?id=45 (accessed 10 February 2017).

International Monetary Fund, *IMF Data Mapper – GDP by Current Prices*, www.imf.org/external/datamapper/NGDPD@WEO/OEMDC/ADVEC/WEOWORLD/AFQ (accessed 30 January 2018).

International Trade Centre (ITC), *Trade Map*, www.trademap.org/Bilateral_TS.aspx?nvpm=1||7||7|TOTAL|||2|1|1|1|2|1|1|1|1, (accessed 1 October 2018).

Kenya's Directorate of Immigration and Registration of Persons, *Information*, www.immigration.go.ke/Information.html (accessed 25 November 2017).

Lamu Port, South Sudan, Ethiopia Transport Corridor (LAPSSET), *Welcome to LAPSSET*, www.lapsset.go.ke/ (accessed 25 November 2017).

Maina, W, *Time for EAC to Lower its Sights; Throw Out Federation Dream*, The East African, 30 May 2017, www.theeastafrican.co.ke/oped/comment/EAC-political-federation/434750-3948146-w43lh8z/index.html (accessed 27 November 2017).

Mugisha, IR, *Nationalism in the Region Could Derail Continental Trade Bloc*, The East African, 27 November 2018, www.theeastafrican.co.ke/business/Nationalism-in-EAC-could-derail-continental-trade-bloc/2560-4870596-td2h1x/index.html (accessed 30 November 2018).

Musisi, F and Muhumuza, MK *Uganda: How Oil Pipeline Deal Slipped Out of Kenya's Hands*, All Africa, 25 April 2016, http://allafrica.com/stories/201604250062.html (accessed 25 November 2017).

Ndege, R, *East Africa Integration: State of Play*, in Africa in Depth, August 2014, www.africapractice.com/wp-content/uploads/2014/08/Africa-InDepth-East-African-integration-State-of-play-August-2014.pdf (accessed 20 February 2017).

Nile Basin Initiative (NBI), *Who We Are*, www.nilebasin.org/index.php/nbi/who-we-are (accessed 5 January 2019).

Northern Corridor Integration Projects (NCIP), *About Us*, www.nciprojects.org/about/about-us (accessed 6 February 2017).

—— *Single Customs Territory*, http://nciprojects.org/project/single-customs-territory (accessed 23 November 2017).

Olingo, A, *Uganda May Join Dar as Kenya Weighs Options of Extending SGR to Malaba*, The East African, 21 May 2017, www.theeastafrican.co.ke/business/Uganda-ditch-Kenya-SGR-route-Tanzania/2560-3935306-phdp9p/index.html (accessed 25 November 2017).

Oluoch, F, *S. Sudan's Push to Join EAC Gains Momentum*, The East African, 7 November 2015, www.theeastafrican.co.ke/news/S--Sudan-s-push-to-join-EAC-gains-momentum/2558-2946330-his9dpz/index.html (accessed 28 November 2017).

Onyango-Obbo, C, *EAC, Just Let Burundi go, We Can Always Remarry*, The East African, 10 December 2018, www.theeastafrican.co.ke/oped/comment/EAC-just-let-Burundi-go-we-can-always-remarry/434750-4889314-8dwp20z/index.html (accessed 28 December 2018).

Opening Remarks by the WTO Director General at the launch of Regional Trade Agreements and the Multilateral Trading System, on 29 September 2016, www.wto.org/english/news_e/spra_e/spra138_e.htm (accessed 18 January2018).

Otuki, N, *Kenya's Power Imports from Uganda now Rise 32 Percent*, Business Daily, 6 September 2016, www.businessdailyafrica.com/Corporate-News/Kenya-power-imports-from-Uganda-now-rise-32-per-cent-/539550-3371092-1xrsap/ (accessed 18 October 2016).

Potekhin, I, *Pan-Africanism and the Struggle of the Two Ideologies*, 1964, South African Communist Party, republished by South African History Online, www.sahistory.org.za/archive/pan-africanism-and-the-struggle-of-two-ideologies (accessed 9 January 2019).

Rwanda Directorate General of Immigration and Emigration, *Information for Applicants Specific to Class T12 East Africa Tourist Visa*, www.migration.gov.rw/index.php?id=233 (accessed 25 November 2017).

Southern African Customs Union (SACU), *History of SACU*, SACU Website, www.sacu.int/show.php?id=394 (accessed 29 January 2018).

The African Union, *Treaty Establishing the African Economic Community*, https://au.int/en/treaties/treaty-establishing-african-economic-community (accessed 4 January 2019).

The Citizen, *Coalition of the Willing Emerges Again in EAC*, 13 January 2014, www.thecitizen.co.tz/News/Coalition-of-the-willing-emerges-again-in-EAC/1840360-2144030-100yaaz/index.html (accessed 15 February 2017).

The East African Community, *Tripartite Transport and Transit Facilitation Programme – Press Release*, www.eac.int/press-releases/150-infrastructure/1244-tripartite-transport-and-transit-facilitation-programme (accessed 29 November 2018).

The East African, *$1.4 Billion Budget Deficit Could Ground EAC Operations*, 4 December 2018, www.theeastafrican.co.ke/news/ea/billion-budget-deficit-could-ground-EAC-operations/4552908-4880340-fu91e0/index.html (accessed 2 December 2018).

—— *Single Tourist Visa: Things to Note*, 22 February 2014, www.theeastafrican.co.ke/news/Single-tourist-visa--Things-to-note-/-/2558/2217586/-/d2xlytz/-/index.html (accessed 24 November 2017).

—— *Tanzania Bans 'The East African' Over Coverage of Govt, Registration*, 24 January 2015, www.theeastafrican.co.ke/news/Tanzania-now-bans--The-EastAfrican--/2558-2600522-ydbvagz/index.html (accessed 27 November 2017).

—— *Uganda Joins Kenya, Rwanda, in Abolishing Work Permits for Professionals*, 13 June 2015, www.theeastafrican.co.ke/news/Uganda-joins-Kenya--Rwanda-in-abolishing-work-permits/2558-2750958-om9sh7/index.html (accessed 24 November 2017).

—— *Country Laws Hampering East African Single Tourist Visa*, 4 June 2016, www.theeastafrican.co.ke/business/Country-laws-hampering-East-African-single-tourist-visa--/2560-3231966-dkumeh/index.html (accessed 24 November 2017).

—— *Magufuli: Tanzania is Not a Grazing Land for Kenya's Cows*, 8 November 2017, www.theeastafrican.co.ke/news/Magufuli-Kenya-cattle-diplomacy/2558-4177942-fkjac7z/index.html (accessed 27 November 2017).

—— *Tanzania Police Burn 6,400 Chicks to Death*, 2 November 2017, www.theeastafrican.co.ke/scienceandhealth/Tanzania-police-burn-6400-chicks-alive/3073694-4166372-q3dus0/index.html (accessed 27 November 2017).

—— *Burundi Accuses Rwanda of Abducting Four Fishermen*, 10 December 2018, www.theeastafrican.co.ke/news/ea/Burundi-accuses-Rwanda-of-abducting-fishermen/4552908-4889312-11r6p78/index.html (accessed 27 December 2018).

—— *EAC Integration in Doubt as Summit Aborts Second Time*, 22 December 2018, www.theeastafrican.co.ke/news/ea/EAC-integration-in-doubt-as-summit-aborts-second-time/4552908-4906704-gwcew6/index.html (accessed 27 December 2018).

—— *Focus on Kagame, Museveni in Simmering Diplomatic Cold War*, 24 March 2018, www.theeastafrican.co.ke/news/ea/Focus-on-Kagame-Museveni-in-simmering-diplomatic-cold-war-/4552908-4355428-e9qiehz/index.html (accessed 28 December 2018).

—— *Jitters in Region as Kagame Fires Military Action Warning*, 12 December 2018, www.theeastafrican.co.ke/news/ea/Jitters-in-region-as-Kagame-fires-military-action-warning/4552908-4892284-e4wry7z/index.html (accessed 27 December 2018).

—— *Kagame Blames Neighbours as Two are Killed in Attack*, 16 December 2018, www.theeastafrican.co.ke/news/ea/Kagame-blames-neighbours-for-deadly-attack/4552908-4897942-43wvpsz/index.html (accessed 27 December 2018).

—— *Nakumatt Eyes Tanzania's Emerging Retail Business*, www.theeastafrican.co.ke/business/Nakumatt-eyes-Tanzania-s-emerging-retail-business-/2560-2405950-4c7cl6z/index.html (accessed 6 December 2016).

——*Nkurunziza meets His Match as Museveni Answers Letter*, 15 December 2018, www.theeastafrican.co.ke/news/ea/4552908-4897182-12sjxww/index.html (accessed 27 December 2018).

—— *Nkurunziza, Now Isolated, Creates Crisis All by Himself*, www.theeastafrican.co.ke/news/ea/Pierre-nkurunziza-now-isolated-creates-crisis-all-by-himself-/4552908-4886924-view-asAMP-m2hqqi/index.html?__twitter_impression=true (accessed 27 December 2018).

—— *Uganda, Rwanda Yet to Restore Cordial Relations*, 4 August 2018, www.theeastafrican.co.ke/news/ea/Uganda-and-Rwanda-yet-to-restore-cordial-relations/4552908-4697068-ubitdrz/index.html (accessed 28 December 2018).

Trade Law Centre (TRALAC), *South Africa Deposits Tripartite FTA Ratification Instrument*, 13 December 2018, www.tralac.org/news/article/13801-south-africa-deposits-fta-ratification-instrument.html (accessed 4 January 2019).

—— *South Africa on Ratification of the COMESA-EAC-SADC Tripartite Free Trade Area*, 14 June 2018, www.tralac.org/news/article/13158-south-africa-on-ratification-of-the-comesa-eac-sadc-tripartite-free-trade-area-tfta.html (accessed 24 November 2018).

Uganda's Directorate of Citizenship and Immigration Control, *Visas and Passes*, http://mia.go.ug/content/visas-and-passes (accessed 25 November 2017).

UN Economic Commission for Africa (UNECA), *MULPOCs, (Multinational Programming and Operational Centres) – Strengthening ECA's Sub-regional Presence*, UNECA website, www.uneca.org/cfm1997/pages/mulpocs-multinational-programming-and-operational-centres-strengthening-ecas (accessed 24 November 2018).

UNECA, *Overview*, at the UNECA website, www.uneca.org/pages/overview (accessed 24 November 2018).

—— *Synergies between the AfCFTA and TFTA will Benefit Africa's Traders and Consumers, Says ECA Chief*, 18 June 2018, www.uneca.org/stories/synergies-between-afcfta-and-tripartite-fta-will-benefit-africa%E2%80%99s-traders-and-consumers-says (accessed 30 November 2018).

WITS – COMTRADE Data, www.wits.worldbank.org (accessed 9 February 2017).

World Bank Data Bank, http://data.worldbank.org/indicator/NY.GDP.MKTP.CD?locations=ZG (accessed 11 October 2016).

—— http://data.worldbank.org/indicator/NY.GDP.PCAP.CD?locations=EU (accessed 11 October 2016).

—— http://data.worldbank.org/indicator/NY.GDP.MKTP.KD.ZG (accessed 10 February 2017).

—— *International Comparison Program Database – Kenya*, available at https://data.worldbank.org/country/kenya (accessed 29 December 2018).

—— *International Comparison Program Database*, https://data.worldbank.org/indicator/NY.GDP.PCAP.PP.CD?year_high_desc=true (accessed 29 December 2018).

—— *World Bank Country and Lending Groups*, https://datahelpdesk.worldbank.org/knowledgebase/articles/906519-world-bank-country-and-lending-groups (accessed 10 February 2017).

—— *World Bank National Accounts Data*, https://data.worldbank.org/indicator/NY.GDP.PCAP.CD?locations=ZG, (accessed 1 October 2018).

—— World Governance Indicators, http://info.worldbank.org/governance/wgi/#reports (accessed 14 November 2017).

—— *World Integrated Trade Solution: Trade Summary for Uganda*, http://wits.worldbank.org/CountrySnapshot/en/UGA/textview, (accessed 22 January 2019).

World Population Review, *Africa Population 2018*, http://worldpopulationreview.com/continents/africa-population/, (accessed 1 October 2018).

—— *China Population 2018*, http://worldpopulationreview.com/countries/china-population/, (accessed 1 October 2018).

World Trade Organisation, *Understanding the WTO: The Agreements – Plurilaterals: Of Minority Interest*, www.wto.org/english/thewto_e/whatis_e/tif_e/agrm10_e.htm (accessed 7 April 2016).

WTO-RTAIS, http://rtais.wto.org/UI/charts.aspx (accessed 16 January 2018).

—— http://rtais.wto.org/UI/CRShowRTAIDCard.aspx?rtaid=148 (accessed 16 January 2018).

—— http://rtais.wto.org/UI/PublicAllRTAList.aspx (accessed 5 September 2018).

—— *Regional Trade Agreements – ECOWAS*, http://rtais.wto.org/UI/PublicShowMemberRTAIDCard.aspx?rtaid=36 (accessed 17 December 2018).

—— *Regional Trade Agreements, EAC*, http://rtais.wto.org/UI/PublicShowMemberRTAIDCard.aspx?rtaid=94, (accessed 17 December 2018).

Index

CPSIA information can be obtained
at www.ICGtesting.com
Printed in the USA
LVHW082109030622
720463LV00006B/248